I0800115

Praise for
Bubba Ephriam

"Roberts has captured the essence and soul of the dying days of segregation and the grudging transition to integration in the 1950s as it played out in Pecos, Texas, around the Lone Star state, and throughout the country. Caught in the middle is modest Black teenage basketball phenom Iria 'Bubba' Ephriam, unaware of the often-uncredited historic role he would play. Ephriam's previously untold story is meticulously researched, and while the book has a sports theme, it's really a highly inspirational tale of history, family, faith, and community."

—**Michael Hurd,** historian and author of *Thursday Night Lights: The Story of Black High School Football in Texas*

"I am guessing, dear reader, that you're familiar with Judge Roy Bean, the legendary law west of the Pecos. However, I'm guessing you may *not* know Iria Ephriam, a young man who decades later made his mark on a different sort of court west of the Pecos. A basketball star in the mid-1950s for the Pecos Eagles in far West Texas, Ephraim—known his entire life as 'Bubba'—was the first African American to participate in the Texas state high school basketball tournament in Austin. A dusty, little town in far West Texas might seem an unlikely place for civil rights history to be made, but made it was. In his fascinating and well-researched account of the trail Bubba Ephraim blazed from Pecos to Austin and beyond, Garner Roberts tells a story that's largely unknown—a story worth telling."

—**Joe Holley,** Pulitzer Prize finalist, *Houston Chronicle*, author of *Slingin' Sam*

"A skillful and thought-provoking account of the dark and angry days of desegregation, viewed through the eyes of a Black West Texas teenager who overcame it all to become a legendary basketball player in a previously all-White world. This is an important, fascinating, and unforgettable tale."

—**Carlton Stowers,** member of the Texas Literary Hall of Fame

"Garner Roberts deals with racial politics, ugly discrimination, and heroic personal triumph in relating a remarkable, little-known Texas high school sports story and its lasting impact and influence."

—**Glenn Dromgoole,** author of *A Small Town in Texas*

"*Bubba Ephriam: Black Texas Basketball Trailblazer* is a powerful book of history about a young man who came through his young life with several struggles from segregation into integration, but he had hope and made a commitment to succeed despite the odds against him. This book is centered around civil rights and the struggle for Black equality."

—**Andrew L. Penns,** pastor and Black historian

BUBBA EPHRIAM

BUBBA EPHRIAM

BLACK TEXAS BASKETBALL TRAILBLAZER

GARNER ROBERTS

Abilene Christian University Press

BUBBA EPHRIAM

Black Texas Basketball Trailblazer

ACU PRESS

ISBN 978-1-68426-123-9 | LCCN 2024937662

Printed in the United States of America

Cataloging-in-Publication Data is on file at the Library of Congress, Washington, DC.

Cover design by Marc English
Cover illustration by Michael Barrett
Interior text design by Sandy Armstrong, Strong Design

For information contact:
Abilene Christian University Press
ACU Box 29138
Abilene, Texas 79699

1-877-816-4455
www.acupressbooks.com

24 25 26 27 28 29 30 / 7 6 5 4 3 2 1

All expletives and racial slurs in the text come from direct interviews and have not been censored so as to retain the stories as told by those who lived them.

Bubba looks at home on this basketball court in Abilene, Texas, in April 2013. (photo by Thomas Metthe)

CONTENTS

INTRODUCTION

Likely, before you discovered this book, you had never heard of Iria "Bubba" Ephriam and didn't know of his story despite its eminent significance. Despite having been born and reared in West Texas and being a somewhat knowledgeable sports fan, I admit that I had never heard of him either. But his story is historic, consequential, and noble.

Bubba Ephriam was the first African American player to participate in the Texas boys high school state basketball tournament in Austin. It was in March 1957 that Bubba and his teammates from Pecos High School journeyed from West Texas to the venerable Gregory Gymnasium at the University of Texas after qualifying for the 37th annual tournament for public schools conducted by the University Interscholastic League (UIL).

Bubba grew up in a migrant farm family of native Texans who endured a hardscrabble life in South and West Texas during pivotal years of segregation and integration. The landmark decision by the US Supreme Court in *Brown v. Board of Education* was announced May 17, 1954, two days after Bubba's sixteenth birthday. There were other parallels between his life and important events in this meaningful period of US history. Bubba's first game with his new high school team was played in Pecos on December 1, 1955—the same day Rosa Parks, a forty-two-year-old seamstress at a department store in downtown Montgomery, Alabama, was arrested for refusing to move to the back of a city bus on her ride home from work in an incident that sparked a 381-day bus boycott. Martin Luther King Jr. called her "ideal for the role assigned to her by history." And the week of Bubba's appearance at the state tournament in Austin was the first week of Jackie Robinson's new job at Chock full o' Nuts in New York City after his retirement from professional baseball. It's well-documented that Robinson was another person ideal for the role assigned to him by history as the first Black player in Major League Baseball.

And Bubba was ideal for his role in Texas history. He was carrying formidable burdens March 8, 1957, when he first stepped onto the court in Gregory Gym in Austin for the Pecos Eagles' state semifinal game. The obstacles he faced included more than just the aspiring players from Nacogdoches High School. "When I got the ball," Bubba said, "the whole gym would be booing. 'Kill him, kill him, trip him, trip him.' There were lots of slurs. I heard everything. I never heard my name called the right way." Sweat mixed with tears on Bubba's face, but he persevered through the pain.

Years later, at a rally for religious freedom and civil rights on the front lawn of the White House on Pennsylvania Avenue in Washington, DC, Bubba said, "I have been discriminated against all my life. Just the other day I was talking about discrimination that I've seen. . . . I told how I was treated in Austin, Texas, at the state basketball tournament. How awful it was being the only Black boy playing in the tournament."

Bubba led coach John Kenner's team to a remarkable fifty victories in two seasons, but after only two years at Pecos High School, he became too old to participate in UIL athletics. So he dropped out of school, left his home in Pecos, and joined the US Navy. He served ten years in the navy, including five years of foreign service. Bubba was a crew member first on the USS *Lexington* and later on the USS *Bennington*, and he served in the Vietnam War, where he earned the Vietnam Service Medal with two bronze stars and the Republic of Vietnam Campaign Medal.

After residing in Los Angeles and Colorado Springs, he found his way to Abilene in the 1980s, where I was fortunate to meet him for the first time in 2013.

And I can confirm what his daughter Loraine Abram says about her father. She refers to him as "a master storyteller." She recalled the days of her youth when Bubba mentored and ministered to his children and their neighborhood friends. "He could pull a story out of nowhere and make the people so real," she said.

Nicole Ephriam agrees. "Uncle Bubba likes to talk," Nicole, granddaughter of his brother, William, said. "That has never changed."

Bubba's courage reminds me of the courage of Benaiah in the Old Testament book of 2 Samuel. He became King David's bodyguard and commander of Israel's army, and the prophet Samuel writes that "he did many heroic deeds," including one time when "on a snowy day, he chased a lion down into a pit and killed it" (2 Sam. 23:20).

Benaiah didn't run away from the things you or I certainly would be afraid of. He wasn't a "scaredy-cat." He chased lions.

Bubba Ephriam didn't back down from things he was afraid of, from obstacles he faced, or from burdens he carried. There were opportunities during his life when he could have given up, abandoned his hopes and dreams, and retired to the sidelines. Instead, he stayed in the game—the game of basketball and the game of life—and played both to the best of his God-given ability.

He had the courage to dream big, as best-selling author Mark Batterson writes in *Chase the Lion*. Bubba's dreams weren't small, and he had (and has) the courage to chase them. His greatest heritage, however, isn't his dreams but the dreams he inspires in others.

—Garner Roberts

ONE

BUBBA HAD THE GUTS TO DO IT

William "Rescues" Bubba from Reeves County Cotton Field

Reeves Ranks Twenty-Second in Nation in Production of Cotton
Pecos Enterprise, Apr. 8, 1954

Reeves Tops 18-County Area in Cotton Totals
Pecos Enterprise, Feb. 17, 1955

Reeves County Ginnings Reach 113,218 Bales
Pecos Enterprise, Jan. 2, 1956

There was no music to distract William Ephriam as he drove south on State Highway 17 in his early '50s GMC pickup. That's because there was no radio in William's otherwise snappy, dark-blue truck. The countryside was quiet this midday. The only sounds were the whir of the tires on the pavement and the roar of the engine as he pressed against the truck's accelerator on the empty two-lane road through the parched West Texas landscape. The azure sky stretched from horizon to horizon.

"Bubba needs to be in school."

The same six words kept tumbling through William's mind. "Bubba needs to be in school." It seemed as if the lives of the two young brothers—the determined William and the unsuspecting Bubba—had been leading to this encounter.

It was another warm day in the middle of September 1955, with the temperature again approaching ninety. School already was in session, and for the first time, African American students were enrolled with Anglo-American students in classrooms at Pecos High School. Instead of sitting at his desk in a classroom, however, Bubba was working for his father in a cotton field—as he so often was during much of his boyhood.

William, twenty, had finished work at eight thirty that morning after his night shift at the Greyhound bus station on one of Pecos's busiest streets, Third Street, the business route for US Highway 80. His wife of eight months, Ophelia, had already left their modest home at 809 South Walnut Street for her job as a domestic laborer in one of Pecos's Anglo neighborhoods. So William spent a couple of hours each at two of his part-time jobs—an animal clinic owned by a local veterinarian, Dr. Bobby Gross, and the local Cadillac automobile dealer, McKinney Motors.

William no longer could delay this visit to the cotton fields in central Reeves County where the Ephriam family was currently working as migrant farm laborers. So he pointed his trusty GMC pickup toward Saragosa with the picturesque Davis Mountains framed in the distance by the windshield of his truck. Because the summer vacation season had passed and school had started, few cars now traveled south on State Highway 17 toward the popular spring-fed swimming pool at Balmorhea State Park. William passed fields white with cotton, windmills, patches of famous Pecos cantaloupe, and cattle and sheep ranches.

As he often did, that morning, seventeen-year-old Bubba had driven one of his father's four trucks to the field just after daybreak and after his mother's generous breakfast of fist-sized biscuits, sausage, bacon, and eggs. He hauled cotton pickers who were unable to provide their own transportation. By now Bubba no longer picked cotton, but instead he aided his grandmother Mattie, known as Big Mama, who served as the Ephriams' weighmaster. Their crew often numbered up to two hundred people who covered two or three fields simultaneously. Each field had to be handpicked two or three times during one cotton season, and there also were chores, such as plowing with a middlebuster behind a horse or mule to create a new seedbed, sowing seeds, irrigating, hoeing weeds, and chopping cotton.

School-age children were among the crews working in the field that day. Black children in rural areas often did not start school until after the cotton was picked, which meant October or maybe November. And they often stopped attending school in April when it was time to plant. Six months of school was a good year. Alwyn Barr's book *Black Texans* says that in 1944–45, when Bubba was six years of age, "Negro schools averaged 147 day terms, compared to 172 for white schools."

Black families, who often picked together in groups, gave the best hours of their days to cotton. They strapped canvas sacks over their left shoulders and carried the sacks on their right hips. They tried to pick as much cotton as possible before the sun got high, because there was no escaping the one-hundred-degree heat. The broiling sun bore down on them and made the cotton fields shimmer like an ocean. They often picked until the sun went down and they couldn't see their hands anymore.

Bubba helped the oldest and youngest workers empty the canvas sacks they had been dragging between the rows, he helped Big Mama weigh and record each person's morning pick (they were paid by the pounds of cotton they picked), he moved trucks to where they next were needed, and he loaded cotton into trucks bound for a local cotton gin. He also was Big Mama's "water boy"—fetching water, ice, bread, and sandwich meat from nearby country stores.

And occasionally, Iria Ephriam would excuse his son Bubba to go hunting and fishing to put meat on the Ephriams' dinner tables.

William arrived at the Ephriam pick that day and quickly located Bubba, but he did not see Cephus, as their father often was called. Both brothers (actually half brothers because they were born to different mothers) were distressed by the ensuing discussion.

"Bubba, you have all these skills." William did most of the talking in this conversation. "You can play basketball, you can play football, you can do it all. You have too much potential. But you need to get your education. You need to be in school. And it's not just about playing basketball.

"You know you can't live with Daddy and not work," William added. "With Daddy, you either work or get out. I know because I had to do the same thing. Remember?"

"I know." Bubba wiped his shirtsleeve across his face, streaking it with sweat and dust.

William swallowed twice, paused a few heartbeats, and continued. "Bubba, I've been bothered by this. You're going to miss out. School has already started. You can come live with me and Ophelia and go to school. You don't have to worry about working. You don't have to go to the fields every day. You don't have to throw your life away in no field.

"Daddy just doesn't understand about getting an education. You know that as well as I do."

With his hands stuck deep in the pockets of his khakis, Bubba listened, nodded his head, and assented in silence. Both brothers knew that convincing their father of what they thought needed to happen would not be easy. "I'll talk to Daddy," William told Bubba before returning to his pickup. "I will. I'll do it today."

Bubba resumed his weighmaster chores with Big Mama, and William walked purposefully to his truck, stirring gentle clouds of dust and scattering jackrabbits and roadrunners, and then drove north to Pecos to the Ephriam homes on East Thirteenth Street. The families of Iria Ephriam and his father, Dan Ephriam, lived in adjacent houses near George Washington Carver School, where William had graduated two years earlier after also leaving home to avoid having to work.

William found his father at home. He expected resistance to what he was about to say. William sucked in his breath as if he had been punched in the stomach, and he slowly began to speak. He talked as if what he was about to say was important. "Daddy, you know school has started." Then those six words again. "Bubba needs to be in school."

Cephus didn't say much. "Bubba don't need no school." It seemed to William as if Cephus didn't care, and he sensed that his father didn't want a confrontation. Saying more might have pushed them both to a place from which they couldn't return.

"Bubba is going to come live with me and go to school," William insisted before quietly leaving his father's house.

Later that afternoon, back in the field before the end of the day's pick, Cephus and Bubba also talked about William and Bubba's resolution. The conversation was unavoidable. "Okay," Cephus said, "if that's what you want to do. Make the best of it. And take care of yourself."

Sixty-one years later, William asserted, "Bubba had the guts to do it."

William had exhibited that same fortitude at about the same age. He was a sixteen-year-old junior in 1952, enrolled in Carver's new building—the school's first permanent home—at 600 East Twelfth Street when Cephus found a job for William. "You're going to have to get out and get a job," Cephus told his oldest son.

"My daddy went and found me a job," William explained. "He wanted me to go to work in a laundry. I was going to have to quit school.

"I told him, 'I can't do that, Daddy. I've got to finish school.' That's the only time he ever said anything negative to me. He was so kind. He was so good. He just didn't understand the value of an education.

"So I went next door to ask Papa Dan if I could stay with him."

"Yes, you can stay with us," his grandfather replied.

A year later in 1953, William graduated from George Washington Carver School a few days before his eighteenth birthday. Two additional classes graduated in May 1954 and May 1955 before Carver's high school students—including Iria "Bubba" Ephriam—began attending desegregated Pecos High School in September 1955.

Sitting in his office in a church building where he ministers in Colorado Springs, Colorado, William can't hide his emotions while talking about his brother, his father, and that pivotal day in a cotton field in West Texas in September 1955. He apologizes to a visitor from his native Texas for his halting language.

"I remember very well that day," he said, blinking away tears. "It was a school day. I think in his heart Daddy knew that Bubba should be in school. But he was trapped back in the day when you worked with your hands and did everything the hard way. He just couldn't get away from that. He couldn't see beyond that. He didn't understand.

"But we knew better," William continued. "The world was changing.

"Daddy was sort of a simple man. He just believed in working. He put a work ethic in me. He taught me how to work. His focus was mostly on working and on his family. He never raised his voice except that one time. He was a kindhearted man. He was so respectful of his parents, and we learned to be respectful.

"But I think Bubba was going to go to school whether Daddy let him or not," William said. "Thank God, he let him go."

TWO

BREAKING THE COLOR LINE IN HIS SPORT

Bubba's Early Years, 1938–55

Dodgers Purchase Robinson, First Negro in Modern Major League Baseball
New York Times, Apr. 11, 1947

Opening Day at Ebbets Field: The Robinson Debut
New York Times, Apr. 16, 1947

Police Investigate Poison Pen Threats to Jackie Robinson
New York Daily News, May 10, 1947

Robinson Reveals Written Threats
New York Times, May 10, 1947

On Tuesday, April 15, 1947, in Brooklyn, New York, Jack Roosevelt Robinson—a twenty-eight-year-old native of Cairo, Georgia, who grew up in Pasadena, California, and excelled at John Muir High School, Pasadena Junior College, and UCLA—made his debut in Major League Baseball. He played first base for the Brooklyn Dodgers at Ebbets Field in Brooklyn against the Boston Braves. It was opening day for the 1947 season. Because of this man's courage, at last, America's pastime was no longer segregated. "I knew I had to do this thing for myself and for my race," Robinson said.

Robinson scored the go-ahead run that day in his very first MLB game, a 5–3 win over the Braves. In his first season he was voted Rookie of the Year, and two years later he was the first Black player to earn MVP of the National League. Six times he played in the MLB All-Star Game, and he helped Brooklyn win six National League titles and one World Series championship.

Jackie Robinson was more than just "a Negro." He was *the Negro* who broke the color line in his sport—a color line that had been drawn as early as eighty years before. In October 1867, the Philadelphia Pythians, one of the nation's most prominent Black baseball clubs, had been denied membership in the Pennsylvania Association of Amateur Base Ball Players. Ryan A. Swanson, in his 2014 book *When Baseball Went White*, calls it "one of baseball's first racial standoffs." Also in 1867, the nominating committee for the National Association of Base Ball Players at its convention on December 11 at Chestnut Street Theatre in Philadelphia "decided not to admit clubs with colored delegates." Swanson writes, "The more organized baseball became, the more thoroughly white baseball leaders were able to enforce segregation rules."

What if Jackie Robinson had not taken that very first step?

On that same day, April 15, 1947, two thousand miles away, Iria "Bubba" Ephriam, an eight-year-old from Mercedes, Texas—a month short of his ninth birthday—was working with his father's crew of migrant farmers in a Reeves County cotton field near their home in Pecos. His future would also include a pioneering feat made possible by a Black man's courage, fortitude, and ambition for something better.

"There were a lot of slurs," Ephriam remembers of his history-making day in 1957. "I never heard my name called the right way. . . . It took me a long time to even sit down and talk about this."

Bubba persevered and succeeded in basketball, his oldest daughter, Iria Loraine Abram, believes, despite "the adults who wanted to deny opportunities." She also explained, "I'm amazed at the hate among adults. He found a way to make peace with it as he got into ministry—knowing that God had a purpose and a plan for him."

On Friday, March 8, 1957, in Austin, Texas, eighteen-year-old Ephriam, known as Bubba to fans of Eagle basketball, made history by becoming the first Black player to participate in the Texas high school basketball state tournament conducted by the University Interscholastic League, the governing body for public school athletics in the state. But Bubba didn't merely "participate." In a dominating performance, he scored thirty points in the Eagles' semifinal victory to propel Pecos High School to Saturday night's championship game for Class AAA.

His achievement required much more than points and rebounds, hook shots and blocked shots. Much like Robinson had experienced a decade earlier, Ephriam was the target of vicious racial slurs, objects were thrown at him from the bleachers, threats were made against him, he was refused service at restaurants, and he endured other forms of discrimination. Ephriam said, "I remember saying to myself, 'If this is what integration is all about, I don't want no part of it.'" But still he was Class AAA's top player that weekend in Austin and the tournament co-leader in scoring despite his team's runner-up finish.

Bubba Ephriam is more than just "a Negro." He is *the Negro* who broke the color line in his sport. Bubba grew up during a time when Black people were moving from farms to cities, securing better jobs and higher incomes and the right to vote, and beginning to wield considerable clout in politics. They benefited from better education, and they acquired resources and expectations with which to challenge the racial status quo and escape the oppressive racial sentiment of the country. The US Supreme Court became more committed to racial equality and invalidated a variety of statutes that had segregated and disenfranchised Southern Black citizens.

What if Bubba Ephriam had not taken that very first step?

On that same day, March 8, 1957, thirty-eight-year-old Robinson ended his first week of work as the vice president and director of personnel at Chock full o' Nuts, a coffee company that operated a chain of small restaurants in New York City and employed more than one thousand people—many of them African Americans. Robinson had announced his retirement from baseball two months earlier, on January 5, after ten award-winning, trailblazing seasons with the Brooklyn Dodgers. "I'm through with baseball because I know that, in a matter of time, baseball would have been through with me," he said. The first-ballot Hall of Famer started work at Chock full o' Nuts on March 4, the Monday of state championship week for Bubba in the capital city of Texas.

On a Friday night in Pecos, Texas, at the Ephriam house on East Thirteenth Street, Loraine Ephriam called her children to come in for dinner from their play outside. Their father, Iria Earl Ephriam, as usual, had arrived home from work and was sitting in his truck, drinking from a can of beer, smoking a cigarette, and watching the neighborhood children play in his yard. "He never did drink or smoke in the house," Bubba said.

That night it was Bubba's turn to wash dishes. He remembers that he was nine or ten years old on this particular night—so likely it was 1947 or 1948 during Robinson's first or second season with the Brooklyn Dodgers. "I had a bad habit of not taking my turn at washing dishes," Bubba admitted.

After dinner, Iria gathered Bubba's sisters into his truck to take them to the local theater for a movie. Bubba didn't want to miss the fun. He hid the dinner dishes in the cabinet under the sink in his mother's kitchen, wiped the table clean, "eased" out the back door, and quietly climbed into the back of his father's truck.

As they arrived at the movie theater, one of Bubba's sisters glanced back and said, "Look, Daddy, there's Bubba."

"Boy, your Mama's going to get you when you get home," Iria said to Bubba as they walked together into the theater to enjoy a movie and popcorn.

After returning home from their evening in downtown Pecos, Iria and his daughters walked inside through the front door, but Bubba "slipped around and went in the back door and went to bed."

Saturday morning, Loraine found the dirty dishes, washed them, and went all day without saying a word about Bubba's negligence. "I thought it was over," Bubba said. "I went to bed. But just before I went to sleep, all of a sudden the covers came off."

Loraine was standing beside Bubba's bed. "She had taken my Dad's belt out of his trousers," Bubba said, "and that's what she had in her hand when the covers came off."

Bubba quickly offered to negotiate. "Mama, I'll wash the dishes."

"I've already washed them," his mother answered—just as quickly—before administering Bubba's punishment with his father's belt.

As Bubba now describes it, "Man, she tore me up."

The youngster she "tore up"—mischievous, but not unprincipled—was born on May 15, 1938, in Mercedes in the Rio Grande Valley a few miles from the US–Mexico border. His parents were Loraine Bernice Williams, eighteen-year-old domestic worker born January 2, 1920, in Yorktown, and Iria Earl Ephriam, twenty-nine-year-old migrant farmer born April 7, 1909, in Egypt, the oldest community in Wharton County, home to many prominent Texans during the state's republic days.

On the Sunday that Bubba was born, Loraine and Iria were across the Rio Grande in Mexico. After Loraine went into labor, the couple began their return trip across the river home to Mercedes, but they were briefly detained at the border for a routine search of their car before Iria convinced the authorities of their urgent need to return to the United States.

Bubba said his father wanted to take his wife to a hospital for the birth of the couple's first child (each had a child from a previous marriage), but Loraine's desire to go home prevailed. "Home" for the couple was a house on a farm owned by a Dutch family for whom Loraine and her mother, Estella Green Williams, worked. "She sent for the Dutch lady," Bubba said of his mother, "and she was the midwife who delivered me."

The couple named their firstborn Iria after his father, but there is no middle name on Bubba's birth certificate.

Loraine was a domestic worker, and she also took turns with other women from her and her husband's families watching Bubba and the young children while the adults and older children picked cotton and worked on nearby farms. "She was real nice," Bubba said of his mother, "and she was well thought of."

Iria was a migrant farmer and sharecropper on nearby farms—working with his brothers Bob, Funny, and Jack and his father, Dan Ephriam, driving a tractor and plowing with mules. "My dad and grandfather were the heads of our family," Bubba said.

"My mom was a Christian," he continued. "She was mind-set and heart-set on being content with what she had, where she was, and what she was doing. She would say, 'If the Lord wanted me to do anything different, he'd let me know.' She used what she had and did what she did to the best of her ability. She would always say, 'I'm blessed.'

"She was very sincere and honest about her church work. And she loved working in her yard and her garden. She always had a beautiful yard."

Loraine raised geese and chickens and sold their eggs, and she owned a Jersey dairy cow named Susie Q and also sold Susie Q's milk, butter, cream, and buttermilk. "People used to buy it from us in bottles," Bubba remembers. And after their move to West Texas, Loraine enjoyed fishing in the freshwater streams flowing from the mountains near Balmorhea.

"She was not afraid of work," Bubba said of his mother. "As long as I could remember, she was always working."

His sister Bernice agreed. "My mom worked all the time," she said. "We never went without anything."

Her home and her family came first for Loraine. Once while she was working as a cook at the bus station in Pecos, one of her daughters became ill at school. "She told her boss she had to go home because one of her children was sick," Bubba explained. "He told her that she wasn't going any place because he needed her there.

"She took her apron off right there in front of all those people in the bus station, tossed it in his chest, and said, 'My children need me more than you do. They come first.' And she walked out of that bus station and came on home.

"That's the way she was about her children," Bubba added. "Her home came first."

Was she strict? Bubba was slow to answer.

Was she lenient? "You know better than that," he promptly responded, laughing. "She had this way of calling my name. I would be out there playing ball, and you would hear that voice. 'Iria Junior.' Man, the marrow in your bones would start curling.

"I would go in there and try to act so good, but they didn't forget nothing," Bubba continued. "She would make you remember before she would 'light in' on you. She would be singing when she came through the door with a strap in her hand or a switch. I caught hold of switches and broke 'em. She would go and get another one. You didn't get away with nothing."

"We did a lot of kids' stuff," Bernice said. "We would play church and cut pictures out of Sears catalogs to make paper dolls. . . . We had two bicycles—one for boys and one for girls. We would have fun riding bicycles. All the neighbors' kids came to our house. We made dolls. We played 'cowboys and Indians.'"

William Ephriam concurred with their memories of Loraine, even though she wasn't his biological mother. "She was so good to me," William said. "She just loved me. She really did. She loved me even after we were grown. I think she loved me more than she did my brother. Somehow or other, the stepmother thing disappeared. There was no stepson.

"When my own mother was gone, she was my mother."

William said Loraine often baked two pans of biscuits—one for him and one for Bubba. "She was so kind," William continued. "She would make me a pan of biscuits, and she would make my brother a pan of biscuits. She was so good to us.

"She was a hard worker. She gave us instruction, and she kept us clean. When I look back on that now, I don't know how she did it. How in the world did she go to work and keep the house clean and keep our clothes clean and cook for us?

"And she was very religious," William added. "She went to church and brought the preacher home on Sundays for dinner. But we weren't going to let him get the last piece of chicken. . . . I didn't understand the sacrifice he made. And all he got out of it was a chicken dinner."

Three years older than Bubba, William Roland Ephriam was born June 17, 1935, in Burr, a small community a few miles from Wharton, to Iria Earl Ephriam and Ora Johnson, a young domestic worker who lived on a farm in Wharton County with her family of migrant farmers. As a boy, William lived with his mother, grew up and started school in Corpus Christi, spent some summers with his father, and moved with his mother to Sweetwater in about 1950 and to Pecos around 1951. He overcame serious injuries from an accident after he was hit by a car on May 13, 1949, while riding his bicycle.

William remembers praying from his hospital bed after the accident. He said a voice told him to "promise him something." The first answer from the thirteen-year-old William was, "I don't have nothing."

Two nights later, he prayed, "'If you let me walk again, I'll live for you.' I was broken and crippled, but I kept saying it. And I heard that voice again, 'Don't worry, William, you're going to be alright.' I knew from that moment on I was going to be okay."

He graduated from Carver High School in 1953, two years before integration in Pecos. He then married Ophelia Gray of Idabel, Oklahoma, on January 13, 1955, in Carlsbad, New Mexico, and worked for Greyhound at the bus station in Pecos. To keep his job, in 1967 he was forced to transfer to Denver, Colorado, where he became Greyhound's first Black ticket agent in its southwest region. He worked for Greyhound until 1977 when he entered full-time ministry in Colorado Springs at the Progressive Church of God in Christ. "I was always interested in the Bible," he said. He and Ophelia were married sixty years before her death in 2015.

William remembers being called into ministry in 1971. He became a pastor for a church in Colorado Springs in 1972 and commuted there from Denver, where he still resided with his family and worked for Greyhound. "The spirit of the Lord said, 'You're not giving enough time,' so I tried to balance it out by moving to Colorado Springs and commuting to Denver. That lasted two or three years. Finally, I had a religious experience and quit my job to devote full time to the church."

William said his maternal grandmother taught him to read, write, and count while they lived in Corpus Christi. He often stayed home while his older sister went to school. His grandmother would say, "Little William, always get an education. They can't take that away from you. They can take everything else, but they can't take away if you get an education.

"You are somebody." William's grandmother mentored her grandson.

"No matter what," he said, "I always knew I was more than what people thought I was. I didn't care if I was digging cesspools; I was somebody. My mother and grandmother instilled in me to get an education. At the end of the day, we had some money and the others were broke."

One of his first jobs in Corpus Christi was shining shoes near the police station on Leopard Street. One day, a man stopped to hire William to shine his cowboy boots—complete with their silver-tipped toes. "You know what the tips on these boots are for?" the man asked William. "To kick a nigger's ass."

Their father, Iria Earl, grew up working, picking cotton, and sharecropping on farms in Wharton County, playing baseball, and later managing Black baseball teams. "He was a quiet type of person," Bubba said. "He, too, was brought up in the church by my grandfather and grandmother. My grandfather was a deacon. They did a lot of singing in church. My dad could train you and teach you how to sing.

"Anything he did, he did it to perfection," Bubba added. "He knew exactly what he was talking about. And he was very strict."

Iria Earl moved his young family from Mercedes to Wharton around 1941 to be near and continue to work with his father, Dan, mother, Mattie, and brothers. A daughter, Ora Lee, the second of the couple's six biological children, was born to Iria and Loraine in Wharton in 1942 before Dan and Iria moved their families to West Texas—first to Balmorhea around 1943 and then to Pecos in about 1945, where Iria, with his brothers and father, helped build St. James Baptist Church.

"My daddy put a work ethic in me," William said, "and I wouldn't trade that for anything. He would say, 'If you take a job, do it right or don't do it.' He taught me how to drive a truck and use tools and how to be a mechanic."

William remembers that once his dad gave him a #2 scoop shovel as a gift. "What is this?" young William asked.

"This is yours."

William's next question: "What am I going to do with it?"

"You're going to use it."

William said his father was an entrepreneur. "He didn't work for nobody," William said. "He worked for himself. My dad was just a worker. If he had a concept of education beyond just working, it would have been a lot different. But he didn't. He would say, 'You need to go to work.'

"And he ain't going to buy you nothing," William continued. "He put you to work to earn money to buy your clothes. He will let you work to earn money. He helped you become independent. He would have us up on the truck at five o'clock in the morning.

"But on Saturday we would have us some money in our pocket. He took time for us. He did things for us. And he didn't criticize us. What he did for us was worth more than money. He gave us his time, and I wouldn't trade it for nothing. We wanted to be with him. We'd rather be with him than anywhere else."

Bernice, one of six children born to Loraine and Iria Earl, said the Ephriam children enjoyed going to the fields. "Daddy, can we go?" they would ask. "Yeah, you can go," he replied.

"My dad would take us to the fields to work," she continued. "We wanted to go. We'd get up early, early in the morning to go to the fields. We picked cotton. We chopped cotton. We even made our own clothes."

Iria played baseball with his sons William and Bubba, he taught them to repair car and truck engines, he took them to movies and to his father Dan's farm on the Pecos River near Barstow, and he enjoyed hunting and fishing with his sons.

"We would sit and talk baseball," Bubba added. "My dad would always tell us, 'You gotta have ball sense.' They taught us ball sense."

Bubba remembers playing baseball as a youngster with his dad and uncles Bob and Funny. "I always wanted to catch," Bubba said. "Uncle Funny would put that stuff on me, and I wanted that mitt to pop like it did for him when Uncle Bob was pitching. You could hear it echo all over the place.

"I remember I would say, 'Throw the ball, Bob.' He was burning me with that ball," Bubba continued. "But I could catch, man."

Iria owned two flatbed trucks to use in his farming business and cotton picking and two dump trucks for his construction business. He contracted for jobs and hired crews to work from each truck. They hauled sand, dirt, and gravel in the dump trucks to install lawns, driveways, and cesspools. Iria's crews dug huge holes in the ground and used railroad crossties to build walls for cesspools as reservoirs for household sewage.

In addition to his dislike for washing dishes, Bubba had an aversion to picking cotton. "Cotton and I just didn't have anything in common," he said. "I just could not pick cotton. I didn't like cotton, and cotton didn't like me."

As a youngster, when he should have been picking cotton, Bubba would carry thread, matchboxes, paperclips, and buttons to the field in his pockets, crawl and play on the ground under the stalks and leaves of the cotton plants, and "build little cities." He would tie thread to grasshoppers and lizards, give them names, and watch them pull matchboxes and sticks along the "streets" of his miniature cities.

"Somehow they would find me under there, and they would 'light in' on me," Bubba said. "I would start hollering, and people knew it was lunchtime. Every day I was getting a whipping. They called me the 'twelve o'clock whistle.'"

Today, Bubba recalls, "I learned something from that. You were born with a gift, but that does not mean your son or daughter will be born with the same gift. The field was the most important job for Black people back then. They could never see where my mindset was. They never thought about that—the ingenuity that I had, the gift that I had. I could build a city down there."

Often at the end of the workday, Bubba said, a field previously white with cotton would now be dark. The cotton had been picked. Except for one white streak—Bubba's row still had cotton on its stalks.

And sometimes the crews made mattresses with their sacks of cotton to rest and sleep. "I barely had enough cotton in my sack for a pillow," Bubba said. "Usually I would be sleeping on two layers of canvas. They would laugh at me about that."

Occasionally, Bubba also was guilty of adding rocks and dirt to his sack of cotton to increase its weight because they were paid per pound of cotton they had picked. William said, "We were asking ourselves, 'How was Bubba getting all this weight for his cotton sack?' Somebody dumped his sack, and he had all these rocks and dirt in it."

Historian Donald Holley, author of the book *The Second Great Emancipation*, calls picking cotton "one of the most backbreaking forms of stoop labor ever known." Picking one hundred pounds of cotton was like picking a hundred pounds of feathers. Holley says it took seventy bolls to make a single pound of cotton, which meant one of Iria Ephriam's pickers had to pick seven thousand bolls to reach one hundred pounds. Their hands cramped, and their fingers were callused and pricked by the barbed, five-point burrs that held each boll. Isabel Wilkerson, in her book *The Warmth of Other Suns*, says, "The work was not so much hazardous as it was mind-numbing and endless. . . . After ten or twelve hours, the pickers could barely stand up straight for all the stooping."

Iria later reassigned Bubba from his cotton-picking duties to help his grandmother Mattie and often permitted Bubba to leave the fields to hunt and fish for meat for their families.

In the 1950s, Texas was the leading cotton-producing state in the nation, and Reeves County emerged as one of the top counties in the state, with more than one hundred thousand bales of cotton processed annually by local cotton gins. Reeves produced more than a hundred thousand bales for at least eight straight years and ranked in the top ten among Texas's 254 counties for at least six straight years.

The 1961–62 *Texas Almanac* says Reeves County produced 118,571 bales of cotton in 1956 to rank seventh among counties (eight of the top ten counties were in West Texas). That put Reeves County at 3.3 percent of the total of 3,615 thousand bales in 1956 in Texas, which was 27.2 percent of the US total of 13,290 thousand bales. Lubbock County led the state in 1956 with 225,802 bales.

The blackland farms of East Texas—many of them tenant farms—produced up to 40 percent of the state's cotton annually in the first, second, and third decades of the century, according to the *Texas Almanac*. But the drought-resistant crop moved south and west, where cotton farmers took cattlemen's best land. The average size of cotton farms increased, the introduction of irrigation improved cultivation, and what was once a hand-labor crop that resisted mechanization began to benefit from power farming.

Bubba started his education in a one-room school for Black students in a small building—he called it "a little hut"—on a back corner of the campus of the public school in Balmorhea, where his family had moved around 1943. Alwyn Barr's book *Black Texans* says 81 percent of African American schools in Texas in 1944–45 had only one or two teachers.

Bubba studied and learned to read from pre-primer readers in Mrs. Shields's classroom with other children of migrant farmers who were working in the area. Their books were "hand-me-downs" from the White children's school, and their book covers were made of paper sacks from local grocery stores.

In her book *Caste: The Origins of Our Discontents*, Isabel Wilkerson says that from the time of Reconstruction to the civil rights era, "southern school boards spent as little as one-tenth the money on black schools as for white schools, openly starving them of resources that might afford them a chance to compete on level ground." Wilkerson adds, "School terms for black students were shorter by months, giving them less time in class and more time in the field for the enrichment of the ruling caste."

Alwyn Barr adds, "Negro schools generally had less funds for counsellors, vocational and science classrooms, health facilities, libraries, cafeterias, gyms, stadiums, and in rural areas buses. . . . Black schools generally cost less for original construction and deteriorated more rapidly as a result of inferior materials. Negro students could expect a much more limited range of courses, both academic and vocational. Thus conditions in Texas as in other southern states bore out the Supreme Court decisions in 1954 and 1955 in the Brown case that segregated schools were unequal and therefore unconstitutional."

Ephriam said of Balmorhea, "The only Blacks there were cotton pickers. When cotton season was over, that's when we went to school."

Ephriam remembers spending one cotton season with his family in Artesia, New Mexico (perhaps after they moved to Pecos about 1945), where his father had contracted for his crew of migrant farmers. It's unlikely that the children attended school that year. "They took us out of school traveling and going on cotton picks," he said. "We missed a lot of school. We got behind."

No records exist today at Balmorhea Independent School District to confirm Ephriam's attendance. An official at the school told him in 2017, "I was unable to locate any documents for you. . . . There was a fire a while back, and maybe it was destroyed."

There is a transcript for Ephriam in the office of the registrar at Pecos High School. It shows that he enrolled at George Washington Carver School in the fall of 1949 at the age of ten, was placed in third grade, successfully progressed through elementary school, and completed eighth grade at Carver at the end of the 1954–55 school year. He attended Pecos High School for two years—as a freshman in 1955–56 and a sophomore in 1956–57.

The transcript lists occupations of his father as "common laborer" and of his mother as "maid," and it says he participated in varsity basketball and baseball as a freshman and varsity football, basketball, and baseball as a sophomore. His academic performance gradually improved in elementary school; by the time he completed eighth grade in 1955 at Carver, he was making B's in all subjects. In two years of high school at PHS his grades were mostly C's with B's in safety education and shop.

Young Bubba Ephriam had a short walk of only one block to Carver each day after the school was moved to East Twelfth Street. His mother dressed him in khaki pants and a pressed shirt—always tucked in. "They put us in nice little clothes, little shirts with collars and pullover sweaters," he said. "They made sure we were clean—not dirty. That was the most important thing—cleanliness." He remembers usually having only one pair of shoes at a time—primarily to wear to church each Sunday. And he carried to school each day a sack lunch with a ham and cheese or bologna and cheese sandwich, an apple or orange, and maybe some banana or bread pudding.

Before the move, classes for Pecos's Black children were held in an old three-room wooden church building on Peach Street, where four Carver teachers taught as many as one hundred students in grades one through twelve. It was heated by burning mesquite roots in a potbelly stove. Later, a former military barracks was added before Carver moved in 1953 to its first permanent home in a new brick building on East Twelfth Street that had been constructed in 1952 by the Pecos school district.

Ephriam said Pecos's school for White students was "on the other side of town. . . . There were segregated sections of town—Black, Spanish and White—with their own schools."

He also participated in Boy Scouts of America (where he was the only Black member of an otherwise all-White troop), earned numerous merit badges, advanced through the ranks to Explorer Scout, and worked several summers as a dishwasher, cook, and wrangler for livestock at nearby Buffalo Trail Scout Ranch in the Davis Mountains under legendary scout leader John Oates.

"He was a marksman with a pistol, shotgun, and rifle," Bubba's son, Ira Earl, said of his father. "He was the best shot you've ever seen. He enjoyed camping, hunting, fishing, and riding horses. He was an all-around sportsman."

Bubba was a candidate for Eagle Scout when his scouting career ended. He said a scout executive in Pecos, Marty Stokes, encouraged him to join the all-White troop. He said Stokes told him, "You're the only colored boy in the state of Texas that's in a White troop."

Bubba added of Stokes, "He was always a nice fellow. I will never forget him. He knew of changes coming. He prepped me. He took me under his wings and helped me."

Bubba's introduction to basketball came after Sidney Lanier Sadler moved to Pecos in August 1949 to begin his teaching and coaching career. He and his wife, the former Billie Kaye Sample, were recent graduates of Samuel Huston College (now Huston-Tillotson University) in Austin, a private, historically Black college established in 1875 as the first institution of higher learning in the Texas capital.

"It was difficult to get teaching jobs because all the schools were segregated, and there were so few Black schools," Billie Sadler, a native of Fort Worth, told the *Pecos Enterprise* in 1993, five years after her husband's death on October 3, 1988. "There were only so many schools where they were hiring Black teachers. . . . Pecos had contacted our college."

The twenty-six-year-old Sidney was hired to teach high school students, and Billie taught grades one, two, and three. There were sixty-nine students at Carver when they arrived.

Sidney Sadler was born on July 4, 1923, in Valley Mills, Texas, was reared and attended school in nearby Waco, served in the US Army during World War II, and competed in basketball, football, and track and field in college. He was a teacher, principal, and coach in Pecos until his retirement in 1986 after a distinguished career. He was a member of the Texas State Teachers Association and the local chamber of commerce, treasurer for his congregation of the Methodist church, board chairman of the Pecos Housing Authority, and president of the Reeves County Retired Teachers Association. He received the prestigious Silver Beaver award given to adult leaders in Boy Scouts of America for his service as scoutmaster of the troop for African American boys where Bubba got his start in scouting.

Twice, he coached his Carver basketball team to the state tournament of the Prairie View Interscholastic League at Prairie View A&M College—in February 1954 and February 1955. As Carver principal, Sadler hired "quality people, educated teachers who were able to teach us and communicate with the kids," Williams said.

Bubba was in third grade when Sadler moved to Pecos, but he vividly remembers this Army veteran, college graduate, principal, teacher, and coach who became so instrumental in his life. "He came when we were real little," Ephriam said. "Coach Sadler introduced me to basketball, but the older guys were more into it than we were.

"We were little tots. He would call to us and say, 'You know what this is? It's a basketball.' It was the biggest thing I had ever seen. He told us to go in there and shoot. I was scared, but over the years, the little ones like us grew up and reached the basket.

"I told my brother, 'It looked like the world,'" Bubba said of the basketball that Coach Sadler held in front of their inquisitive faces. "My brother told me, 'He did give you the world.' I accomplished a lot of things."

Donnie Lee Hall, who also played for Sadler at Carver, said, "There was talent here. We just needed some coaching. He took over." Young Donnie Lee sat beside Coach Sadler in the team photograph of the 1953–54 Carver Wildcats, Sadler's first team to qualify for the PVIL (Prairie View Interscholastic League) state tournament.

Bubba said while he was still in primary grades, Sadler would come to his house, get him and William, and take them to play baseball or basketball. "Alright, you two, come on," he would say.

Carver's first court was actually a half-court with a dirt surface. The backboard and goal were nailed to a telephone pole. The first goal was a bicycle wheel. Later, when the school's new building was built in 1952, Carver students got their first official basketball court with regulation boundary lines, goals, and backboards—although it was still outdoors with a concrete surface adjacent to the school building.

"He organized baseball and basketball teams for us," Ephriam said of Sadler. "He'd get out there with us. He taught us the rules and how to play. We had sandlot football. He would get us out on the basketball court and talk to us.

"He inspired us," Ephriam added. "He believed every boy had ability. All he had to do was apply himself. He would paint them a picture of themselves doing these things.

"He walked around through the halls at school with a paddle and a piece of rawhide on it around his wrist. He maintained discipline. He didn't tolerate misbehavior from the first grade to seniors in high school. We called him Prof. He was a father, a friend, and a brother."

Bubba said that before Sadler came to Pecos, "We had no place, nobody to go to. We really didn't have anybody to take our problems to."

"Sidney Sadler took us under his wing," Hall said. "He made us into good basketball players. Bubba was lazy, but Coach Sadler could see something in somebody. Bubba was ready when he went to Pecos High School.

"Coach Sadler stayed on Bubba's butt all the time," Hall continued. "Bubba was draggin', but he finally got it out of him. Coach Sadler groomed him."

"When I first met him," William said of Sadler, "me and my brother were driving a truck for our daddy. When harvest time rolled around in the fields, we worked. We couldn't go to school.

"One year I missed sixty days of school," William continued. "Prof knew we had to work in the fields. He would bring our school work to us to do at home, and he would count it for our grades even though we weren't in class."

R. C. Christopher, a teammate of Ephriam's at both Carver and Pecos high schools, said that for many years he had photographs of four people on the wall of his dental office in Austin—his mother, Coach Sadler, and two presidents of Austin's Huston-Tillotson College, where he graduated in 1960. "I had the utmost respect in my life for that man," Christopher said. "He was somebody who wanted people to better themselves. He was interested in us as people.

"He knew our names, but he called all of us 'son,' and he called all the girls 'sister.' When he said 'son,' that was to let us know that he cared about us. And he wouldn't take no crap out of us. He was a father image to many of us. He dang sure was to me.

"He was what all the Black kids in Pecos in those days aspired to be, because we had no such person in our immediate family. . . . Prof was my first real positive image of something that I could aspire to. He was important to me in my life."

Christopher remembers Sadler's customary Stetson hat and his strict discipline. "Anything that went on at school, Mama knew about it, because he done called Mama. Prof would get me in his office and say the same words to me my Mama said. I understand them now."

In addition to introducing them to basketball, Sadler introduced to them the idea of finishing school. "Before that," William said, "most folks didn't think about finishing school. Finish for what? If you finished third grade, you were doing good.

"He invested himself in us," William continued. "He would teach you the basics. He would get out there and play basketball with us and watch us. He picked his kids out and trained us. You could understand what he was saying. He could communicate, and he was obsessed with raising the level of our lives.

"He saw the condition we were in. He knew life was better than that."

Sadler taught them "the science of basketball" and took them to see the Harlem Globetrotters play in nearby Odessa. "You could blindfold us," Bubba said, "and we could still run the figure eight. Pass and move, pass and move. . . .

"Anywhere in the key, even when his back is to the goal, the big man is supposed to know where that goal is," Bubba continued. "Prof taught us this. What are the markings on the floor for? I studied the science of the court."

Bubba perfected his hook shot through hours of practice and by studying Goose Tatum of the Harlem Globetrotters. "I never had to look at the goal to shoot," Bubba said. "I knew where I was at all times. I learned the science of basketball. That's why the Harlem Globetrotters wanted me."

Christopher explained, "Basketball is an offensive game. Mr. Naismith invented the game for you to put that ball in the hoop—not see who could hold the ball the longest. And I don't understand coaches today running up and down the sidelines. Prof didn't do that. He would say, 'Son, you forgot what we practiced?' If he's running up and down the sideline, you can't look over there and see what your coach is saying."

Christopher said when he started school "there was no such thing as a jump shot. Prof taught us to spin the ball in your fingers. He physically taught us how to shoot the basketball and shoot a jump shot. 'Son, you don't want to be shooting those flat shots. Shoot it high and let it roll off these two fingers. Move this hand out of the way. Flick your wrist.' I can remember it like it was yesterday.

"He taught us well," Christopher continued. "Offense, five-man wheel, variations, break off that wheel and get to the basket. He taught us how to use both hands, how to screen for teammates. He taught us how to handle the basketball. Prof was a good teacher, a good person, and a good coach."

William described Sadler as "one of a kind." He added, "I'll never forget him. . . . He was our principal, our policeman, and our friend all at the same time. He had a heart. He would take time with you. You could talk to him. You could carry on a conversation with him. He was somebody who cared about you. He was more than a principal. You weren't just a student."

Sadler became their mentor, father figure, and friend, and he molded and coached them into a skilled basketball team that challenged and defeated teams from much larger schools across West Texas. "Nobody in this area could touch us, a little Class B school," Bubba said. "We played Pecos High School, but their team was no match for ours."

Ephriam and Christopher were both members of Sadler's teams that made back-to-back trips to the PVIL state tournament—Ephriam as a seventh grader in 1954 and an eighth grader in 1955. The 1953–54 season was the first year that Class B teams could qualify for the PVIL state tournament; previously, they played only for district championships. "This is the first year the league has set up a playoff for Class B Negro schools," the *Pecos Enterprise* reported.

The PVIL was founded in 1920 as the Texas Interscholastic League for Colored Schools, and it existed until 1970.

In January 1954, Sadler, who had organized the Carver team about five years earlier, told the *Enterprise* that his team "has the material to go a long way toward the championship." This team included all but two players from his 1952–53 team that had won the district title.

According to the *Pecos Enterprise*, the 1953–54 Carver Wildcats started the season with a six-man varsity of two seniors—the high-scoring Raymond Minter and Curtis Johnson—junior Harvey Bailey, sophomore R. C. Christopher, and freshmen Bubba Ephriam and Willie Wright. Seven other freshmen played on the Carver B team.

Sadler believed in playing "the toughest teams around" early in the season to prepare his squad for the district tournament. So after wins over Black teams from Borger and Lubbock and losses to teams from Lubbock, Odessa, Amarillo, and Midland, the Wildcats improved their record to 3–4 in their seventh game—a 66–41 triumph on January 11 over a Midland squad with Minter, Sadler's senior center, scoring twenty-two points and the fifteen-year-old Ephriam leading with twenty-three points.

Later came wins over Hobbs, Littlefield, McCamey, and Slaton and losses to El Paso and Odessa before the PVIL District 2-B tournament on February 5–6, 1954, in Midland. The top eight teams advanced to Midland from among district members that included Ballinger, Big Spring, Brady, Brownwood, Coleman, Colorado City, Hamlin, Lamesa, McCamey, Pecos, Slaton, Stamford, and Sweetwater.

The *Enterprise* reported that Sadler's starting lineup for the district tournament was composed of seniors Minter and Johnson along with Christopher, Wright, and Eddie Walker. Minter scored twenty-one points in the Wildcats' opening game—an easy 63–26 win over McCamey—and he followed with eighteen points in a 60–36 win over Coleman and twenty-four points in a 58–43 come-from-behind win over Sweetwater in the final game. Carver outscored Sweetwater 15–3 in the third quarter to overcome a 30–24 halftime deficit and take their eleventh win of the season. Ephriam scored eleven points in the final.

At the PVIL state tournament two weeks later, the Wildcats were eliminated in their opening quarterfinal game, 55–51, by Cushing Mount Grove before 2,300 fans in the gymnasium at Prairie View A&M. The game was tied at forty-seven points to start the fourth quarter and at fifty late in the contest before Cushing pulled away for the win. The six-foot, three-inch Minter scored twenty points before leaving the game with five fouls. He was later named PVIL Class B all-state and committed to play college basketball at Prairie View A&M. Christopher (who scored twelve points in the final) and Wright (eighteen points) were selected honorable mention all-state.

The *Enterprise* reported that "the failure of senior Curtis Johnson and lanky Iria Ephriam to play up to their usual form cost the Carver team considerable points."

Sadler told the *Enterprise*, "The boys played well in spots and ragged in others. Cushing had a real fine team though, and our boys simply could not get used to the big crowd and excitement that goes with a championship tournament. They did a good job, however, considering everything, and we are proud of them."

The 1954 Class B trophy went to Malakoff Lincoln, which defeated Plainview 61–49 in the PVIL championship game. The other winners were Houston Wheatley in AAA, Paris Gibbons in AA, and Palestine Green Bay in A.

Meanwhile, as Bubba and his teammates were playing at Prairie View, in Missouri, three White high school teams announced they were withdrawing from the high school playoffs "because Negro schools are competing for the first time." The *Houston Informer* reported that thirty Negro schools—six in Class B and twenty-four in Class A—were eligible for the first time in 1954 in the Missouri State High School Activities Association. But parents of players at Keytesville voted seven to three to withdraw from the playoffs, and school boards at Huntsville and Deering decided to withdraw their teams.

The following year, despite the loss of Minter, Sadler's Carver team reached the PVIL state semifinals before ending its season. Christopher, the six-foot-three Ephriam, Walker, and Bailey returned and were joined by Billy Alsobrooks, Earlie Wilson, Sammy Brown, Willie Dixon, Charles Brown, W. A. Wright, and Donnie Lee Hall. Christopher was selected to the 1955 all-state team.

The Wildcats had warmed up for the February 4–5, 1955, district tournament in Midland with wins over teams from Black schools in Crane, El Paso, McCamey, and Midland and losses to teams from Crane, El Paso, Lubbock, and Odessa. At the district playoffs, they whipped Colorado City in the quarterfinals and Big Spring in the semifinals before taking down Sweetwater again in the final.

At the PVIL tournament on February 18–19, 1955, Carver knocked off defending state champion Malakoff Lincoln with a score of 70–38 in its quarterfinal game before falling again to Cushing Mount Grove in the semifinals, ending at 64–59. Cushing, coached by J. W. Moreland, went on to claim the Class B state title with a 60–52 victory over Detroit.

Houston Wheatley in AAA and Palestine Green Bay in A repeated as PVIL champions in 1955, and Victoria Gross was the AA winner with a 71–48 win over Odessa Blackshear. It was the sixth straight title for the Wheatley Wildcats and coach Collin Briggs with all-state players Roy Lee Washington and Carlton "Ding Dong" Bell.

Sadler's young team had come within five points of reaching the final game. With most of his players returning the following season, the Carver coach was already thinking about another PVIL appearance in 1956. "I shall return," he reportedly said as he was leaving.

So it's evident that Sadler and the Wildcats never imagined that the PVIL semifinal loss would be Carver's final basketball game. Six months later—in August 1955—the Pecos school board voted to integrate Pecos High School the following month. That decision closed Carver's high school and sent those students to PHS, leaving Carver to educate Black children only in grades one to eight.

Also, it ended the basketball coaching career of Sadler, who later was symbolically reunited in the Hall of Fame of the Prairie View Interscholastic League Coaches Association in 2014 in ceremonies in San Antonio with two of his former players, Christopher (inducted in 2010) and Ephriam (also inducted with Sadler in 2014).

And it marked the final game as teammates for Christopher and Ephriam wearing Carver uniforms. But their playing careers resumed the following season in 1955–56 as teammates at Pecos High School. They were the only two Carver Wildcats ever to play for the Pecos Eagles varsity basketball team.

THREE

THE "PROBLEM OF INTEGRATION" IN PECOS

Pecos School Board Votes to Integrate, August 4, 1955

Integration at High School Is Scheduled This September
Pecos Enterprise, Aug. 8, 1955

Area School Desegregation Policy Varies
Odessa American, Aug. 14, 1955

Segregation, Old Tradition, Broken Today
Odessa American, Sept. 1, 1955

Record Enrollment Expected in School Opening Wednesday
Pecos Enterprise, Sept. 5, 1955

The 1955–56 school year was a historic one for public schools in Pecos. Created in 1915 during the 34th session of the Texas legislature, the school district officially reached an enrollment of at least three thousand for the first time when 3,111 students registered for classes for its fortieth year.

Pecos was a growing city, the largest in Reeves County, and a regional commercial center for ranching, oil and gas, and agriculture. Farmers grew cotton, grain sorghum, cantaloupes, and other crops. It was located on the treeless, arid, rolling plains of West Texas and was once an important river crossing. The population in the county was 8,006 in 1940 and 11,745 in 1950, but it jumped 50.2 percent in 1960 to 17,644, including 12,728 residents in Pecos. The city and the county experienced rapid growth in the 1950s because of the expanded use of irrigation, increased cultivated acreage, and exploration and production of crude oil and natural gas.

Records in the superintendent's office show that school enrollment reached at least one thousand (1,096) for the first time in 1939–40 and at least two thousand (2,005) eleven years later in 1950–51. But it took just five years to gain another thousand students, growing 55.2 percent to reach an official count of 3,111 in September 1955. (In 1968–69, the district consolidated with Barstow and eclipsed four thousand with 4,108 students. Its record enrollment of 4,585 came in 1970–71.)

But the 1955–56 school year was historic for another—and more significant—reason. It was the first year of desegregation in Pecos, putting Black students in high school classrooms with White students for the first time.

It was fourteen months and two weeks after *Brown I* and just sixty-five days after the *Brown II* decision of the US Supreme Court that the Pecos Independent School District school board gathered on August 4, 1955, for a regular meeting in the office of superintendent Ray H. Whitley, a forty-one-year-old graduate of Southwest Texas State University in San Marcos (now Texas State University) who was in his tenth year as superintendent in Pecos.

Dr. Byron Lackey, a forty-eight-year-old local dentist, was presiding officer. According to minutes of the meeting, all seven board members were present, including J. E. "Jimmie" Hagar, vice president, and T. A. Robison, secretary. The other four trustees were Dr. I. G. Lunday, William R. "Bob" Bickley, Guy E. Walker, and Al Cook. Dr. Lunday and Hagar had just been elected four months earlier in April.

Dr. Lackey had moved to Pecos in 1934 after receiving his DDS degree from Baylor School of Dentistry. A native of Fort Worth, he graduated from Texas A&M University in 1930, earned all-Southwest Conference honors as a catcher for the Aggies, and played professional baseball with Houston in the Texas League and Omaha in the Western League before entering dental school in 1931. During his forty-two years as a dentist in Pecos before his retirement in 1976, he also was a member of the city council, active in the chamber of commerce, and president of West of the Pecos Museum.

Dr. Lackey's fellow board members had elected him president in April 1954.

The sixth item on the agenda that Thursday night was what the board minutes referred to as "the problem of integration." At least five people met with the board to discuss the issue—Mike Allison, George Barton, Reverend R. M. Montgomery, Sidney Sadler (principal, teacher, and coach at George Washington Carver, Pecos's school for Black students), and Banky Stocks.

The minutes included one paragraph about the board's consideration of integration—only one hundred words.

Dr. Lunday, a local doctor of chiropractic medicine, made a motion for the "integration of white and colored pupils," and his motion was seconded by Bickley. The motion called for a three-part desegregation plan—the integration of the high school in the upcoming school year of 1955–56, then the junior high school in 1956–57, and the elementary school in 1957–58.

A graduate of Mount Calm High School and Texas Chiropractic College, Dr. Lunday was also active in the Pecos community. He was a member of the volunteer fire department and served as the doctor for the Pecos High School Eagles football team. The 1951 PHS yearbook was dedicated to Dr. Lunday, "who has unselfishly and willingly devoted his services and time to our football team and school." The students wrote, "Our hats are off to 'Doc,' whom we have come to love through his loyal service and friendship that he has so kindly given us."

The board secretary recorded in the minutes that Dr. Lunday's motion carried by a narrow margin of four to three with Dr. Lackey, Dr. Lunday, Bickley, and Robison voting for the motion and Hagar, Walker, and Cook voting against.

The following Monday, August 8, 1955, the *Pecos Enterprise* reported: "Pecos Independent School District's board of trustees voted 4–3 Thursday night in favor of integration of Negro and white students in the local high school this September.

"The action is the first step of a gradual, three-phase integration program through which the entire school system will be desegregated within three years. . . .

"This makes the Pecos school system the first in the Trans Pecos or Permian Basin area to desegregate their system in accordance with a recent US Supreme Court ruling calling for national desegregation of school students."

The *Enterprise* said that at the meeting there was a discussion of "an apparent preference among the city's Negro population to keep their school, George W. Carver, on a segregation basis."

The newspaper added, "The members reached a majority agreement, however, that since the Supreme Court had made the ruling, it was not up to the board to decide whether or not integration should be exercised here. The court's decision made desegregation a law, and consequently it must be carried out." (In its account, the local newspaper did not identify who voted for and against Dr. Lunday's motion.)

Board members could not agree when to start integration—in September 1955 or September 1956—according to the *Enterprise*, but a majority favored immediate integration. The Carver School was maintained for Black students in grades one through eight at least for the 1955–56 school year.

Registration for high school students began eighteen days later, on Monday, August 22, 1955. Principal L. R. Hudson told the *Pecos Enterprise* that school officials were expecting a sizable increase in enrollment in the city's growing school system. Two additional classrooms were being built at South Pecos Elementary School because of overcrowding.

Classes began Wednesday, September 7, with officials "expecting one of the largest enrollments in the Pecos Independent School District's history." The *Enterprise* said the two new classrooms for South Pecos Elementary would not be ready for the start of school, so "two classes of South Pecos students will have to be taught at Pecos Elementary School."

Superintendent Whitley told members of the Lions Club one week later that enrollment reached 3,081, including 539 students in Pecos High School. Enrollment had increased 5.5 percent from 1953 to 1954, Whitley said, but it jumped 11.8 percent from 1954 to 1955. PHS previously was the smallest school in its Class AA district, but the *Pecos Enterprise* said September 15 that it "now ranks as the largest high school."

The *Enterprise* added, "In fact, there is a good possibility that Pecos may be forced to jump from its present AA football classification to the higher AAA classification before too long."

Pecos ISD had to hire thirty-four new teachers for 1955–56, bringing the total to one hundred thirty-four teachers in the school district. "I am proud of the teachers in our school system and of the work they are doing," Whitley said.

After two weeks of classes, the *Enterprise* reported enrollment had climbed to 3,149.

The school district was outgrowing even its newest facilities. In 1952, Pecos ISD built new buildings for East Pecos Junior High School, North and South Pecos elementary schools, and George Washington Carver School.

The growth was occurring under the leadership of Whitley, who worked for thirty-five years as the superintendent in Pecos after serving ten years as a teacher and coach. A graduate of Hallettsville High School, he served on the executive committee of the Texas State Teachers Association and was a member of the Texas Association of School Administrators. Whitley was named outstanding citizen of Pecos in 1973 by the chamber of commerce. (He died on September 26, 2006, at the age of ninety-two.)

Enrollment growth led Whitley and the school board to call another bond election for the following spring. On March 27, 1956, local voters approved more upgrades costing four hundred thousand dollars by a margin of 304 to 173, including a new auditorium at the high school, nine more classrooms at South Pecos Elementary, two new classrooms at North Pecos Elementary, and repairs to the junior high school. It was the fifth bond election in the past ten years, according to the *Enterprise*, resulting in $1.5 million in improvements.

On May 10, 1956, the board voted to delay the implementation of the second and third phases of its integration plan "because of the lack of facilities and the expense involved in the integration of children in the elementary and junior high grades and the numerous attendant problems in connection therewith."

Bubba Ephriam was seventeen years of age in September 1955 when he began attending classes as one of the first African American students at Pecos High School. Today he says he does not recall immediately hearing the news of the 1954 US Supreme Court decision or the vote on August 4, 1955, by the Pecos school board to integrate the local high school.

When classes ended at Carver in May 1955, Ephriam and his classmates and teammates assumed they would be returning to Carver in the fall. Most members of the same Wildcats basketball team that had just made its second straight appearance in the PVIL state tournament at Prairie View A&M College were expected to return in the fall of 1955.

Ephriam said his parents "weren't up-to-date about stuff like that. They didn't understand. They didn't know." But he said they were in favor of his move to PHS despite the fact that some parents wanted their children to remain at Carver. "Some of that was because of fear," Bubba added. "People told my parents of threats, and some feared they might not get jobs [if their children attended schools for White children]."

Bubba's grandmother Mattie Ephriam, who was a schoolteacher before she married, realized the value of continuing their education. "When this started happening," Bubba said, "she was informing our family about the importance of education. There was never anything negative from my parents about the school being integrated. My grandmother prepped them."

Donnie Lee Hall, one of the youngest members of Sadler's PVIL playoff teams at Carver, acknowledged that Ephriam "broke the ice for the boys who came behind me." But Hall was one of the many former Carver players who never played for Pecos High School. "I attended Pecos High," he explained, "but I didn't stay long. You know how it is."

Bubba's brother, William, a 1953 graduate of Carver who was married at the time of integration and working at the local Greyhound bus station, believes Sidney Sadler "had a lot to do with [the decision to desegregate]. Our community had tremendous respect for him. He felt it was necessary for progress. He told me, 'They are going to integrate the school, William.' So I got involved because of my brother.

"Prof was responsible for the smooth transition," William added. "I don't remember any violence or anything like that happening in Pecos."

R. C. Christopher, Bubba's teammate on basketball teams at both Carver and Pecos high schools, also remembers hearing the news from Sadler. "R. C., you'll be going up to the high school next year," Sadler told Christopher.

"I wonder if they are going to let me play basketball?" Christopher responded.

Integration meant the seventeen-year-old Christopher would be changing schools—leaving George Washington Carver School for the first time—for his senior year. He said his parents, Roscoe and Emily Christopher, who followed his grandfather John Christopher to West Texas about 1941, were "unwitting victims of the time" and unaware of the decision by the Pecos school board.

"My parents didn't know things about history," Christopher said. "If my daddy had his way about it, we'd be just like him. He finished third grade and could barely write his name.

"My mama was concerned about keeping clothes on our back, not school board stuff," he continued. "Pecos was just a nondescript little ol' town. There were no Black activists. There weren't any die-hard, active, nigger-hating White folks in Pecos, either."

Billy Jim Simmons, Bubba's teammate for two seasons at PHS, agreed. "Pecos was a good town to integrate," he said. "We were lucky in Pecos. It wasn't the kind of town that would cause problems. I would have been real surprised if we had that sort of thing.

"I don't think the kids at Pecos High School looked at [Black students] any different than they did Whites. We were a town that just didn't have a problem with Black people. There weren't these smart-aleck Blacks that would try to cause trouble or Whites that caused trouble. We didn't have that situation.

"I was around," Simmons continued. "We would see them around Pecos. They had their part of town, and we had our part of town. . . . The coloreds may have been worried about how they were going to be treated, but I don't know why. I don't know where it would have come from. It wouldn't have come from the kids."

Sadler's wife, Billie, added, "We thought it went pretty well. We did get along in Pecos."

Bubba and William said many African Americans in Pecos believed Sadler should have been hired to coach basketball at the newly integrated Pecos High School. William explained, "The problem we had with it was we felt he should have been the coach of the basketball team." Sadler had coached the Carver basketball team to the Prairie View Interscholastic League state tournament the previous two years, in February 1954 and February 1955. His wife, a former Pecos elementary school teacher and kindergarten principal, later served on the Pecos ISD school board.

"We thought the only reason they wanted us was for the basketball team," William continued. "Prof had a *team*. He had brought them along since they were little guys, so now we wondered what would happen."

Today William remembers, "We thought we wanted integration. . . . We had our own stores, little groceries, little shoe shops. But we lost our community with integration."

Bubba concluded, "Integration took me away from the Black kids."

But his daughter, Iria Loraine Abram, said he "opened the door and helped to integrate basketball in Texas—and not just to the leagues for Black students. He recalls those days with a lot of love for basketball and the camaraderie with the guys without all the politics."

Eight months after the board's decision to integrate Pecos schools, three of the four trustees who favored integration were voted off the board. In volume 2 of *Pecos: A History of the Pioneer West*, Alton Hughes writes, "Byron [Lackey] was a casualty of the anti-desegregation sentiment and failed to be reelected. Time has proven that the board on which Byron served made a wise decision, although unpopular at the time."

Three members of the school board were to be elected or reelected to three-year terms in an election held on April 7, 1956. Minutes of the board show that 2,160 people came to the polls that day, and the top three of at least eleven candidates were board newcomers Tommy Wheelis (25.6 percent), William A. Honaker (24.7 percent), and Richard L. Toll (19.0 percent).

Failing to win reelection were Dr. Lackey (11.5 percent), Bickley (10.4 percent), and Robison (8.4 percent).

(Later that same year, Wheelis and Honaker resigned and were replaced by board appointment with Norman Eisenwine and Floyd Brownlee Jr. Wheelis resigned, according to board minutes, because he was a director of the bank that held the Pecos ISD account. Guy Walker was elected president of the new board after Dr. Lackey's departure.)

The speculation by the *Pecos Enterprise* that Pecos High School would be forced to move to Class AAA proved to be true. The very next year, 1956–57, enrollment at PHS grew to 561 students (among the record 3,168 in the district). And despite the fact that it had just left Class AA and now was in its first year in Class AAA, already it was the largest school in its new district.

After a disappointing end to the 1955–56 season, its last in Class AA, the Pecos Eagles basketball team—with Bubba Ephriam in his second year in a starring role—was ready for the challenge of Class AAA in 1956–57 in what proved to be a memorable season.

FOUR

SUPREME COURT DECISIONS INVALIDATE TEXAS LAWS

Desegregation in Texas Public Schools

High Court Bans School Segregation; 9–to–0 Decision Grants Time to Comply
New York Times, May 18, 1954

Shivers to Fight Ruling for Negroes in Schools
Abilene Reporter-News, June 22, 1954

Ruling Gives Green Light to Schools' Integration
Odessa American, Aug. 26, 1955

Schools Will Receive State Funds as Usual
Odessa American, Sept. 22, 1955

Court OKs Funds for Mixed Schools
Fort Worth Star-Telegram, Oct. 13, 1955

One week after the US Supreme Court issued its landmark decision in *Brown v. Board of Education*, Dr. J. W. Edgar, Texas's commissioner of education, sent a letter to the superintendents of all public schools in the state. After conferring with John Ben Shepperd, the Texas attorney general, Dr. Edgar told the superintendents that all public schools in the state should continue to operate as segregated schools during the 1954–55 school year. In his letter dated May 24, 1954, Dr. Edgar said the state's system of public schools was obligated to continue to operate under the state constitution and laws adopted by the state legislature.

Commissioner Edgar was supported by a resolution of the State Board of Education, which stated that until a final decree was handed down by the US Supreme Court implementing its decision, Texas segregation laws would remain in effect.

According to the United States Commission on Civil Rights, in one of a series of reports in 1963 on the progress of civil rights in public schools in the South, "The doctrine of separate schools for white and Negro children was enshrined in Texas both by custom and by law." The Texas Constitution, article 7, section 7, stated, "Separate schools shall be provided for the white and colored children, and impartial provision shall be made for both."

And the Texas Revised Statutes, article 2900, further declared, "No white children shall attend schools supported for colored children, nor shall colored children attend schools supported for white children."

Certainly, the governor, Allan Shivers, was complicit. The day Chief Justice Earl Warren announced the Supreme Court's decision, Governor Shivers told the *Austin American-Statesman*, "Sometimes those who seek reforms go so far that the evils of the reform movement are more onerous than the evils they're trying to remedy."

Of the court's decision, Governor Shivers said, "It will require years to comply with the order for integration of schools. I hope that it can be worked out so as not to cause damage to the school children and that the children themselves will not be placed at a disadvantage." He said the problems were "too big to be solved in days or weeks or months. Just saying we abolish segregation doesn't cure it. It doesn't accomplish anything. What is done about enforcing it is the important thing."

The following day, he added, "The problem would be more acute in east Texas than in other sections of the state." (In the early 1950s, African Americans composed 13 percent of the population in Texas, but 90 percent of them lived in eighty-eight counties in the northeast and east-central areas of Texas. Robyn Duff Ladino, historian and social scientist, says in *Desegregating Texas Schools: Eisenhower, Shivers, and the Crisis at Mansfield High*, "In general, East, Central, and Coastal Texas strongly opposed integration. West Texas held a more liberal attitude, accepting that changes toward integration seemed inevitable.")

Shivers, who was elected lieutenant governor in 1946 and took office on January 21, 1947, unexpectedly became governor about two years later on July 11, 1949, upon the death of Governor Beauford H. Jester. Shivers, a veteran of the US Army and former state senator who was born in Lufkin and graduated from the University of Texas, developed a powerful political machine to run the state and the Democratic Party, the dominant political party in Texas at the time. Three times, he was elected by an overwhelming margin to serve as governor in 1950, 1952, and 1954.

In September 1954 (four months after the Supreme Court's *Brown I* decision), the Texas Democratic Party, at its convention in Mineral Wells under the leadership of Governor Shivers, adopted a platform that resurrected the doctrine of "separate but equal" and pronounced the *Brown* decision an "unwarranted invasion of states' rights."

(In 1953, while the Supreme Court was considering the case, Governor Shivers had written to President Dwight D. Eisenhower, "There is nothing more local than the public school system.")

In his campaign for reelection in 1954, during his Democratic primary campaign against Ralph W. Yarborough, Shivers promised to contest the US Supreme Court's decision in Texas. Speaking on June 21 in his hometown of Lufkin, according to the Associated Press, he said, "We are going to keep running the public schools of Texas as they are today."

Ladino says in *Desegregating Texas Schools* that in Lufkin, Shivers "began to take a more defiant stand against the decision." The governor said,

> All of my instincts, my political philosophy, my experiences and my common sense revolt against this Supreme Court decision. It is an unwarranted invasion of the constitutional rights of the states. . . .
>
> My administration has already told the local school districts that, as far as the state of Texas is concerned, there are no changes to be made. . . . We are going to keep the system that we know is best. No law, no court, can wreck what God has made. Nobody can pass a law and change it.

Shivers declared that integration would not take place in Texas while he was governor.

Attorney General Shepperd joined the governor in his clash with the Supreme Court, which had invited Southern states to file briefs and present oral statements in *Brown II* implementation arguments. As Ladino quotes, Shepperd told the court, "It is clear that any attempt to effect immediate or too-sudden mixture of white and colored pupils, especially if made by an authority outside the individual school district, would be rash, imprudent, and unrealistic. . . . It is our problem—let us solve it."

The 54th session of the Texas legislature opened on January 11, 1955. Governor Shivers's speech to the assembled senators and representatives included a recommendation that "no change be made in our system of public education until—and maybe not then—the Supreme Court gives us its complete mandate."

And the legislature followed his direction; no changes were made in the first legislative session to be conducted in Texas after the Supreme Court decision.

Southern School News, in its review of the decade following *Brown v. Board of Education* published in May 1964, said that "the transition from segregated to desegregated schools followed three patterns in the region: Compliance, tokenism and defiance." The *School News* added,

> Several districts, usually larger cities in the border area, immediately accepted the rulings in the School Segregation Cases and admitted large numbers of Negroes to schools with whites. Other districts desegregated on a token basis—admitting a small number of Negroes to biracial schools as an indication of good faith, but resisting anything more.
>
> The third approach to the decisions—defiance—usually consisted of officials employing every means available to prevent Negroes from entering the public schools with whites.

The chief means of achieving delay in compliance, the *School News* said, were legislation and litigation. Dozens of laws were passed in Southern states that delayed desegregation or made it difficult.

Within the first two school years after May 17, 1954, according to the *Southern School News*, only three Southern states—Arkansas, Tennessee, and Texas—had some biracial classes. No additional states acted in 1956–57, then a single Southern state acted in each of the next five years: North Carolina in 1957–58, Virginia in 1958–59, Florida in 1959–60, Louisiana in 1960–61, and Georgia in 1961–62. In that first decade, most school districts that desegregated acted voluntarily.

In Texas, El Paso became the first large city to decide to desegregate when its school board voted six to one in June 1955, according to the United States Commission on Civil Rights, to bring its 501 Black students and 24,916 White students together in September 1955.

The following month, July 1955, El Paso superintendent Mortimer Brown called Rodney James Kidd, the UIL director, to inform him that El Paso schools were desegregating and to ask if "certain colored students" transferring to previously all-White schools would be eligible to compete in UIL athletics. According to Bobby Hawthorne—writing in "The University Interscholastic League and the Integration of Texas High School Athletics" in *The Texas Book*—Kidd said, "It was the first time our committee had before it the eligibility of Negro students representing white high schools."

Kidd convened members of the UIL executive committee, who released a statement that concluded, "The state executive committee of the Interscholastic League interpret the language 'public white school' as not excluding any public school in Texas which has previously limited its enrollment to white students, but which has modified its rules so as to admit students of the Negro race."

Hawthorne, journalist and former UIL director of academics, noted in *The Texas Book* that "the League took pains to assure schools that the ruling would not permit black schools to enroll a couple of white students and then petition for UIL membership."

After Friona became the first (and only) school in Texas to integrate in 1954–55, various publications (including the Associated Press, the United States Commission on Civil Rights, and Ladino's *Desegregating Texas Schools*) reported that Pecos, El Paso, and about sixty other school districts in the state followed with either full or a gradual system of integration in the 1955–56 school year. They included San Antonio, Austin, Corpus Christi, Waco, Kerrville, Denison, Hillsboro, Harlingen, and Pecos's West Texas neighbors in Big Spring, Odessa, Lubbock, Andrews, San Angelo, Monahans, Fort Stockton, and McCamey.

The Associated Press reported on September 6, 1955, "Integration of white and Negro students went smoothly where it was tried."

In Big Spring, 135 miles east of Pecos, the school board voted to integrate the first six grades of its elementary school in 1955–56. But a group of four local taxpayers, including a school trustee, and the Texas Citizens Council sought injunctions to stop the payment of state funds to desegregated schools in an attempt to prevent integration. But the 118th District Court, in a decision announced on August 26, 1955, in Big Spring by Judge Charlie N. Sullivan to a crowd of about 150 people, denied the injunctions, ruled void the segregation portions of the Texas school finance laws, and said in effect that public schools could go ahead and immediately desegregate if they wanted.

The Associated Press called it "the first clear test of the state's school laws." Attorney General Shepperd had asked that no state payments be made to desegregated schools, and he specifically said the Big Spring ISD disqualified itself from receiving state funds by integrating. Judge Sullivan said he would enter an order declaring that all provisions of the school finance laws pertaining to segregation were null and void.

The Texas Citizens Council, formed to fight desegregation in the state and represented by Dallas attorney Ross Carlton, said it would appeal the decision to the Texas Supreme Court. Carlton argued, "State funds may only be apportioned and used in separated white and Negro schools." The Big Spring board and superintendent W. C. Blankenship were represented by attorney Guilford Jones.

The state's supreme court cut short its summer vacation and began meeting September 16 to hear oral arguments for the appeal in *R. E. McKinney et al v. W. C. Blankenship et al.* The Associated Press said, "The court's ruling is expected to have a strong effect on how soon integration is accomplished across the state."

(Dr. Edgar, the state's commissioner of education, said on September 22 that state payments were being mailed to schools throughout Texas, according to the Associated Press, "without reference to whether a school has integrated Negro and white students." He told reporters that pending litigation before the supreme court concerning the use of state aid in integrated schools would not delay September payments. "No one has enjoined us from doing so," Dr. Edgar said. "We certainly don't feel we have authority to withhold funds.")

On October 12, 1955, the nine-man Supreme Court of Texas unanimously upheld the lower court's decision, denied the injunctions, and ruled that the laws on segregation in the state constitution and statutes were invalidated by the decision of the US Supreme Court. Ladino writes, "Texas segregationists received a blow from the state supreme court."

In a piece titled "Texas Supreme Court Knocks Out School Segregation Law," the *Southern School News* reported in November 1955, "In the Texas court's main opinion, Associate Justice Few Brewster labeled as 'utterly without merit' the argument that Texas segregation laws were unaffected by the U.S. Supreme Court decision." On record as concurring were Justices Meade F. Griffin and Ruel C. Walker.

Governor Shivers and Attorney General Shepperd took the ruling as final. They considered an appeal to the US Supreme Court futile. As *School News* recorded, Shepperd said, "This settles the law in Texas on a statewide basis, but integration will still be a district-by-district matter. As attorney general I will, of course, as I have in the past, uphold the law as declared by the court or such new laws on the subject as may be passed by the legislature." Governor Shivers remained combatant. According to the Associated Press, he said, "In light of these decisions, no school district should feel compelled to take hasty or unnecessary action."

Southern School News said in November 1955 that twenty-one Black students were eligible to attend White schools in Big Spring. Of those, seven decided to enroll, and fourteen chose to continue at the segregated school.

With the fear of possibly losing state funds alleviated, voluntary desegregation in South and West Texas continued. The civil rights commission said that by the end of the 1956–57 school year, 145 school districts in Texas had either desegregated completely or had initiated programs of gradual compliance.

It was apparent, however, that resistance to desegregation still existed in many other communities, especially those with larger African American populations. The commission said in those cities, "No voluntary action to desegregate the schools would be taken and that Negro students would be required to resort to the federal courts to have their constitutional rights vindicated."

Mansfield was the first school district in the state to be ordered to desegregate by federal courts. The US District Court for the Northern District of Texas and the Fifth Circuit Court of Appeals declared on August 27, 1956, the right of the Black plaintiffs to attend Mansfield High School in September 1956 and prohibited school authorities from refusing the plaintiffs' admission to the school.

But during the first two days of registration, August 30–31, 1956, an estimated 250 to 400 people gathered at the school to protest the court order and confront the three Black students who were expected to enroll. "Militant segregationists seemed to be in control," the civil rights commission said in its report. Local law enforcement officers were in attendance, but reportedly made no move to enforce the desegregation order.

The commission said Mansfield was "the only community in the state to react with violence to an order to desegregate its public schools." Ladino says an effigy packed with straw and with its head and hands painted Black was hung downtown (with a sign that said "THIS NEGRO TRIED TO ENTER A WHITE SCHOOL") and another was hung on the flagpole at the high school.

Governor Shivers ordered Texas Rangers to help preserve the peace, and the civil rights commission said he urged Mansfield school authorities to "transfer out of the district any scholastics, white or colored, whose attendance or attempts to attend Mansfield High School would reasonably be calculated to incite violence."

In the face of this opposition and intimidation, the commission said, no Black students appeared at the school to register. And neither did they appear September 4 for the first day of classes. Ladino says in *Desegregating*

Texas Schools, "The African American parents chose not to subject their teenaged children to the hatred and animosity exemplified by the radical segregationists."

Mansfield operated a separate school for its Black elementary students, but Black students of high school age were required to travel about twenty-five miles daily to Fort Worth to attend Terrell High School. Ladino says Mansfield High School remained segregated for nine more years; African American teenagers from Mansfield were not allowed to attend classes in their hometown until 1965.

The next session of the Texas legislature, the 55th, convened January 8, 1957, under the direction of a new Democratic governor, Marion Price Daniel II, a Baylor University graduate and former US senator from Dayton, Texas, who also was opposed to desegregation and who would be elected governor a total of three times (1956, 1958, and 1960). As a US senator, he had joined eighteen other senators and eighty-two members of the US House of Representatives in signing the 1956 Southern Manifesto, which condemned the Supreme Court's 1954 *Brown v. Board* decision, encouraged states to resist implementing it, and accused the US Supreme Court of "clear abuse of judicial power."

A former Texas attorney general, speaker of the Texas House of Representatives, and later a member of the Texas Supreme Court, Governor Daniel assured the legislature that he favored continued segregation.

The Texas legislature passed several laws aimed at preventing desegregation in 1957. The primary one prohibited desegregation by a school district without prior approval from a majority of its voters. The stated penalty included the loss of state funds and fines of up to one thousand dollars against officials who took such action.

Southern School News said the penalties never were invoked, but the act did slow desegregation. In its 1963 report on the progress of integration in Texas, the United States Commission on Civil Rights said, "The referendum law had the immediate effect of bringing voluntary desegregation to a virtual standstill. Prior to this time, the local boards were often able quietly to establish a policy of desegregation while arousing a minimum of public emotion; it now became necessary to throw the question open to public debate."

According to the Texas Association of School Boards, Pleasanton ISD was the first district to hold an election to integrate its schools under this law. The measure passed by a four to one margin.

In the five years the referendum law was in effect (from 1957 until it was declared unconstitutional on December 10, 1962, by Attorney General Will Wilson), ten school districts in the state—out of the fifteen that held referendums—were desegregated after voter approval. According to the civil rights commission, all were relatively small and had few African American students.

Wilson advised the Texas Education Agency that it could pay state funds to school districts that desegregated by board action or court action without the need for a referendum. He quoted a ruling by the United States Court of Appeals for the Fifth Circuit in *Boson v. Rippy*: "Recognition and enforcement of constitutional rights cannot be made contingent upon the result of any election."

According to *Southern School News*, no effort was made by court action to overturn Wilson's opinion. Wilson's successor, the newly elected Attorney General Waggoner Carr, said he would abide by his predecessor's ruling.

In the state's two largest cities, Houston and Dallas, federal courts became the principal battlegrounds in the legal struggle for equal rights in public schools. Protracted litigation resulted in court decrees to desegregate under grade-a-year plans beginning in September 1960 in Houston and September 1961 in Dallas.

A decision by the federal government also accelerated the progress of desegregation. According to the civil rights commission, the federal government said that "after September 1, 1963, segregated public schools would be considered 'unsuitable' for dependents of military personnel living on base." School integration would be required "to retain Federal funds for the education of such children." The civil rights commission said the Abilene Independent School District "began desegregation in January 1963, when its school board authorized the admission of 38 Negro pupils to a previously all-white elementary school serving the children of personnel from a nearby air force base."

According to a historical marker on the Dyess school campus prepared by the Texas Historical Commission, "African American military families living on Dyess Air Force Base in Abilene previously were forced to send their children [across town] to the segregated Woodson School." The Abilene school board voted unanimously on January 14, 1963, to begin integrating schools in Abilene ISD. Dyess Elementary School was selected as the first campus in Abilene ISD to integrate kindergarten through sixth grade, with Black students beginning to attend one week later on January 21.

Other Abilene ISD schools gradually began integrating kindergarten through sixth grade in the fall of 1963. All Abilene public schools were integrated by 1970—sixteen years after the *Brown v. Board of Education* ruling.

The Civil Rights Act of 1964 also was a landmark civil rights and US labor law that outlawed discrimination based on race, color, religion, gender, or national origin. Signed into law on July 2, 1964, by President Lyndon B. Johnson, it prohibited unequal application of voter registration requirements and racial segregation in schools, employment, and public accommodations. It came 101 years after Abraham Lincoln signed the Emancipation Proclamation, which granted rights to African Americans that would have to be reiterated many times long after Lincoln was gone.

The US Supreme Court is the top layer in a three-tiered federal court system. Below it are the federal courts of appeals, which hear appeals from federal district courts, which constitute the first, or trial, layer of the system. The federal court system is the proper venue when plaintiffs assert that a state has violated the US Constitution by depriving them of their federal right for equal treatment.

The decision of the US Supreme Court announced on May 17, 1954, applied to five separate cases that were combined for arguments before the court. These were cases originally filed in 1950 in Clarendon County, South Carolina, and in the District of Columbia and in 1951 in Prince Edward

County, Virginia, in New Castle County, Delaware, and in Topeka, Kansas (*Oliver Brown et al v. Board of Education of Topeka, Kansas, et al*). They were pooled together by the court because of their similarities and became known under one common title, *Brown v. Board of Education.*

The plaintiffs said segregation violated the equal protection clause of the Fourteenth Amendment. They challenged school segregation on all levels and the US Supreme Court's ruling from May 18, 1896, in *Homer A. Plessy v. John H. Ferguson* that "equal but separate accommodations for white and colored passengers" on trains in Louisiana were constitutional—a ruling that would stand for nearly sixty years.

That vote was seven to one to maintain separate train cars for Black and White passengers in Louisiana. One justice, David J. Brewer, took no part in the consideration or decision of the case for what Richard Kluger says, in *Simple Justice: The History of Brown v. Board of Education and Black America's Struggle for Equality*, are unknown reasons. The author of the majority opinion in *Plessy* was Henry Billings Brown, and the lone dissent came from John Marshall Harlan, a descendent of a Kentucky slave-owning family who wrote, "The destinies of the two races in this country are indissolubly linked together, and the interests of both require that the common government of all shall not permit the seeds of race hate to be planted under the sanction of law."

According to Kluger, Harlan added in his dissent:

> "The white race deems itself to be the dominant race in this country. And so it is, in prestige, in achievements, in education, in wealth and in power. . . . But in view of the Constitution, in the eye of the law, there is in this country no superior, dominant, ruling class of citizens. There is no caste here. Our Constitution is color-blind, and neither knows nor tolerates classes among its citizens. In respect of civil rights, all citizens are equal before the law. The humblest is the peer of the most powerful. The law regards man as man and takes no account of his surroundings or of his color when his civil rights as guaranteed by the supreme law of the land are involved."

The 1896 decision of the Supreme Court was loathed by Black people across the nation, but it remained the disgraceful law for fifty-eight years. Peter Irons, in his book *A People's History of the Supreme Court*, says *Plessy v. Ferguson* is "second only to *Dred Scott* [1857] in Supreme Court infamy." NAACP counsel Charles Hamilton Houston (1895–1950) was the dean at Howard University School of Law where he trained a generation of lawyers, including Thurgood Marshall, to fight for civil rights. According to Peter Canellos in *The Great Dissenter*, Houston believed that "Black people could never improve their lot unless they learned to make the legal fight themselves. Waiting until whites woke up would get them nowhere."

"In the early 1950s, twenty-one states and the District of Columbia still had mandatory or optional school segregation. . . . Precedent strongly supported it. Of forty-four challenges to school segregation adjudicated by state appellate courts and lower federal courts between 1865 and 1935, not a single one had succeeded," according to Michael J. Klarman in *From Jim Crow to Civil Rights*. Justice Felix Frankfurter reportedly said in a conference, "Plessy is right."

Klarman adds, "Lower courts were not blazing new trails on this issue as they often do before the high court's momentous constitutional rulings. . . . *Brown* was not inevitable in 1954."

The first federal court case to hold that separate schools for children of color were not equal and that such conduct violated their constitutional rights was *Mendez v. Westminster School District et al* (1946) and its appellate case *Westminster v. Mendez* (1947) in California. The case provided an important link in a series of school desegregation cases that culminated in *Brown v. Board of Education*. The judges found that the El Modena, Garden Grove, Santa Ana, and Westminster school districts in Orange County systematically and intentionally segregated Mexican American children into separate schools based on their surname and/or the color of their skin. *Mendez* is not cited in *Brown*, but the NAACP filed a friend of the court brief in *Mendez* and used it as a test case in its attempt to end the separate but equal practice in public education.

Dr. Philippa Strum, professor at City University of New York and global fellow at the Woodrow Wilson International Center for Scholars, writing in her book *Mendez v. Westminster*, says the *Mendez* case began in September 1945 when three children of Gonzalo and Felicitas Mendez were denied enrollment at the nearby 17th Street School, also known as the Westminster Main School, the school their father had attended as a child. Busy tilling fields on forty acres of land he had leased, Mendez asked his sister Soledad Vidaurri to enroll his three children as she enrolled her two children, Alice and Virginia. School officials told Mrs. Vidaurri her children (who were fair-skinned and whose last name did not "sound" Mexican) could be enrolled, but Sylvia, Gonzalo, Jr., and Jerome Mendez (who were dark-skinned with a Mexican-sounding last name) would be required to attend Hoover School, whose 152 students were all Mexican or Mexican American.

Outraged and appalled that their children were denied admission, Gonzalo and Felicitas, both US citizens, consulted with Los Angeles attorney David C. Marcus. He advised the couple that California did not have a state law that required separate schools for Mexican American or African American children (although "separate schools for 'Indian children . . . and for children of Chinese, Japanese or Mongolian parentage'" were lawful). Families of children in three other school districts joined Mendez in a suit filed March 2, 1945, in a federal district court in Los Angeles based on the guarantee of equal protection of the laws in the Fourteenth Amendment of the US Constitution. Dr. Strum says all the petitioners were US citizens of Mexican or Latin descent. Their attorney demanded that the school districts be enjoined from maintaining separate public schools for Mexican American children. Marcus said his clients had been deprived of their rights as US citizens.

According to Frederick P. Aguirre, superior court judge in Orange County writing in the *Journal of Hispanic Higher Education* in October 2005, "a jury was not selected because an injunction was demanded; therefore, Judge Paul J. McCormick ruled on all matters of fact and law in a two-week trial that began July 5, 1945."

Among the twenty-five witnesses for the petitioners was nine-year-old Sylvia Mendez, who testified in perfect English that she was ready to attend her neighborhood school. One expert witness, Dr. Ralph L. Beals, chair of the UCLA Department of Anthropology, testified that separating Mexican American children from White children "would stamp the Mexican American children with a badge of inferiority and the white children with a badge of superiority and that such practice would lead to unproductive Mexican American citizens." According to Strum, he said that "neither learning English nor becoming Americanized was best accomplished by segregation. . . . The best way to learn a language was through immersion with people who spoke it." Segregation impeded "the assimilation of the child to American customs and ways."

Another expert witness, Marie M. Hughes, PhD candidate at Stanford University who specialized in research about Mexican American children, said, "Segregation by its very nature is a reminder constantly of inferiority, of not being wanted, of not being a part of the community."

Court documents show that James L. Kent, superintendent at Garden Grove, testified that he considered Mexican American children "inferior," and he said all students of Mexican ancestry had to attend Hoover School "because of language problems." Frank A. Henderson, superintendent at Santa Ana, testified "that students were assigned to the city's elementary schools solely on the basis of their last names. . . . Exceptions were sometimes made by the four districts for Latino children who 'looked' white or had European names."

Seven months later, on February 18, 1946, Judge McCormick ordered an injunction, restraining the four districts from segregating children of Mexican or Latin American descent in separate public elementary schools. As recorded by Strum, he declared:

> The equal protection of the laws pertaining to the public school system in California is not provided by furnishing in separate schools the same technical facilities, text books and courses of instruction to children of Mexican ancestry that are available to the other public school children regardless of their ancestry. A paramount requisite in the American system of public education is social equality. It must be open to all children . . . regardless of lineage.

Judge McCormick added, "It is also established by the record that the methods of segregation prevalent in the defendant school districts foster antagonisms in the children and suggest inferiority among them where none exists." He said school segregation impeded learning instead of enhancing it.

The school districts filed an appeal to the Ninth Circuit Court of Appeals in San Francisco, and among the amicus briefs filed was one from the NAACP authored by Thurgood Marshall, Robert L. Carter, and Loren Miller. According to Phillipa Strum, Carter told Aguirre that *Mendez* was a "test case" for the NAACP in its attempt to overturn *Plessy v. Ferguson* and that the brief was very similar in content to the first brief that the NAACP filed in *Brown*. "I used it as a trial run for *Brown*," Carter said later. In their brief, they wrote, "Segregation on a racial basis in the public school system is a type of arbitrary and unreasonable discrimination which should be forbidden under our laws."

The Ninth Circuit court unanimously (7–0) upheld the trial court's decision April 14, 1947, and the four school districts accepted the decision and did not appeal to the US Supreme Court.

The *Mendez* case also exposed the California law mandating separate schools for Native American and Asian children. Governor Earl Warren recommended to the state legislature that they repeal that section of the state's education code, and he signed the resulting bill into law on June 14, 1947.

At least two other legal cases—one in state courts, another in federal courts—played prominent roles in this chapter of Texas history about civil rights, discrimination, and the US Constitution's equal protection guarantee in the Fourteenth Amendment. Principals in these cases were I. H. "Sporty" Harvey and Peter "Pete" Hernandez, two names that are not well-known in Texas history. But these two men—one an African American boxer from Hallettsville, the other a Mexican American farmworker in Jackson County—made headlines in 1954, a monumental year for racial equality in the state. Harvey and Hernandez were appellants in landmark cases that reached the supreme courts of Texas and the United

States. In fact, *Hernandez v. State of Texas* immediately precedes *Brown* in volume 347 of the official Supreme Court Reporter.

Professional boxing was lawful but strictly regulated in Texas in the 1950s. One of the restrictions, adopted into article 614 of the state's penal code in 1933, prevented boxing or wrestling matches "between any person of the Caucasian or white race and one of the African or Negro race."

Twenty years later, Harvey challenged that law. A native Texan who was born July 21, 1925, in Halletsville, Harvey moved to nearby San Antonio with his family in 1937. At age eighteen he was working for W. F. Littleton Tire Company, and at one time while serving in the US military, he was stationed at Fort Sam Houston in San Antonio. According to historian Ryann D. Garza of Texas A&M University–San Antonio, the earliest record of Harvey's participation in boxing was 1950 in mixed-race matches at Fort Sam and also against Hispanic fighters in Mexico. Later, the journeyman fighter worked in the trucking and freight business and continued to box professionally as a means to supplement income for his family, which eventually included four children. But his income was limited because he was prohibited from fighting White boxers.

Garza says Harvey told the *Los Angeles Herald Examiner* in 1988 that Black boxers in Texas trained in backyards and fields and used cotton sacks filled with rags for punching bags. "Speed bags, we didn't have that," he said. "It was terrible. The only ones who helped me were the Spanish people. They didn't have any more equipment that I did. The white man had everything."

In July 1953, this muscular, well-dressed Black man walked into the law office of Maury Maverick Jr., an attorney and member of the Texas House of Representatives, in downtown San Antonio. The thirty-two-year-old Maverick, great-grandson of a rancher who signed the Texas Declaration of Independence, had introduced a bill in 1953 in an unsuccessful attempt to repeal Texas's ban on mixed-race boxing and wrestling. According to the *San Antonio Express-News*, Harvey told Maverick, "I want to file a lawsuit with you. I want to talk to you about dignity for my people."

At Maverick's request, Harvey wrote a letter on July 20, 1953, to M. B. Morgan, Texas commissioner of labor statistics who had jurisdiction over professional boxing in the state, for permission to fight a White boxer.

Morgan denied Harvey's request on July 28, 1953, "due solely to the fact that plaintiff is a Negro." And less than a month later, August 13, 1953, Maverick filed a lawsuit on behalf of Harvey in 126th District Court of Travis County in Austin. The basis of Harvey's suit, as disclosed in his pleadings, was that "the statute and rule of the commissioner prohibiting white-Negro fights constitute state action denying him rights guaranteed by the Fourteenth Amendment to the constitution of the United States as well as civil rights guaranteed by the federal Civil Rights Act."

The NAACP and another of Harvey's attorneys, Carlos Cadena, believed that cases of minority plaintiffs, especially in Southern states, would best be adjudicated in federal courts for a fairer trial, but Maverick reportedly wanted to win this civil liberty case in state court "to change the mind-set of Texas juries and jurists." He told Jan Jarboe Russell, as reported by *Texas Monthly* in July 2003, "I wanted to whip 'em in a Texas court."

A jury trial was waived, and evidence was presented January 26, 1954, in the courtroom of Judge Jack Roberts. Among the witnesses who testified was James "Jimmy" Scaramozi, a White boxing promoter and trainer, who, according to Ryann Garza, said Harvey was "forced to fight the same small group of African American boxers over and over again and therefore receiving smaller earnings than white boxers." Commissioner Morgan testified, "Citizens of Texas are satisfied with our present law and think it would be best to keep the law on our books."

Harvey, the only Black man in the courtroom that day, told the judge he would never have a chance to win a championship in Texas because of his race. "The guys I want to fight I can't fight because I'm a Negro," he said, according to author Cary Clack. Maverick added, "If Sporty could box he would make more money. Thus, because he was black, he was being denied an equal opportunity to make a living."

But Judge Roberts ruled against Harvey on February 3, 1954, and the resulting appeal for Harvey by Maverick—aided by funds from the NAACP—reached the Third Court of Civil Appeals of Texas in Austin on October 13, 1954. At the appeals court, the controlling question became "whether the statute proscribing white and Negro boxing exhibitions violates the Fourteenth Amendment to the federal constitution." Clack says Maverick argued, "We have this nation holding itself up as a democracy to the colored peoples of the world, and yet we have this law here where a Negro man can't even have a professional fight with a white man."

The appeals court ruled in Harvey's favor, reversed the state district court's decision, and said:

> Professional boxing being a lawful calling in this State, we believe that statutes which regulate it fall within the inhibitions of the Fourteenth Amendment within the rule that "If some persons engaged in a calling or business are subjected to special burdens or favored by special privileges while others engaged in the same calling or business are not so treated, the legislation is based upon unconstitutional discrimination.' . . .
>
> When we consider this record and the Fourteenth Amendment, as interpreted by the United States Supreme Court, which we and all other officials of this State are sworn to preserve and defend, we have no hesitancy in declaring Sec. 11(f) of Art. 614, Texas Penal Code, to be in violation of the Fourteenth Amendment to the Constitution of the United States and is null and void.

A rehearing was denied November 17, 1954, by the state appeals court, and January 19, 1955, the Supreme Court of Texas sustained the judgment of the Third Court of Civil Appeals of Texas.

Just over a month later, February 24, 1955, Harvey fought twenty-one-year-old Reagan "Buddy" Turman in the Sportatorium near downtown Dallas. It was the first professional boxing match between an African American and a White fighter conducted by Texas state boxing officials. Turman, a former Texas amateur light heavyweight champion from the East Texas rural community of Noonday, won the unanimous ten-round decision. According to Cary Clack, writing in "The Bout" in digital magazine *Truly*Adventurous* in 2020, Turman told the *Dallas Morning News*, "I'd sparred a lot with black fighters. I was just thinking about trying to win. That whole thing about not allowing blacks and whites to fight seemed stupid. But it was that way all over the South."

Clack said the amazing fact was that Harvey was still on his feet at the end of the fight. "What had knocked him down again and again was not as powerful as what lifted him up," Clack wrote. "And what lifted him up, leaving him standing, was a strength scorecards could never gauge." Harvey believed his loss in the ring was payback for beating the state in court. "They got back at me and gave the decision to Buddy," he said.

"The only thing I know is that I did my best," he told his wife, Hazel. "I thought I put up a good fight." (Clack reported that Turman also won a rematch in Tyler in June 1955 by unanimous decision.)

Harvey had a few more fights in Texas against White fighters, but he lost most of them and finished his career in the state with a losing record. He moved to Los Angeles in 1957 and fought a few times in Long Beach and Santa Monica.

Despite never making much money and his poor boxing record, he told the *Herald Examiner* he was proud of his fight against "Jim Crow." "I'm very happy about that," he said. "I figured there would be kids coming along who didn't have the problems that I had. . . . I did something to make me feel good."

Harvey died from heart disease on June 5, 1997, in Los Angeles at the age of seventy-one.

The case of Pete Hernandez reached the United States Supreme Court in 1954, where it overturned a longtime practice in Jackson County and at least seventy other counties in Texas of systematically excluding people of Hispanic descent from serving on juries—which, like voting, is a primary duty and privilege of US citizenship. *Hernandez v. State of Texas* was the first Mexican American civil rights case heard and decided by the US Supreme Court during the post–World War II period. And it was the first case in which Mexican American lawyers had appeared before the US Supreme Court.

Hernandez, a migrant farm worker and cotton picker, was accused of murdering Cayetano "Joe" Espinosa in a bar in Edna, Texas, a small town in Jackson County where no person of Mexican origin had served on a jury in at least twenty-five years. He was indicted by a grand jury in September 1951, then convicted and sentenced to life in prison by a petit jury. Gustavo

"Gus" Garcia, an experienced Mexican American civil rights attorney, had agreed to represent the accused without fee.

Garcia reportedly was not surprised when Hernandez was found guilty. The Hernandez legal team appealed to the Texas Court of Criminal Appeals, the highest court in Texas to consider criminal matters, and the lower court decision was upheld on June 18, 1952.

Carlos A. Soltero, writing in *Latinos and American Law: Landmark Supreme Court Cases*, says, "Texas' highest criminal court rejected his appeal in part because it found that Mexicans 'are not a separate race but are white people of Spanish descent,' and since other white people served on the juries, the absence of people of Mexican ancestry did not violate equal protection."

The US Supreme Court accepted the appeal of the case, heard arguments January 11, 1954, and announced its unanimous verdict on May 3, 1954, to reverse the conviction.

According to Soltero, Chief Justice Warren began the opinion with the proposition that the court's precedent held that criminal prosecutions in cases where persons of the defendant's race or color have been systematically excluded from the grand or petit jury violate equal protection.

Warren continued, "The State of Texas would have us hold that there are only two classes—white and Negro—within the contemplation of the Fourteenth Amendment. The decisions of this court do not support that view." The verdict came just fourteen days before his more well-known announcement of the *Brown* decision. Warren made this frequently cited statement in the *Hernandez* opinion:

> Throughout our history differences in race and color have defined easily identifiable groups which have at times required the aid of the courts in securing equal treatment under the laws. But community prejudices are not static, and from time to time other differences from the community norm may define other groups which need the same protection. Whether such a group exists within a community is a question of fact. When the existence of a distinct class is demonstrated, and it is further shown that the laws, as written or as applied, single out that

> class for different treatment not based on some reasonable classification, the guarantees of the Constitution have been violated. The Fourteenth Amendment is not directed solely against discrimination due to a "two-class theory"—that is, based upon differences between "white" and Negro.

Hernandez and his pro bono legal team, which included Carlos Cadena from *Harvey v. Morgan*, "established, to the satisfaction of the Supreme Court, that Mexicans were a distinct group, at least in Jackson County. Although 14% population of the Jackson County were persons with Mexican or Latin American surnames, Texas stipulated that 'for the last twenty-five years there is no record of any person with a Mexican or Latin American name having served on a jury commission, grand jury or petit jury in Jackson County.'"

The court added, "It taxes our credulity to say that mere chance resulted in their being no members of this class among the over six thousand jurors called in the past 25 years. The result bespeaks discrimination, whether or not it was a conscious decision on the part of any individual jury commissioner."

The Supreme Court said Hernandez and others were entitled to a fair process, not a particular result. According to the court, Hernandez

> did not seek proportional representation nor did he claim a right to have persons of Mexican descent sit on the particular juries which he faced. His only claim is the right to be indicted and tried by juries from which all members of his class are not systematically excluded—juries selected from among all qualified persons regardless of national origin or descent. To this much, he is entitled by the Constitution.

The Supreme Court's decision secured equal civil rights for Latinos in a struggle that somewhat parallels the struggles by African Americans at the time. Texas chose not to re-try Hernandez, and he was released from prison.

In Topeka, Kansas's capital where there were eighteen elementary schools for White students and four for Black students, thirteen families filed a class action lawsuit on February 28, 1951, on behalf of twenty of their children against the Board of Education alleging that its segregation policy was unconstitutional. The names on the case were listed in alphabetical order, and Oliver Brown, the father of student Linda Carol Brown, was listed first ("he was no longer willing to accept second class citizenship"). The lawsuit was filed eight days after her eighth birthday. The oldest daughter of Oliver and Leola Brown, Linda reportedly said, "I couldn't understand why I couldn't go to school with my playmates." They attended Sumner School for White children four blocks from her house, but she was bussed across town to Monroe School for Black children after being denied admission to Sumner.

Original arguments before the Supreme Court were conducted in December 1952. Peter Irons says in *A People's History of the Supreme Court* that when the first round began on December 8, more than half the seats in the chamber were occupied by African Americans who came to hear Marshall and other lawyers "give voice to their grievance against segregation." But the court was unable to reach a solution by June 1953 (the end of its 1952–53 term), and it ordered additional arguments on five questions that it posed (including Justice Felix Frankfurter's fundamental question: Did the framers of the Fourteenth Amendment intend to outlaw school segregation?). The re-arguments followed in December 1953 after being postponed from October 1953 after the death of the chief justice.

The first of the court's five questions for the parties to the litigation was "What evidence is there that the Congress which submitted and the state legislatures and conventions which ratified the Fourteenth Amendment contemplated or did not contemplate, understood or did not understand, that it would abolish segregation in public schools?"

Lead counsel for the plaintiffs and the NAACP was Thurgood Marshall, a native of Baltimore, Maryland, who attended Lincoln University in Pennsylvania and Howard University School of Law and later was appointed to the US Supreme Court by President Johnson in 1967. He told the court, "Segregation of Negroes as practiced here is universally understood as imposing on them a badge of inferiority."

He reminded the nine justices that the Fourteenth Amendment, ratified July 9, 1868, declares: "No state shall make or enforce any law which shall abridge the privileges or immunities of citizens of the United States; nor shall any state deprive any person of life, liberty or property without due process of law; nor deny to any person within its jurisdiction the equal protection of the laws."

And seventeen months after the first round of arguments began and five months after arguments concluded December 10, 1953, Chief Justice Earl Warren—former attorney general and popular governor of California who was appointed chief justice by President Eisenhower after the sudden death of Chief Justice Fred Vinson, Jr., on September 8, 1953—in a "firm, clear, unemotional voice" read the court's unanimous decision:

> Does segregation of children in public schools solely on the basis of race, even though the physical facilities and other tangible factors may be equal, deprive the children of the minority group of equal educational opportunities? We believe that it does. . . .
>
> Segregation of white and colored children in public schools has a detrimental effect upon the colored children. The impact is greater when it has the sanction of the law, for the policy of separating the races is usually interpreted as denoting the inferiority of the Negro group. A sense of inferiority affects the motivation of a child to learn. Segregation with the sanction of law, therefore, has a tendency to retard the educational and mental development of Negro children and to deprive them of some of the benefits they would receive in a racially integrated school system. . . .
>
> We conclude unanimously that, in the field of public education, the doctrine of "separate but equal" has no place. Separate educational facilities are inherently unequal. Therefore, we hold that the plaintiffs and others similarly situated for whom the actions have been brought are, by reason of the segregation complained of, deprived of the equal protection of the laws guaranteed by the Fourteenth Amendment.

The word *unanimously* did not appear in the court's printed opinion. Irons, in *A People's History of the Supreme Court*, says Chief Justice Warren inserted it for emphasis during his reading of the majority opinion. Irons says that during the five months after the final arguments, Warren was determined to forge a unanimous decision with a brief, forceful opinion. Irons says Warren believed that "only if the justices spoke with one voice, in words the American people could understand, would the Court be able to help the nation heal its racial wounds." Warren did not want dissents or concurrences. Kluger writes in *Simple Justice*, "He wanted a single, unequivocating opinion that could leave no doubt that the Court had put Jim Crow to the sword."

Warren reportedly added, "We decided not to make up our minds on that first conference day, but to talk it over, from week to week, dealing with different aspects of it—in groups, over lunches, in conference. It was too important to hurry it." Justice Robert H. Jackson reportedly left his hospital bed, where he was recovering from a heart attack, to join his fellow judges on the bench when the decision was announced to illustrate the importance of demonstrating their unanimity.

Klarman, in his book *From Jim Crow to Civil Rights*, quotes Warren: "The 13th, 14th and 15th Amendments were intended to make equal those who once were slaves."

On that decisive day in May 1954, according to Irons, Chief Justice Warren—in a Supreme Court chamber described as packed, but not crowded, and quiet—stressed "the importance of education to our democratic society." What the cases really involved was the psychological impact of enforced separation on Black children. He said nothing about reading, writing, and arithmetic. Warren said the primary role of public education is fostering "cultural values" and "good citizenship" among children.

The chief justice thought the primary vice of segregation was not bad schools for Black children, but the bad lessons it taught them. He concluded, "To separate them from others of similar age and qualifications solely because of their race generates a feeling of inferiority as to their status in the community that may affect their hearts and minds in a way unlikely ever to be undone."

With its *Brown* decision, the Warren court launched a new chapter in US legal history that has been described as revolutionary. Lucas Powe Jr., in his book *The Warren Court and American Politics*, says:

> Scholars seem agreed that the Warren court consisted of a group of powerful, talented men who were more sympathetic to claims of individual liberty while being simultaneously more egalitarian than their predecessors, more willing to intervene in contentious controversies, more prone to ignore the past and more convinced that national solutions were superior to local solutions.

Judge Aguirre, writing in the *Journal of Hispanic Higher Education*, said *Brown* and *Mendez* "exemplify the best in our American cultural values: courage and fairness." He added:

> The cases display the courage of Gonzalo and Felicitas Mendez, of Reverend Oliver Brown and of all the other parents in the *Mendez* lawsuit and the *Brown* lawsuit to challenge the racist educational system through the courts for the benefit of their children and all other children. These cases also show the courage of the judges in rendering unpopular yet morally and legally fair opinions. . . . Justice ultimately prevails.

After *Brown I* was announced on May 17, 1954, the US Supreme Court ordered no remedy, and it ordered the cases to be returned to the docket for further argument on implementation and enforcement of its decision and to hear from schools and states requesting relief concerning the task of desegregation. In its decision announced May 31, 1955, which became known as *Brown II*, the court delegated the task of carrying out school desegregation to district courts. The Supreme Court said:

> The courts will require that the defendants make a prompt and reasonable start toward full compliance with our ruling. Once such a start has been made, the courts may find that additional time is necessary to carry out the ruling in an effective manner. The burden rests upon the defendants to establish that such time

> is necessary in the public interest and is consistent with good faith compliance at the earliest practicable date. . . .
>
> The judgments below are remanded to the district courts to take such proceedings as are necessary to admit to public schools on a racially nondiscriminatory basis with all deliberate speed the parties to these cases.

Supporters of the earlier decision were displeased with *Brown II*. Critics of the second decision said the phrase "with all deliberate speed" was too ambiguous, and many Southern states and school districts used it as legal justification for resisting, delaying, and avoiding integration. Segregated school districts in the South, Ladino writes, interpreted it to "mean 'go slow,' 'stall,' 'delay' and, in the most conservative sense, 'never.'"

Klarman says justices remanded cases to district courts to issue decrees in accordance with "local conditions" while keeping in mind the "flexibility" of traditional "equitable principles." They required a "prompt and reasonable start toward full compliance" with additional time allowed if "consistent with good faith compliance at the earliest practicable date." The court approved "gradualism" and imposed no deadlines for beginning or completing desegregation.

One county in Virginia, Prince Edward County, closed its school system for five years in 1959–64 rather than integrate. Isabel Wilkerson, in her book *Caste—The Origins of Our Discontents*, says the White school board in Prince Edward County, one of five involved in the 1954 US Supreme Court *Brown* case, "delayed integrating as long as it could and then shut down the school system entirely rather than allow black students into classrooms with white students." This lawsuit originated in the spring of 1951 when Black students at segregated Moton High School began a strike to protest overcrowding and other unequal conditions at their school.

Wilkerson says parents of both races in Prince Edward County were forced to find alternatives for the education of their children. She writes, "Local whites diverted government funds to private academies for white students, while black parents whose tax dollars were now going to the white students had to make do on their own."

Certainly, there were legal battles still to be won, but African Americans had secured a victory in *Brown* that would bring them closer to full equality than they had ever been in the United States.

FIVE

MAKING HISTORY IN FRIONA, TEXAS

Friona Is First in Texas to Integrate Its Public School

Negro Tots in School with Whites
Dallas Morning News, May 5, 1955

Negroes Accepted in Texas School
Miami News, May 5, 1955

Friona Led Way in School Integration
Los Angeles Mirror, May 9, 1955

Texas Brothers Began a Reform, Peacefully
Dallas Morning News, May 16, 2004

Friona Receives Marker: School Was First in State to Enroll Black Children
Amarillo Globe-News, Nov. 19, 2006

The tiny West Texas town of Friona thrust itself onto the pages of America's newspapers in 1955. Americans from Miami to Los Angeles, at their breakfast tables or on their morning commutes to work and school, read about Friona—not because of how accurately it represented life in rural Texas in the 1950s, not because it was originally plotted from the famous XIT Ranch, not because it courageously survived blizzards and droughts to become the most populated town in Parmer County.

Friona made the front pages of America's newspapers because its school was the first in Texas to integrate African American students with Anglo-American students in 1954—just weeks after the US Supreme Court decision. Pecos was *among* the first a year later, but it was not *the* first. That distinction belongs to another small farming and ranching community of about twelve hundred people in the Texas Panhandle.

And it happened quietly with no fanfare. A newspaper in Los Angeles called it "an example of America's vast potential for common decency."

Three sons of Mary Louise and Robert Walker Jr. were the first African American children to attend public schools with Anglo students in Texas. For about a year, the migrant family lived and worked on a farm owned by Elthie and Johnny Hand near Friona, a market and shipping point in the small county named for a signer of the Texas Declaration of Independence. The Hands, who had worked their land since 1943, grew cotton, wheat, milo, and seed corn on about a thousand acres.

The Walkers lived adjacent to the Hands' home in a small farmhouse that reportedly did not have electricity. It's possible the Walkers were not aware of the Supreme Court decision that declared segregation unconstitutional, announced on May 17, 1954, by Chief Justice Earl Warren.

But within a few weeks, in the fall of 1954, Robert, Ray, and Jimmy Walker were attending Friona Elementary School after moving to Texas from California.

Elthie Hand talked to Mary Walker and to the superintendent, Dalton Caffey, about sending the Walker children to school. In May 2004, at the age of eighty-one, Mrs. Hand told the *Dallas Morning News*, "I didn't know whether to send them to school or not. They had no money, no nothing. I just felt like I needed to take them. And Mr. Caffey said, 'We have to take them. Bring them over.'

"We took care of these little kids because that's just what people do around here," Mrs. Hand continued. "They lived 10 feet from us, and they were like part of the family."

At the time, many towns and cities in Texas had separate schools for African American children, but Friona did not. To attend a school for African American students, Robert, Ray, and Jimmy Walker would have had to commute twenty-two miles northwest from Friona on US Highway 60 each day to Hereford, another small town in adjacent Deaf Smith County.

"We don't have many Negroes living here," Caffey, at the age of forty-four, told reporter Paul Coates for an article published May 9, 1955, in the *Los Angeles Mirror*. "Most of them are farm laborers, and they move on when the cotton season is over. . . . We don't have a Negro school here. I figured my job is to see that any child gets the education he's entitled to. And I couldn't see why they shouldn't be admitted to our regular school.

"I talked to those folks and told them there'd likely be some trouble from the people in town," Caffey continued. "But if there was going to be any, we might as well have it over with now. I told them, 'Send your children to school.'"

The superintendent told the *Amarillo Globe-News*, "With the Supreme Court ruling on segregation, it looked as if we would have to do it eventually anyway, and we felt we'd rather do it of our own volition rather than have it crammed down our throats later."

Coates wrote in the *Mirror* of his telephone conversation with Caffey: "I called Friona and talked to a country school teacher whose sense of human dignity helped put the town on the front pages of America's newspapers."

Caffey said he enrolled the Walker children in Friona Elementary School without conferring with the school board "because I couldn't reach them," according to Coates's account in the *Mirror*. The *Friona Star*, on the occasion of the dedication of a Texas historical marker in 2007, said Caffey did call D. C. Herring, president of the Friona school board, to tell Herring of his decision.

"When I did get together with the board," Caffey continued, "they all agreed with me."

He added, "People gathered around downtown to discuss it, but all they said was it's the common sense thing to do."

Caffey's son Kim told reporters later that his father didn't consider himself a pioneer. "He was a school man, and it didn't matter what color they were," Kim Caffey said. "They needed to be educated."

"It was that simple," the *Friona Star* added, "and without bureaucratic fanfare in September 1954 the Friona Independent School District became the first white school district in the state of Texas to accept Black students."

The *Morning News* said the Walkers had lived in several other towns in the Texas Panhandle—including Abernathy, Morton, and Muleshoe—and Jimmy, Ray, and Robert went to school in each town. But Friona was the only White school they attended.

There are conflicting reports of how well the Walker boys were treated at Friona Elementary School and why they withdrew.

Their attendance apparently didn't become news outside Friona until the following spring when in Austin on May 4, 1955, Caffey and Dr. Bascom Hayes, assistant commissioner at the Texas Education Agency, revealed the subsequent enrollment of three other African American students in Friona.

By then, the Walker boys were no longer enrolled in Friona, but three other Black children, brothers Marvin and Donnie Smith and Mozelle Lemmon, were attending classes at Friona Elementary School. Their families had also moved to Friona and were working on nearby farms.

Caffey told reporters the integration occurred without incident, although there were complaints from "a few parents when the Negroes first came to class. . . .

"The Negro youngsters have been accepted by the other children," Caffey said. "They are very congenial. In fact, the white children seem rather proud of the Negroes. They are good students."

The historical marker, which was approved by the Texas Historical Commission, says the Walkers moved from Friona during the school year. (The marker was dedicated on February 8, 2007, and installed near the elementary school at the intersection of Eighth Street and Euclid Avenue.)

In their interviews with the *Dallas Morning News* in 2004, Mary Walker and her fifty-nine-year-old son Robert, residents of nearby Clovis,

New Mexico, recalled no such easy transition. Mrs. Walker said that by spring, she was teaching her children at home.

Robert said his teachers ignored him and "always sided with white students in disputes. . . . When I knew something, I'd raise my hand, but they'd never call on me." Mrs. Walker said that "a white woman at the school who sold soda and candy" refused to take money from her children, and Robert remembered another time when he shared his lunch with a classmate, but "a white girl ran up and warned the boy that he'd die of poison."

Robert added, "It bothered us, but we just kind of got used to it. We just sort of moved along, turned the other cheek and didn't cuss about it. They just did things that made us feel disliked."

Kim Caffey, still a resident of Friona in 2007, according to the *Star*, said reporters from across the nation called his father, but the superintendent declined most of the requests for interviews. There were threatening calls and mail—"most of which came from the deep South."

Dalton Caffey eventually told his children not to answer the phone.

The *Morning News* said there are no official records at Friona ISD to document the attendance of the Walkers, but the *Amarillo Globe-News* reported in 2006, in an article about the historical marker, that the 1954–55 Friona yearbook shows a picture from the school Christmas program that includes the Walker children. (Mrs. Hand told the *Morning News* she made robes for her daughter Wessie and the Walker boys for the Christmas program.)

In 2004, the *Amarillo Globe-News* reprinted the Coates article from 1955 with this editor's note: "We have discovered no article in the *Star* discussing the situation, and Superintendent Hal Ratcliff said there wasn't even a notation in the school board minutes, although it apparently was discussed."

Robert, who told the *Morning News* none of the three brothers graduated from high school, said he never contemplated his place in the history of Texas civil rights.

"It's something that we just put behind us and got on with our lives," he said. "Do you think we'll go down in history?"

The historical marker resulted from a student project in a class taught by Patsy Allen at Friona High School in 2005. Pedro Ramos, a 2006 graduate of Friona High School and the student who led the project, told the *Amarillo Globe-News* that Friona's role in allowing children of all cultures, races, and backgrounds to attend public schools gave Friona High School students a source of pride.

"A small town had a big part in history," Ramos said. "We were researching how Friona got established and how it all came together."

Darla Bracken, director of the Friona Public Library, showed the students a book that stated Friona ISD was the first in Texas to integrate in the 1954–55 school year. "People have actually always known it," she said. "The kids saw that. . . . I thought it was great that it touched them that way. They saw it with new eyes."

Allen's students researched the story and interviewed former students, teachers, and Walker family members who still resided in the Friona area. "It makes you grateful now," another student, Angelica Arellano, said. "I can't imagine how it was, going to different restrooms, and being treated so badly."

The marker from the Texas Historical Commission arrived in the fall of 2006 in Friona. A dedication ceremony was planned for early 2007.

"It makes us more proud of our community," Anayeli Ramos, another of Allen's students, said.

Mary Louise Walker, Robert Walker and two of his other brothers (Freddy and Jerry, who were too young to attend school in 1954), Elthie Hand, D. C. Herring, Kim Caffey, and Pedro Ramos were among the people who attended the ceremony, according to the *Friona Star*.

Superintendent Jim Parker welcomed the crowd, and Mayor John Taylor proclaimed Equal Education Day in Friona. Gladys Spring, chair of the Parmer County Historical Commission, also attended.

The text on the marker reads:

> **Friona Schools**
> Friona has the distinction of being the first town in Texas to integrate its schools. The first school opened on this site in 1908 in a one-room frame building with Roxie Witherspoon

teaching 18 pupils. A two-story brick school finished in 1911 burned after being struck by lightning in 1922. A new two-story brick high school opened in 1924. Attendance grew in the 1940s, when rural schools at Lakeview, Messenger, Black and Rhea consolidated with Friona.

The school achieved its greatest fame in 1954. Racial segregation of schoolchildren was considered legal in the 20th century, reaffirmed by the U.S. Supreme Court in 1896 in the case of *Plessy v. Ferguson*. On May 17, 1954, the court overturned its decision, declaring segregation unconstitutional in *Brown v. Board of Education*. Chief Justice Earl Warren wrote, "We conclude that, in the field of public education, the doctrine of 'separate but equal' has no place." Federal and state government moved slowly to implement change, but in Friona, progress would not wait.

The Robert Walker Jr. family came to town in September 1954. When Superintendent Dalton Caffey chose to enroll Walker's three African American sons in Friona's only school, he quietly achieved the first integrated public school in Texas. Caffey then informed the school board of his decision, and things generally went smoothly for the school and the new students. The Walkers moved away during the school year, and in the spring of 1955 three more African American students attended school here. Since that watershed year, Friona schools have continued to uphold Caffey's wish for equal educational opportunity.

Yes, Robert Walker, you did make history.

SIX

NEW PLAYERS, NEW COACH FOR PECOS

Bubba, R. C., and Coach Kenner Arrive at PHS in 1955–56

Sonora Coach Hired as Cage Mentor for Pecos High School
Pecos Enterprise, Apr. 28, 1955

Eagles Smother Wink in Basketball Opener 57–6
Pecos Enterprise, Dec. 5, 1955

Seminole Downs Eagles, 49 to 45, in 6-AA Opener
Odessa American, Jan. 8, 1956

Pecos Upsets Tribe, 64–59
Odessa American, Jan. 29, 1956

Eagles Drop 78–59 Playoff Game to Title-Bent Indians
Pecos Enterprise, Feb. 20, 1956

Iria Ephriam Sr. was returning to his home in Pecos after an afternoon of work near the small community of Pyote. It was dusk in West Texas—the brilliant sky once again the color of a rose petal. Soon after Ephriam turned west on US Highway 80, he noticed the flashing lights of a highway patrolman in the rearview mirror of his truck, which was filled with red sand. He had loaded the sand with his #2 scoop shovel at a friend's farm north of Pyote on State Highway 115 near the Ward–Winkler county line. Ephriam needed sand for his construction and landscape business to level and condition the soil as he installed lawns for his customers.

Bubba's father stopped his truck along the busy highway as he drove toward Pecos. He already had turned on the lights of his truck.

"You probably don't know why I pulled you over," the trooper said. "You have a taillight that's flickering so it looks like you're trying to turn. You might want to check it out.

"Can I see your driver's license?" the trooper asked before he walked back to his patrol car. Ephriam could hear the radio playing in the trooper's car.

The patrolman returned to Ephriam's truck. "You any relation to this Bubba Ephriam playing basketball on the radio now?"

"Yes, sir, he's my son."

"Your son!" The patrolman was surprised to hear Ephriam's response. "What are you doing out here with a truckload of sand, and he's there playing basketball? If I didn't have to be out here, I would be at that game."

Ephriam answered, "I would be there, too, if I didn't have to get this sand in by tomorrow morning."

"I'm going to let you go this time," the officer said. "But the next time you're out here and he's in there playing basketball, I am going to give you a ticket."

Ephriam lingered a few minutes listening with the officer to Bubba's game on the radio before continuing toward home with his truckload of red sand.

It was early in the 1955–56 basketball season, Bubba's first with the Eagles after enrolling at Pecos High School in September 1955. Bubba and his new team were already enjoying success. The Eagles won their first eight games and had a record of nine wins with only one loss when District 6-AA games started January 3, 1956, in Crane.

There were big expectations for the Eagles. Before their opening game of the season—Thursday, December 1, 1955, in Eagle Gymnasium against Wink—the *Odessa American* said, "The Pecos Eagles launch an ambitious campaign [aimed] at dethroning defending state basketball champion Seminole." The 1955–56 district race between Seminole, the 1955 Class AA state champion, and Pecos, district runner-up to the Indians the previous year, was expected to be "a wild battle."

Four starters returned for Pecos, the *American* reported, "plus a couple of Negro hotshots who were outstanding in their league last year." The returning starters were center Billy Jim Simmons, one of the top scorers in West Texas the previous season, along with forwards Dick Patrick and Richard Cothrun and guard Bill Kelley.

The newcomers, the *American* said, were "guard R. C. Christopher, an all-state selection in pre-integration circles, and tall Bubba Ephriam." The newspaper continued, "Height will be the outstanding characteristic of this year's Eagle outfit. Ephriam towers six feet, seven inches. Patrick is six feet, four. Simmons is six feet, three, and Cothrun is six feet, two inches." A tall lineup, indeed, despite the fact that the *American* added about three inches to Ephriam's stature.

The first game gave Eagles fans a glimpse of what was ahead. Pecos trounced Wink fifty-seven to six in a game in which the Wildcats failed to score against the Eagles after the opening quarter. Simmons scored twenty-one points to lead the Eagles, and in his first game in his new purple-and-gold uniform, Ephriam hit six field goals and three free throws for a total of fifteen points.

The Eagle defense limited Wink to only two field goals and outscored the visitors 17–0 in the second quarter, 9–0 in the third, and 22–0 in the fourth. According to the *Pecos Enterprise*, the starting five did all of the scoring—as they often did—for Pecos (Kelley had nine points, and Patrick and Christopher added six points each).

One thousand miles away, in Montgomery, Alabama, the historic first appearances by African American students Bubba Ephriam and R. C. Christopher for the Pecos High School basketball team December 1, 1955, in West Texas did not make headlines.

Instead, on that same Thursday in Montgomery, the major newsmaker was a forty-two-year-old woman. A seamstress at Montgomery Fair, a department store downtown, Rosa Louise Parks left work soon after five o'clock for a short walk to a nearby store and bus stop at Court Square for her ride home. She allowed the first bus to pass because it appeared to be full, but she entered the next bus, paid her ten-cent fare, walked past the first ten seats that on Montgomery city buses were reserved for White passengers, and sat in an empty seat on the aisle beside a Black man. Seated across the aisle from Parks were two Black women.

At a subsequent stop, in front of the famous Empire Theatre, several more riders entered the bus. One White male rider did not find an empty seat, so he stood quietly in the aisle without complaining. The bus driver, James F. Blake, noticed that the White man was standing, went to Parks's row, and demanded that all four Black passengers vacate the row. Mary Hull, in her book *Rosa Parks: Civil Rights Leader*, says that Alabama state law "gave bus drivers virtually unlimited discretion in enforcing segregation on their buses."

The two women and the man to Parks's right did as Blake requested, but Parks declined. She slid to her right to the window, looked out at the theater, and remained seated in the racially neutral, unreserved middle section of the bus. Blake repeated his demand, but Parks again calmly refused. After conferring with his supervisor, Blake summoned Montgomery police. Officers F. B. Day and D. W. Mixon responded, arrested Parks, and took her to city hall. "Why do you push us around?" she asked as the police officers took her away.

In her autobiography, *Rosa Parks: My Story*, Parks said, "People always say that I didn't give up my seat because I was tired, but that isn't true. I was not tired physically or no more tired than I usually was at the end of a working day. I was not old, although some people have an image of me as being old then. I was forty-two. No, the only tired I was, was tired of giving in."

Parks was fingerprinted and photographed at the city jail on North Ripley Street and placed in a cell with two other women. She was held for about two hours before Edgar Daniel Nixon, former leader of the local chapter of the NAACP, and family friend Clifford Durr paid her bail bond of one hundred dollars. Her husband, Raymond, a barber at nearby Maxwell Air Force Base, came with other friends to take her home.

The following Monday, December 5, the first day of the historic 381-day bus boycott in Montgomery sparked by her arrest, Parks appeared in a city court at nine in the morning. She was found guilty of violating segregation laws in a five-minute trial before Judge John B. Scott, paid her ten-dollar fine (plus four dollars in court costs), and returned home.

Civil rights advocate Martin Luther King Jr. said Parks was "a victim of both the forces of history and the forces of destiny." In his autobiography, he wrote, "Mrs. Parks was ideal for the role assigned to her by history. Her character was impeccable and her dedication deep-rooted. All of these traits made her one of the most respected people in the Negro community."

In an interview on NPR radio in 1992, Parks explained, "There was opportunity for me to take a stand to express the way I felt about being treated in that manner. I had not planned to get arrested. I had plenty to do without having to end up in jail. But when I had to face that decision, I didn't hesitate to do so because I felt that we had endured that too long.

"The more we gave in, the more we complied with that kind of treatment, the more oppressive it became."

In addition to new African American players, also new to the 1955–56 Pecos Eagles basketball team was its coach, twenty-eight-year-old John Woinder Kenner, a graduate of Navarro Junior College and East Texas State University (now Texas A&M–Commerce) who was in his fifth year of coaching, with previous stops in Klondike at West Delta High School for one season in 1951–52 and in Sonora for three seasons in 1952–55.

In addition to coaching Sonora's high school basketball varsity team, Kenner coached junior high school football and track and field teams. He became reacquainted with Garland Matthews, the director of athletics and the football coach at Pecos High School, at the Comanche Relays in Fort Stockton on March 5, 1955. Matthews was searching for a new basketball coach for the Eagles.

Previous Pecos coach R. C. "Dick" Burris, who announced his resignation on February 11, 1955, with two games remaining in the season, had guided the Eagles to consecutive district runner-up finishes with a combined record of 30–14 in his two seasons (12–8 in 1953–54 and 18–6 in 1954–55) after arriving from McCamey. He was a native of Los Angeles, California, veteran of the US Air Force, and graduate of Hardin-Simmons University in Abilene, Texas, who resigned as the Eagles' basketball coach to accept a position with the US Federal Bureau of Investigation in Washington, DC.

Matthews had been coaching in Corsicana when the six-foot-four Kenner played at Navarro Junior College for coach Kenneth Clark, a Baylor University graduate who played football and basketball for the Bears. "Would you be interested in leaving Sonora and coming to Pecos High School?" Matthews asked Kenner as they became reacquainted during the track and field events in Fort Stockton.

"Well, yes," Kenner replied.

Matthews invited Kenner and his wife, Helen, to visit Pecos and meet with the superintendent, Ray H. Whitley. It was during this meeting on Sunday, April 24, according to Kenner, that the superintendent asked, "Do you know how to handle Black people?"

Kenner thought to himself, "Is this a loaded question or not? Here I am, not thirty years old. How am I to answer this?"

"Yes, sir, I do," Kenner responded to Whitley.

"Well, how?" the superintendent said.

As Kenner recalled that conversation, he believed Whitley may simply have been asking for information. The prospective coach answered, "Mr. Whitley, just like everyone else. You don't expect any more; you don't expect any less. We all just live together."

"Oh," Whitley offered.

Kenner remembered, "We got off to a good start right there."

Two days later, according to the *San Angelo Standard-Times*, Whitley offered the job to Kenner during a telephone conversation, and he accepted. "It's my loss and Garland Matthews' gain," Joe Turner, Sonora's director of athletics, told the *Standard-Times*. "We hate to see him go." Kenner had coached a young Broncos basketball team to third in District 6-A in his final season as Sonora's varsity head coach, and his junior high school teams were undefeated in football and district champions in track and field.

In Kenner's third season at Sonora in 1954–55, the Eagles were 6–4 in District 6-A after winning only one district game in his first season (1–9 with the lone win over Junction) in 1952–53 and two district games in his second season (2–8) in 1953–54.

The 1954–55 Broncos were led by a young sophomore, George Johnson, who averaged 21.2 points per district game (with a record forty points in an overtime win over Junction), finished runner-up in 6-A in scoring, and earned unanimous all-district and third-team Class A all-state. Kenner's team led 6-A in scoring (63.5 points per game), but it couldn't overcome coach Swede Pelto's Ozona team that won its fourth straight district title.

Kenner did not come to Pecos with an impressive record. His three Broncos teams had a combined 9–21 record in district games. Most of the sports headlines in Sonora's weekly newspaper, *The Devil's River News*, were claimed by the Sonora High School girls team coached by legendary Dr. Jewell G. Pye, whose team in 1955 captured its fourth straight District 6-A title.

Born April 12, 1927, Kenner grew up and played high school basketball in the small East Texas community of Powell near Corsicana. His father ran the local cotton yard, and Kenner grew up handling 520-pound bales of cotton. "When I was thirteen years old, I started that," he said. "I was raised around this cotton gin in Powell. The cotton yard was going big then."

At that time, Kenner said, two Black families lived on his family farm, where he also resided in his retirement years with his wife, Helen, before his death on December 3, 2019, at the age of ninety-two. "South of here, there were nothing but colored people," he said. "I was raised here. This was all cotton country. All my friends were colored people. They had a high school about two miles from our place.

"We chopped cotton together, picked cotton together, sang together, swam together, and played ball against one another all the time," Kenner continued. "That's what I told Mr. Whitley. He didn't know I was born and raised with them. I knew them. All of them are our good friends. Always have been."

As a college student and later as a coach, Kenner studied the offensive and defensive strategies and systems of basketball coaches Branch McCracken of Indiana, Adolph Rupp of Kentucky, and Milton Jowers of Southwest Texas State (now Texas State University). He said his coach at East Texas State, Jack Woodroof, taught him how to get along with people.

"I wish I could go back and teach young men who are trying to be coaches what they mean to their community and to the kids," he said. "You've got to be the role model. Don't *play* the role model; *be* the role model. There's a heck of a difference between playacting and being the real thing.

"He told us exactly what we needed to know about how to be a success in the classroom and what people expected out of us and how to get along. And this is where some kids need advice today."

Kenner's preference for the 2-1-2 formation on defense dated back to his days at Powell High School under coaches Charles W. Meeker and Dolph Tillison, who both also served as superintendents of the small school in the East Texas community.

"That defense is still used today," Kenner explained. "If you watch your colleges, they will fall back in the 2-1-2. . . . The reason we ran the 2-1-2 was our superintendent who moved to Powell was a Baylor man. He put that in and taught us all the fundamentals about how that thing worked.

"The 2-1-2 bends like a box. Wherever the ball goes, you face it with a 2-1-2. You keep your eye on the ball. You need to be looking. It has to be 2-1-2. So if you keep that up and no one gets out of position, then it will hold up under a lot of stress. It gives you a rebound advantage, and you're also in position for a fast break from it because of the position everybody is in. And also, if you do not have many people, it keeps the foul count down."

Kenner also learned what he called the "basketball stance" or "athletic stance" from his Powell coaches. "Knees bent, ready to move, rather than standing there straight-legged."

He adopted the 1-3-1 offense from Jowers at Southwest Texas State—"One man out front, one high post, one low post, and two forwards." Kenner added, "That's what broke us open to start doing so well out in West Texas. That thing was unseen. I did a lot of playing out of that. We started scoring like I don't know what after we went to that."

He said the 1-3-1 offense also made it more difficult for opponents to double-team his two premier players, Ephriam and Simmons. With Ephriam at the high post, Kenner played Simmons on one wing with the other forward at the low post (Dick Patrick in 1955–56 and Eugene Walker in 1956–57) to "force someone to stay back there. If they don't stay back there with him, we'll just lob the ball back there, and he'll make it.

"They could not double-team both [Ephriam and Simmons]," Kenner continued. "One of them would be loose most of the time."

He challenged his players to look for options from the 1-3-1 offense. "It's not the play that you start; it's the options that you do," he said. "The danger with the kids is they want to run the options. I said, 'Guys, if you don't run the play, the options will never show. That's what makes the options go is the play you run. So get that in your head.' They liked the options. . . .

"Everybody had to be looking," he added. "Whose man had screwed up? If your man screws up, the rest of you have got to make it cost 'em."

Another feature of Kenner's first season at Pecos was moving Simmons from center to forward. "Billy Jim was the center the year before," Kenner said, "and Billy Jim weighed about a hundred sixty-five pounds. So when they integrated, I had Bubba. I told Billy Jim, 'You're going to play forward.'

"Uh-oh. That's where it hit the fan," Kenner continued. "Here's this Black boy coming in, and ol' Coach Kenner is going to put a Black boy at center. Which I did. I played basketball all my life, so I could recognize who needed to go where. I made Bubba the center. Billy Jim got out there [at forward], and his talent showed up better. He was built for that better than he was the post, for crying out loud. Anybody with any basketball knowledge would know that just looking at him.

"That had its effect the first year with the public and the school system, but not with the kids," Kenner explained. "The kids understood. I never had any trouble with the kids at Pecos at all. But I didn't allow anything to go on that I didn't think should. I was from 'the old school,' so to speak."

Kenner said his team's winning record "took care" of most of the resistance that resulted from moving Simmons to forward. "Had we lost," he said, "it would have been a different story."

Kenner quickly recognized that Ephriam knew the game of basketball when he came to Pecos from Carver, where he had played for coach Sidney Sadler. "He knew, but he was raw with it," Kenner said of the Eagles' new center. "He had it, but he didn't know how to completely fit in with the group and be a cog, even though he was the main cog with Billy Jim. But these cogs have to fit together. . . .

"It took Bubba a while to learn the footwork to be the post man. That's what I was all the time so I knew all the little steps and everything else that it took to be a post man. He caught on to that real quickly, but he had a little trouble with the footwork."

Ephriam believes Kenner did not know how to coach Black players ("he ruined our game") and didn't understand what Ephriam calls the "freelance" style of play he learned from Coach Sadler at Carver. Ephriam came to Pecos already equipped with a hook shot. "Kenner hated my hook shot," he said. "I mastered the hook shot at Carver. When I went to Pecos High, the hook shot was just part of my makeup."

Sadler's teams enjoyed success using a fast-paced offense, running and moving, and man-to-man defense. "You stay in your opponent's face at all times," Sadler told his defensive players. Ephriam added, "Coach Sadler stopped using the zone defense when we were B string for Carver." Ephriam described Kenner's zone defense as "standing around waiting on a play to develop."

"I don't regard him as a coach," Ephriam said of Kenner. "I never learned anything from him. . . . I have searched my mind, heart, and soul trying to come up with something good that he taught me. The answer is always nothing."

Simmons said Kenner "walked into a hell of a deal my junior year. We had our best team. All of those guys played all sports. They were good football players. Our starting guard, Bill Kelley, was the starting quarterback on the football team. We were just close all the way through. We went to school together."

He said Kenner "wanted to beat everybody. He wanted to beat 'em bad. . . . He wasn't a meek coach. He ran the show. There were one or two times coach made us practice after we got in from the game at ten or eleven o'clock at night. We didn't get beat; we just didn't play up to what he thought our standards should be.

"I don't remember him getting on me or telling me things I should have done. He inherited me as a guy who was third-team all-state as a sophomore. I was going to be the heart of his team.

"He didn't know what to think of Bubba or R. C. He didn't want to step on any toes.

"I was very coachable," Simmons continued. "I'd do anything. I wasn't going to be a problem."

Simmons said he was surprised when the school board hired Kenner, because "I don't know what credentials he had to show. He was a young guy when he came to Pecos. . . . I liked the guy. He was a good guy, really, but I didn't like the way he liked to show off and he liked the glamour. He had a couple of good years here."

Simmons said he wasn't aware of the sentiment among some people in Pecos for Sadler to replace Burris. "That would have been awful hard to do it looks like to me," Simmons said. "Keep in mind we had no Blacks in our school at that time if you're talking about when Kenner got the job" (in April 1955 before PHS was integrated in September).

"But it wouldn't have surprised me," Simmons continued. "I knew him a little bit. They all respected him. I didn't know that was even in the cards. I certainly wouldn't have minded it."

In addition to teaching Ephriam footwork and his preferred way to play center in the high post of his 1-3-1 offense, Kenner said he talked to Ephriam about what to expect as an African American player during the first year of integration in Pecos. "I sat Bubba down," Kenner recalled. "I knew how people were because I was from East Texas. I wasn't that way, but I knew how everybody was.

"I said, 'Bubba, I'm going to tell you. You're a Black person, and people are going to find it mighty hard to accept the situation we're going through now. One day it'll all work out. But here's the thing. You're going to hear things that are terribly upsetting to you. I can understand it, but here is what I want you to think about and what I want you to do for me. I don't care what you hear, I want you to show no emotion whatsoever. When you make a real good play, show no emotion whatsoever. You just jog back down the floor or run back down the floor like everybody ought to. Can you think about that and do that?'"

"Yes, I can," Ephriam answered, according to his new coach.

"And it actually worked, because he never let me down," Kenner continued. "He never showed any emotion that anything like that upset him. He knew we cared for him. He never let me down in any way. 'Bubba, you can be the best ambassador to your people. This is a great opportunity for you to show what you can do. Don't put on when you make these big, nice plays.'

"I didn't allow any showboating at all," Kenner added. "It was strictly business. Bubba never let me down. I've never seen anyone so unselfish as he was, because he let Billy Jim have the limelight. But when we really needed help, he could take over and dominate."

One week after the season-opening thrashing of Wink, Pecos warmed up for a more challenging trip to Monahans with an easy 62–25 victory at Grandfalls. The *Odessa American* said Pecos was favored to capture the eight-team Monahans tournament held December 9–10. "Tall, talented Eagles rule as a heavy favorite to romp to the championship," the *American* wrote. "The Eagles boast four starters off last year's team that finished second to Marfa in the tournament plus a pair of hotshot Negro stars in their first season with the Eagles after Pecos integrated the races last fall."

Pecos was matched against the host, Monahans, in Friday's tournament opener, and Kenner's team came away with another easy victory, 71–33. In the semifinals Saturday morning, as expected, Pecos topped Kermit, 54–49, and Alpine also advanced with a five-point win, 55–50, over Crane in its semifinal game.

In the championship game, Pecos held a slim advantage of 32–31 at intermission, but the Eagles scored the first nine points of the third quarter while holding the Bucks scoreless for six minutes to take a ten-point lead at 41–31. "After that, it was all Pecos as Bubba Ephriam, Billy Jim Simmons and Dick Patrick took command of both backboards," the *American* reported. "Ephriam, 6'7" Negro sensation, registered 26 points—all from the field. At least nine of his 13 field goals came on tip-ins as he leaped high in following up teammate shots." Pecos came away with a 48–41 decision over Alpine in "a well-played championship game."

And again, the five starters did all the scoring as Ephriam outscored the combined efforts of his four teammates. Simmons and Christopher each had eight, Patrick, four, and Kelley, two. Ephriam, Simmons, and Patrick were named to the all-tournament team.

The Eagles returned home for a rematch with Grandfalls on December 13 before another weekend tournament. As they did on several occasions, Simmons (thirty points) and Ephriam (twenty) outscored the entire opposing team in a 77–28 win over Grandfalls.

Twelve teams entered the fifth annual Andrews tournament held December 15–17, with Seminole, Odessa, El Paso Jefferson, and Pecos rated as the top four contenders for the title. In the feature game of the first day, reigning tournament champion Odessa handed Seminole, defending Class AA state champion, its first loss of the season, 64–55, before a capacity crowd of nearly two thousand fans. Pecos defeated Tahoka, 61–43, on Friday and Kermit, 68–53, early Saturday to take an undefeated record of 8–0 into the semifinal game Saturday afternoon against El Paso Jefferson.

Behind six-foot-eight sophomore center Albert Almanza, who was named the tournament's outstanding player, Jefferson turned back Pecos, 40–35, to hand the Eagles their first loss of the season and advance to the championship game against Odessa, which had qualified with a 73–51 win over San Angelo. The Jefferson Silver Foxes won the final game, 80–62, with four players in double figures (led by twenty-three from Almanza, a native of Mexico who later played on a Southwest Conference championship team at the University of Texas and led Mexico's national team in scoring at the Olympic Games in 1960 and 1964).

"Man, those jokers were tall," Ephriam said of the Jefferson players. "They were huge. I don't see why they didn't beat us more than they did."

Again, three Eagles were members of the ten-man all-tournament team—this time Ephriam, Simmons, and Christopher.

Kenner's team concluded play for the month of December with another home game—December 20 against Van Horn—before a holiday break to prepare for the District 6-AA season. Ephriam's twenty-three points and eighteen from his former Carver teammate Christopher paced the Eagles in their 61–46 win over Van Horn for Pecos's ninth win in ten games. In addition to the 6-AA opener against Crane, also awaiting the Eagles during the first week of district play in January 1956 was a much-anticipated game against their nemesis Seminole.

From all outward appearances, the Eagles' season was progressing nicely with their first-year coach, the return of scoring-leader Simmons and three other starters, and the addition of two talented Black players to their roster. Pecos carried a record of 9–1 to the beginning of district play along with the Monahans tournament championship trophy and a lone five-point loss to a good Class AAAA team, El Paso Jefferson. But the relationship between the new coach, Kenner, and the new center, Ephriam, wasn't always congenial.

One of his teammates occasionally had to step between Ephriam and Kenner during practice to prevent confrontations from escalating. "Tempers flared up," Ephriam said. "He didn't like my style of play. He called me a 'showboat.' . . . He had never coached Black guys before."

Ephriam recalled an incident that likely occurred in December after the Eagles' first game. On a Saturday, two days after the opener, Bubba, his mother, and his sister Ora Lee were downtown on South Oak Street at Fonville Jewelry, John F. Fonville's new store that the *Pecos Enterprise* called "one of the most modern jewelry stores in West Texas," shopping for Bubba's Christmas gift, a new watch.

Kenner also happened to be downtown and saw his starting center, who introduced his mother and sister to his new coach. "Mother and sister, my eye," Bubba said the coach responded, rolling his eyes. Bubba added, "He didn't believe that was my mother and sister."

The following Monday, Kenner required Ephriam to run laps in the gymnasium during practice. According to Ephriam, Kenner told the assembled team, "I guess you all are wondering what this is all about. Mr. 'Big Star' Bubba Ephriam was walking downtown Saturday with two girls on his arms."

"He was punishing me because he didn't believe," Ephriam said. Christopher came to Ephriam's defense at practice, but Kenner denied him. "Nobody asked you," the coach told Christopher as Ephriam continued to circle the gym floor.

Kenner said once he used the lanyard attached to his whistle to whip Ephriam's legs in practice after he told the coach, "I can't jump."

Simmons remembers Kenner ordering Ephriam to run laps around the gym during practice with the coach following behind and striking his legs with the lanyard. "He would kind of run around the court with Bubba," Simmons explained, "but I don't think it was a mean thing. I don't think Bubba took it that way. If you looked at it like a principal coming in the gym, he might think something. But I even believe they were laughing while they were doing it. I may be wrong. . . .

"I don't think Kenner would have done anything to hurt Bubba," Simmons said. "I think Kenner liked Bubba a lot. . . . I think Bubba would have told me things because we were close. I think I would know a lot of things that Bubba had going on, but I don't think there was anything bad. Bubba might have felt like that.

"Kenner could have been the type that would make you think that he might not like Blacks," Simmons continued. "He might be the type that might make you think that. When I think about him taking the initiative to beat Bubba going around the gym, that's sort of a sign of something. He's the coach, and he's the player. Bubba might have taken that as something more. I just don't think there was something going on there. There could be things that certainly I didn't know about."

"Bubba was a helluva basketball player," Donnie Lee Hall, an Eagles fan and former teammate of Ephriam at Carver, said. "When Bubba came to Pecos High, he was ready to play basketball. Kenner would get on him all the time. He was hard on him."

News of Kenner using his whistle lanyard to whip Ephriam's legs reached the superintendent's office. Whitley called the coach into his office.

"John, have you been whipping Bubba's legs with that lanyard on your whistle?"

"Yes, sir, I have," Kenner answered the superintendent.

"Well, what for?"

"Bubba said he wasn't able to jump in practice, and I was convincing him that he could. That's the only way I could. I've asked him to. No, he just can't."

Whitley listened to Kenner's answer and responded, "Can you stop that?"

"Yes, sir, I can. If you tell me not to do that anymore, I won't do it."

Whitley asked, "What effect is that going to have?"

"Mr. Whitley, he's going to drop from about twenty points a ball game down to about ten."

"Oh, well, just try not to do it so much."

Like Simmons, Ephriam believes the 1955–56 Eagles were potentially a better team than the 1956–57 squad that won district and regional titles and advanced to the state tournament. "We could have had a better team if Kenner had opened up and used the Black guys that were there," Ephriam said. "We could have went to state the first year we were there and won the championship, but he didn't know how to use the players he had."

Another one of Ephriam's teammates at Carver in 1954–55, Al Wilson, joined him at Pecos High School, but he played on the B team in basketball at Pecos in 1955–56.

"Anybody who stepped into this position who knew anything about basketball could have won state both years," Ephriam added. "That's how good of a team we had. But somehow he held us back. Several Black guys could have made the varsity team that first year, but he held them back and played them on the B team. He just didn't have the basketball knowledge and experience of Coach Sadler."

Ephriam said Sadler taught his Carver teams "the science of the court." He said Sadler's teams could run plays blindfolded.

"Goose Tatum never looked at the goal. He knew where it was. That's the way he practiced. And that's the way I used to do it." Ephriam said he often practiced alone or with another teammate or two after dark, sharing the outdoor court at Carver with June bugs aplenty under the moonlight of the clear West Texas sky.

"Black teams were much better than White teams back then," Ephriam said. "They were more athletic. But I guess he did the best he could."

Bubba's son, Ira Earl, who goes by Earl, remembers hearing William Ephriam and their cousins talk about Coach Kenner. "He wasn't a fair man," Earl said. "He would lean more toward the high-profile people."

Christopher added, "When Bubba and I were on the varsity basketball team together at Pecos High School, they won more games than they had since the 1920s.

"The thing that stopped us from being better was racism of the time in the person of John Kenner. . . . If they had made [Sidney Sadler] the high school coach, we would have walked away with the high school state championship that year." He also believes Carver transfer Al Wilson should have joined him and Ephriam in the starting lineup in 1955–56.

Christopher remembers that in his only year at PHS—the first year of integration—during the Eagles' away games "the police had to escort us to the city limits to keep them from throwing rocks at the bus. They brought us food on the bus because they wouldn't serve us. When we would pull into a service station, we couldn't drink out of the water fountains. They had a little tin cup out there for us. Those things were still segregated back in those days."

Pecos traveled to Crane on Tuesday, January 3, 1956, to start the District 6-AA season against the Golden Cranes with what the *Odessa American* labeled as a "do or die" game looming three days later against Seminole. But the Eagles were able to avoid that potential distraction and easily disposed of Crane with a 66–47 triumph. Five Eagles played for Kenner, five Eagles scored in the double figures, and Pecos improved to 10–1 for the season with the important victory.

The two former Carver teammates, Ephriam and Christopher, each scored fifteen points to pace the Eagles, Simmons and Kelley each scored thirteen, and Patrick added ten points. Pecos never trailed (although there was a 12–12 tie early in the second quarter) and led 28–18 at the half. Crane, led by twenty-two points from center Bill Preslar, got a late start to basketball because its football season was extended by the playoffs.

The *American* called Friday's game "an early showdown . . . for what is expected to be the wildest District 6-AA basketball race in history. . . . The league's co-favorites, Seminole and Pecos, collide head-on Friday night in Pecos. The winner of that one will automatically become the title favorite, and the loser will face an uphill struggle to get back into the scramble."

Seminole, a veteran team with a strong bench, was "a razor-thin choice to repeat against the tall, talented Eagles, who picked up unexpected strength when Pecos became the first integrated high school in the Permian Basin last fall," sportswriter Ben Peeler said.

Coach Metz LaFollette's team had lost only once during its first fourteen games of the season (to Odessa High School), and seven different players had led the team in scoring at least once. The Indians owned wins over Midland, Lubbock, and El Paso high schools, and they trounced three-time reigning Class A champion Avoca.

Center Edwin Young (6'4") was the only "tall boy" on the team, the *American* said, but "the Tribe is a deadly shooting unit that last year overcame that handicap with ease." Seminole reportedly was also quicker than the Eagles. "Seminole is much faster afoot and has a better shooting percentage," the *American* added.

Seminole was reigning Class AA state champion. In March 1955, the Indians knocked off Atlanta 60–52 in their semifinal game in Austin and followed that with a narrow 50–49 triumph over San Marcos in the championship game.

Pecos's starting lineup (6'4" Ephriam at center, 6'3" Simmons and 6'4" Patrick at forwards, and 5'10" Christopher and 6'0" Kelley at guards) "has little to fear from anybody, but there aren't any reserves to equal those of Seminole." (Returning starter Richard Cothrun apparently never joined the PHS team because of injuries sustained during the Eagles' football season.)

The gymnasium at Pecos Junior High School on Third Street, where the game was to be played, held only about seven hundred fans. Three times that many were expected to attempt to jam their way into the building for the "showdown" Friday, January 6. Pecos High School officials warned fans to arrive early, and an additional one hundred people lined the east end of the court in temporary seats and a standing-room-only area.

A roaring crowd of an estimated nine hundred fans, including two hundred from Seminole, squeezed into the gym. Hundreds of fans were turned away, so they didn't get to witness the Indians' 49–45 victory before what the *Pecos Enterprise* said was "probably the largest crowd ever to witness a basketball game in Pecos." The visitors roared to leads of 20–8 after the opening period and 32–16 at intermission with "fantastic" shooting before Pecos rallied in the third quarter. The Eagles outscored Seminole 14–13 in the third period and 15–4 in the fourth, but the sixteen-point halftime deficit proved to be too much to overcome.

Young, Seminole's lanky pivot man who was all-tournament in Austin the previous season at the state meet, led his team with twenty points before leaving the game with five fouls. Ephriam again led the Eagles with seventeen points, and Simmons added twelve, but the Eagles (10–2, 1–1) were now looking up in the district standings at Seminole (14–1, 2–0).

Before the rematch three weeks later on January 27 in Seminole, Pecos faced five district opponents and a home-and-home series with the Odessa High School B team. And Kenner's team remained in contention by winning all seven games, including a 23–12 home win over winless Monahans on January 10 when the Loboes went into a stall for three quarters in their upset bid. Monahans led 8–6 after the first quarter, but the visitors scored only four points in the final twenty-four minutes. Simmons scored twelve points in the Eagles' victory, with Ephriam held to a single point, the fewest in his two years playing for PHS.

"Stalling on the part of the visitors became boresome to the fans," the *Enterprise* reported, "who began to throw paper on the court. Only a threat of a forfeit to Monahans calmed the fans."

Pecos defeated Brownfield 62–45 on the road on January 13 (Ephriam 22, Patrick 12, Simmons 11 points), and the Eagles braved a West Texas snowstorm on January 17 to travel to Alpine for a "surprising" 51–37 win over the previous year's District 7-AA champion now competing in 6-AA (Simmons 19, Patrick 13 points).

The district schedule for Friday, January 20, called for Alpine to visit Seminole in another upset bid as Pecos entertained Kermit, still winless in district at 0–5. The Indians took care of Alpine, 55–50, to maintain the lead in 6-AA.

In Pecos, Kenner said his team was leery of its third meeting of the season against Kermit. The Eagles had beaten Kermit in the Monahans and Andrews tournaments, but Kenner said this time his team was "afraid." The coach told his players, "Good night, guys, this is terrible. Go out there and get just as relaxed as you can and you play this game as best as you can, and I don't care what the score gets; I won't pull you out and you can go all the way."

Kenner continued, "Well, it got worse, and it got worse, and it got worse. When we got right next to that one hundred, I said, 'Guys, don't you think it's time to come out and let some of these other guys play?' And they said, 'Coach, you know what you told us.' I said, 'Yes, okay.'"

After Pecos's overwhelming 125–46 victory, the *Odessa American* reported, "Pecos could do no wrong against winless Kermit as the tall Eagles broke every school, district, area and possible state record in a remarkable outburst." Pecos built leads of 31–7 after the first quarter, 57–21 at intermission, and 88–35 after three periods in route to its seventy-nine-point win.

The *Enterprise* later called it an "unnecessary 125–46 clobbering of Kermit" and said Kenner was not "winning a popularity contest in cities in the 6-AA loop." The Eagles' hometown newspaper added, "Repercussions are very likely at the spring meeting of coaches and superintendents when that group meets to set up fall football schedules. We have been told by one who will be attending the meeting that Kenner is due for a 'dressing down.'"

Simmons's thirty-five points led the winners in the "clobbering," but he got plenty of help from Ephriam (29 points), Patrick (23), Christopher (20), and Kelley (18). With another district game remaining—at home on January 24 against Andrews—the Eagles appeared ready for their rematch with Seminole on the road on January 27.

Four days after their 125-point outburst, the Eagles held off the deliberate Andrews team 28–19 (Patrick 12, Simmons 11 points) in another attempt by an Eagles' opponent to win by stalling. Coach Vernon Johnson's strategy was somewhat successful in the first half; the Mustangs trailed by only a point (14–13) at intermission. But the visitors scored only six points in the final two quarters of the Eagles' victory. Ephriam was scoreless from the field with only three free throws.

That set the stage for Friday's rematch between district-leading Seminole (7–0) and challenger Pecos (6–1). Jim O'Brien of the *Pecos Enterprise* called it "a battle of nerves" and added, "A loss to Seminole will put an end to all district hopes and to plans for a trip to Austin and the state playoffs. No one knows this better that the Eagle cagers. They have had this game on top of the agenda for the past couple of weeks."

Since their "Cinderella" season of 1954–55 when they took their opposition by surprise, the Indians had picked up what O'Brien called "a great deal of polish that goes into making a well-rounded basketball team."

And just like the first game on January 6 in Pecos, the visiting team took the win (as predicted by O'Brien, who said that "Pecos has the stuff to turn the trick"). This time, the Eagles handed Seminole a 64–59 loss to break the Indians' eleven-game winning streak. Seminole again shot well early and led 19–13 after the first quarter, but Pecos rallied to tie the score at 33–33 by intermission.

Pecos's inspired play continued, and the Eagles held a slim one-point lead, 49–48, entering the final quarter. Scoring by Patrick had given his team leads of 39–38 and 46–42 in the third period.

The score was tied four times in the fourth quarter. The *American* said the fourth quarter was "a wild scramble," and the *Enterprise* said "the final frame was a 'dilly.'" The Eagles once held a six-point lead before settling for the five-point victory. Ephriam gave his team leads of 55–53 and 56–55, and he scored with 1:15 to play for an advantage of 60–57. Patrick and Kelley scored Pecos's two field goals in the final minute to turn back the Seminole threat before a capacity crowd of more than one thousand people.

Both teams were now 7–1 in district play (with six games left to play). For the season, Seminole was 18–2 and Pecos 17–2.

Pecos closed January with a 90–23 win over Crane as Ephriam erupted for a career high of thirty-seven points. He hit thirteen of his twenty-one field goal attempts (62 percent) along with eleven free throws. The *Enterprise* said he was both "cool as a cucumber" and "hot as a pistol" with "an amazing 37 points, enough to conquer the Cranes single-handed."

O'Brien wrote in the *Enterprise*, "Watching Bill Simmons, Dick Patrick and Bubba Ephriam go high for the rebounds and blocking shots that might go for two-pointers is really something to see. It is hard to figure that any team can beat the combination. The floor work of Bill Kelley and R. C. Christopher—intercepting passes, stealing the ball from the opposition, and being pesky in general—is enough to drive a rival coach to drink. Defensively, it is without a doubt the best team we've seen this season, bar none."

The Eagles seldom were threatened in their five district games in the final month with wins of 74–52 over Brownfield on February 3 (Simmons 25, Ephriam 13 points), 73–42 over Monahans on February 7 (Ephriam 30, Simmons 18), 75–51 over Kermit on February 10 (Simmons 26, Ephriam 18),

60–37 over Alpine in the final home game on February 14 (Ephriam 20), and 26–15 over Andrews on February 16 in another attempt at stalling (Simmons 8) in the regular season finale that left the co-leaders with identical District 6-AA records of 13–1.

The *Odessa American* had reported on Sunday, February 12, "The torrid District 6-AA basketball race roars into its final week with powerful Pecos and defending state champion Seminole still deadlocked for first place."

The Seminole team overcame a setback in early February, according to the *American*, when Johnny Speer—the team's second-leading scorer (12.7 points per game), its co-MVP, and all-tournament in Austin the previous year when Seminole High School won the state championship—quit after being moved from the starting lineup to the bench for the role of a substitute player by Coach LaFollette in favor of senior Charlie Benson, who had returned to the team after missing the 1954–55 season with injuries. Benson had been the team's leading scorer as a sophomore in 1953–54.

"As long as he feels like that, I guess it was the best thing to do," LaFollette told the *American*. "I hoped Speer would come along and change his attitude, but since he's decided to quit I'm glad he did before the situation got worse. His loss will hurt us in the matter of manpower, although I don't believe it'll hurt our first team any."

As District 6-AA co-champions, Pecos and Seminole now faced each other in a one-game playoff to determine the league's lone playoff representative. Both head coaches wanted to play on Saturday, February 18, at Odessa High School, but the OHS gymnasium was already scheduled for a playoff game.

Pecos favored Kermit as host for the playoff, and Seminole preferred Hobbs, New Mexico. A coin flip set the game in Kermit's gym, which seated about 1,500 fans, just two days after the regular season ended because that was the final day for districts to declare a playoff representative to UIL officials in Austin.

Seminole scored the first five points of the game, but Pecos recovered to take the lead. Kelley's steal and ensuing layup gave his team a cushion of 13–8 before Seminole added the final two points of the opening period to trail 13–10. Then the Indians, behind the scoring of Charlie Benson and Rupert Combs, took control in the second quarter. They tied the game at

14–14 and then scored the next five points before taking a margin of 31–27 to the dressing room at intermission.

Seminole outscored Pecos 47–26 in the second half, shot 54 percent from the field for the game, and won 78–59 to end Pecos's hopes for its first-ever playoff spot. Seminole was leading by ten at 52–42 just two minutes into the fourth quarter when Ephriam left the game with five fouls after scoring fifteen points.

O'Brien wrote, "Whatever chance the Eagles had of pulling this one 'out of the fire' was dashed against the backboards of the capacity-filled Kermit gym." One minute later, Seminole's tallest player, Young, also fouled out with the margin still at ten at 57–47 after scoring eight points.

The *Odessa American* reported, "The Eagles stayed close until early in the fourth period when they lost their big Negro center, Bubba Ephriam, via the foul route. After his departure, the Indians pulled safely away."

O'Brien added, "The loss of Ephriam was a bitter pill."

Simmons led Pecos with seventeen points, and Christopher matched Ephriam with fifteen. Benson led the winners with thirty-one points (he was fourteen of twenty-two from the field) before a standing-room-only crowd.

The *Seminole Sentinel* said, "Those two colored players on the Pecos team are good sports and would be a credit to any team. They have the respect of the Indians and a big majority of the Seminole fans."

Suddenly, the Eagles' season—their first with Ephriam in the lineup for a new coach—came to a disappointing end before what the *Odessa American* said was a capacity crowd of 1,600 fans, reportedly the largest crowd ever at the Kermit High School gym.

"That White boy could shoot," Christopher said of Benson. "He just sat out there and beat the hell out of us. Kenner didn't know how to defense him. Prof would have known. Al [Wilson] would have been in that game instead of Billy Jim Simmons or Dick Patrick. Kenner didn't know how to coach against that one guy, and we lost that game."

With Sadler as coach, Christopher said, "We'd have put a box-and-one on his butt in a minute. Four men in a zone, and Al Wilson would have guarded Benson. That son of a gun wouldn't have been able to get the ball. Prof would have told Al to stay between him and the ball. He would have had hell getting the ball. They just whipped the ball around, he sat out there with that set shot, and he tore the bottom of the net up. They whipped our butts good. . . .

"Nearly everybody we played, we were outcoached," Christopher added. "A lot of those games we played and won. I'm convinced today, we wouldn't have won if it hadn't been for me and Bubba."

The Indians (with a season record of 27–2) had won for the second and decisive time in three meetings with Pecos (24–3) that season and earned the right to meet Abernathy in bi-district competition. (Seminole was later eliminated by Phillips, 70–69, in the Region I-AA tournament in Lubbock in only its third loss of the season.)

The co-champions each placed two players on the all-District 6-AA team as selected by the *Odessa American*—Ephriam and Simmons from Pecos and Seminole's Young and Benson, who shot better than 60 percent from the field. They were joined by district scoring leader Donnie Benham of Andrews. The *American* said, "The first team, if playing together, likely could overwhelm any high school five in the United States. They would carry a collective scoring average of almost 90 points per game [and] boast exceptional height, good speed and tremendous defensive ability."

Simmons averaged 17.7 points per game and "made the transfer from center to forward with his usual grace," the *American* said. "He moved to forward this year to make room for Ephriam and still led the team in scoring.

"Ephriam, the giant Negro star, averaged 17 points a game, dominated most backboards as if they were personal property and proved himself a fine defender as well." Christopher and Patrick of Pecos were named to the second team.

The *San Angelo Standard-Times* named Simmons the district MVP (for the second straight season), and he was joined on its all-district team by teammate Ephriam, Benson of Seminole, Benham of Andrews, and Don Burgess of Alpine. Christopher was named second-team all-district by the *Standard Times*.

Jim O'Brien, writing in the *Pecos Enterprise*, said, "When it comes to floor work, where in the district will you find two better than Bill Kelley or R.C. Christopher? The dribbling of R.C. reminds one of a junior

Globetrotter. Where did he learn the art? From none other than his former cage tutor, a top basketball player in his own right."

Simmons finished the season with 461 points after scoring a record 424 as a sophomore in 1954–55, and Ephriam was narrowly behind him with at least 452 points. At the team's annual P Association awards banquet at year-end, radio station KIUN named Simmons as the basketball team's outstanding player.

The starting five accounted for all but 34 of the Eagles' 1,602 points for the season, which included 280 by Patrick and 233 by Christopher.

In the first season at Pecos High School that its varsity basketball team included two Black players, Coach Kenner, superintendent Whitley, Ephriam, and his teammates apparently didn't have to contend with what occurred in the communities of Wharton and Beeville. Just four days after Pecos's season ended with a playoff loss to Seminole, Wharton superintendent C. Graves Sivells Jr. said the school board directed Wharton High School to forfeit its girls bi-district basketball game because "of the fact that there is a colored girl on the Beeville team." Writing in *The Texas Book*, Bobby Hawthorne said the board's vote on February 22, 1956, was unanimous even though coach Meta "Mickie" Holesovsky's team was undefeated with a win over Angleton, the eventual state champion.

And it wasn't the first time Wharton declined to play against a team with African American players. Hawthorne, a journalist and the former UIL director of academics, said Wharton forfeited a football game to Port Lavaca in fall 1955 "to keep its white kids from playing against blacks."

According to Hawthorne, Sivells told Boyd Tingle, the WHS director of athletics and football head coach, "You can't play that game. Get yourself another ball game." Tingle's wife, Pat, a fourth-grade teacher, told Hawthorne, "People don't understand how ugly it was back then. They don't believe it. But I remember what they told me when it came up about playing Port Lavaca. Sivells said, 'We'll never play those black bastards.'"

Doris Housworth Teague, a sixteen-year-old Wharton basketball player, attended a meeting the following day to hear the board's explanation for its decision. She told Hawthorne, "I can remember Thomas Abell [a lawyer who was a member of the school board] saying . . ., 'If we let you do this, we will have those niggers knocking down the doors to get into this school. And we're not going to have that.'"

Wharton officials received a letter dated April 13, 1956, from UIL director Rodney James Kidd that the state executive committee was studying the incident to determine if Wharton had violated UIL rule 27, which said that "any school failing to participate or complete the official schedule of games, unless excused for valid reasons by the State Executive Committee (SEC), shall be guilty of a breach of contract and suspended for one year."

Sivells and four Wharton school board members attended a meeting on April 24 in Austin to argue their case. According to Hawthorne, Sivells told the committee that since the Wharton school was segregated, "the school board and administrators didn't consider it wise to play a game with a desegregated school because the colored folk in his community might not understand how a black child from Beeville or some other school was allowed to play in the white high school gymnasium against the white players . . . but their children were not. They weren't even allowed to attend games in the white gym. They darn sure weren't going to open the doors to outsiders."

Despite Sivells's pleas, the executive committee voted on April 27 to suspend Wharton's girls basketball team from UIL competition for one year beginning on September 1, 1956. A few days later, May 9, the Wharton board authorized Abell to bypass the UIL and appeal the suspension to the Board of Regents of the University of Texas. In his letter on June 15, Abell said, "Wharton has not integrated the Negroes and whites in its school system and has no intention of doing so." He said UIL rule 27 was written "at a time when segregated schools were required by law, hence it was not the intention that forfeiture of a game for racial reasons be a violation of the rule." Avoidance of an integrated situation, Abell said, "was certainly valid."

UT regents chairman Tom Sealy of Midland, in a letter dated July 31, acknowledged that the regents "do not have any direct jurisdiction over this matter," but he suggested that the executive committee reconsider its decision.

In a follow-up letter to Sealy from UIL reiterating its position, Kidd and R. D. Eddy noted that the university had not objected to the league's

1955 interpretation of what constituted a "white public school," nor had the university "objected to the possibility that a Negro child might play in the state basketball tournament, might even use the Gregory Gym dressing rooms and other facilities."

Eddy, a member of the executive committee, said, "The state executive committee recognizes that the ruling of the US Supreme Court on segregated schools has created many new and unusual problems not covered by existing policies."

A series of letters between Sealy, Kidd, Sivells, and UT president Dr. Logan Wilson continued until September 23, 1956, when the UIL legislative advisory council gathered in Austin for an emergency meeting. Regents chairman Sealy said, "I also devoutly hope and anticipate that the council . . . will so amend its rules as to relieve Wharton from the penalty inflicted upon it. Please do whatever you can to see that this is accomplished."

Hawthorne said no newspapers covered the meeting attended by twenty-one of the twenty-three council members at the Driskill Hotel in downtown Austin. The council amended UIL rule 27 so that in the future, schools unwilling to play teams with Negroes would forfeit the game and rebate privileges, but they would not be suspended. But the council refused to overturn Wharton's suspension, and the Wharton school board filed no further protests or appeals.

Basketball was Ephriam's first varsity sport at Pecos High School, he explained, because his birth certificate from Hidalgo County did not arrive in time to prove his age to make him eligible for varsity football in the fall of 1955. So he played on the Eagles' B team in football, and after basketball, he played baseball for coach Weldon Boggus and competed in track and field for coach Garland Matthews in the spring.

Long-time friend Christopher, now a seventeen-year-old high school senior, was his teammate in varsity basketball, baseball, and track and field. And after the athletics seasons ended, Christopher made history in another way. He was among the first seven African American students who graduated from Pecos High School.

Reginald Claudius Christopher was born August 20, 1938, in a small community named Reklaw ("that's Walker spelled backward," he said) between Rusk and Tyler in East Texas. His family members were cotton pickers and cotton farmers. "Don't call 'em sharecroppers," he said. "They weren't sharing in much." Sharecropping, slavery's replacement, kept African Americans in debt and still bound to the owners, farms, and plantations for which they worked.

His parents, Emily and Roscoe Christopher, followed Roscoe's father, John, to West Texas about 1941. R. C. said his mother was a high school graduate who insisted that their children attend school and get an education. "I heard my mama tell my daddy, 'They aren't going to no cotton patch. They're going to school, and they're going to finish school.'

"My mama is my hero," he continued. "She was as mean as a snake, but she took care of us. She saw to it that we stayed in school, and she kept food on the table and clothes on our back. She was purposeful. 'You respect people.' If my daddy had his way about it, we'd be just like him. He finished third grade, could barely write his name, shining shoes, driving cotton-farming machinery."

R. C. attended George Washington Carver School with other Black children in Pecos from grades one through eleven and competed in PVIL sports, then enrolled in Pecos High School in September 1955 for his senior year. He was a member of the school choir and male quartet, and he ranked seventh in the graduating class of ninety-four seniors with a grade point average of 93.58. (He would have been valedictorian if he had been allowed to graduate from Carver's class of 1956.) The *Pecos Enterprise* said the PHS class of 1956 was "the largest graduating class in the school's history."

Six other Black students graduated with Christopher in Pecos Junior High School gymnasium May 24, 1956. They were Odessa Bailey (who ranked nineteenth with a grade average of 91.23), Ruth Ella Bradford, Eddie Ferguson, Gracie Lee Lewis, Audry Lee Pendleton, and Velma Walker.

Valedictorian was Bill Kelley (95.97), senior class president and four-sport letterman who starred in basketball with Christopher and Ephriam and as a quarterback in football. Dr. Harold G. Cooke, the president of McMurry College in Abilene, was the commencement speaker.

Four years later in 1960, Christopher graduated from Huston-Tillotson College in Austin and returned home that summer to begin his job search. "I figured a college graduate ought to be able to get one of them jobs," he said. "I went to the employment office," but he said they told him, "Boy, we ain't got nothing for you. Mr. Anderson needs some cotton pickers."

Christopher said, "I'm thinking, 'Man, I'm a college graduate. What is he talking about?' I spoke very harsh to the man. I talked bad to that man. Black kids have been killed for less."

Christopher recalled that five years earlier, almost to the exact day, Emmett Louis Till, a fourteen-year-old African American boy whose family had immigrated to Chicago, Illinois, was murdered on August 28, 1955, while on a return visit to Money, Mississippi, for what he allegedly said that offended a White woman, Carolyn Bryant, in her family's grocery store.

Till's mother, Mamie, had sent Emmett to Mississippi to spend the summer with his cousins, aunt, and uncle Mose Wright. But she never saw him again. He was abducted, tortured, and killed a month after his fourteenth birthday, and three days later, his swollen and disfigured body was found by fishermen in the Tallahatchie River—with a seventy-five-pound fan from a cotton gin tied around his neck. Two defendants, Roy Bryant and his half brother J. W. Milam, who later admitted to the killing in an article in *Look* magazine, were acquitted by an all-male, all-White jury on September 23, 1955. The case attracted widespread attention and became emblematic of racial injustice.

Till's murder occurred just 103 days after the announcement of the Supreme Court decision in *Brown v. Board of Education*. Michael J. Klarman, in his 2004 book *From Jim Crow to Civil Rights*, says, "Connecting these killings [Till in 1955 and George Lee and Lamar Smith in Mississippi in 1957] to *Brown* is speculative, but the timing suggests a possible linkage, and some contemporaries inferred a causal connection. The *Herald* of Yazoo City, Mississippi, declared that the blood of Till was on the hands of the justices. . . . One Mississippi white declared, 'There's open season on the Negroes now. They've got no protection, and any peckerwood who wants can go out and shoot himself one, and we'll free him.'"

Isabel Wilkerson, in her book *The Warmth of Other Suns*, says Mamie held the funeral with an open casket so people could see what had been done to her son. *Jet* magazine published a photograph of Emmett's mutilated body, and thousands stood in line for hours to view the body at Roberts Temple Church of God in Christ. One of those, a migrant named Ida Mae Brandon Gladney, said she was unprepared for what confronted her. "The undertakers had done what they could," Wilkerson writes, "but an eye was out of its socket, and the face so disfigured that it did not resemble a human being's. She had to look away."

Reverend Wheeler Parker Jr., a cousin of Emmett Till, told American author and moral philosopher Susan Neiman, "There's an old saying, 'If I was Catholic and I lived in the South, I'd be worried. If I was Jewish, I'd be packing up. If I was black, I'd be gone.'"

And according to Klarman, Mississippi was not the only Southern state to become more racially violent after Brown. For example, Birmingham, Alabama, became known as "Bombingham" when African Americans were the targets of twenty-one bombings between 1955 and 1963—none of which the police solved.

When R. C. returned home from the employment office that summer day in 1960, his mother had already heard of his conversation there. "What in the hell is wrong with you?" she asked. "Them White folks down there say you were talking smart."

"Mama, I wasn't talking smart. I just told them I'm a college graduate. I'm not picking no damn cotton. . . .

"They wanted to keep Black people subservient."

Instead of finding a job, Christopher joined the US Army, served three years, including some time in Germany, and returned to Austin to work at Huston-Tillotson as a men's counselor for one year. He taught and coached three years at Blackshear, a school for Black students in Odessa, then applied and was accepted to attend the School of Dentistry at Meharry Medical College in Nashville, Tennessee.

He graduated from dental school in 1972, served as a dentist in the US Air Force until 1982, and had a dental practice in Austin for seventeen years until his retirement in 1999. In his retirement years, he studied gerontology and earned a master's degree in human development and family studies from Texas Tech University in 2010. He died on April 18, 2023, at the age of eighty-four.

Christopher believed he was the first Black athlete to graduate from a UIL school in Texas after integration. Certainly, he was among the first. "I called the UIL a few years ago," he said, "but they told me they kept no records on that kind of stuff."

(Christopher's claim to be the first Black athlete to graduate from a UIL school could be accurate. According to published reports, many of the approximately sixty schools that integrated in 1955–56 started with elementary grades, leaving Pecos as one of the very few with Black students in high school in the first year of integration.)

He recalled those long rides to out-of-town games across West Texas, eating meals on the bus with Bubba because "they wouldn't serve us," and occasionally needing a police escort to the city limits.

"A lot of us were victims then," Christopher continued. "We didn't understand the effect that racism had on us—not just the Black kids, but the White kids too. Bill Kelley and the rest of those White kids were just as much victims of the times as I was, and we didn't understand it.

"Some of them still don't."

District 6-AA Playoff

Kermit, Texas

Saturday, February 18, 1956

Seminole 78, Pecos 59

	1Q	2Q	3Q	4Q	Total
Pecos	13	14	14	18	**59**
Seminole	10	21	19	28	**78**

Pecos	Field Goals Made	Free Throws Made	Total Points
Billy Jim Simmons	7	3	17
Dick Patrick	2	3	7
Bubba Ephriam	7	1	15
R. C. Christopher	6	3	15
Bill Kelley	2	1	5
Charles Patillo	0	0	0
Team Totals	***24***	***11***	***59***

Seminole	Field Goals Made	Free Throws Made	Total Points
Edwin Young	2	4	8
Charles Benson	14	3	31
Donnie Wilson	4	0	8
Leland Cathey	5	5	15
Rupert Combs	6	0	12
Harry Walker	2	0	4
Team Totals	***33***	***12***	***78***

SEVEN

CAPACITY CROWDS CHEER THE EAGLES

Non-District Basketball Games at PHS in 1956–57

Workouts Start for Pecos Cagers
Pecos Enterprise, Nov. 19, 1956

Cage Wars Begin for Pecos
Odessa American, Nov. 27, 1956

Pecos Spoils Big Lake Mark
Odessa American, Dec. 19, 1956

Pecos Eagles Win Own Cage Tourney
Odessa American, Dec. 23, 1956

Two bits, four bits,
six bits, a dollar,
all for Pecos,
stand up and holler.

Expectations were high for the Eagles' basketball team before the 1956–57 season at Pecos High School. Three starters were gone from the previous year's team that had won twenty-four of its twenty-seven games and shared the District 6-AA championship with Seminole in John Kenner's first year as head coach. But the Eagles' leading scorers, Bubba

Ephriam and Billy Jim Simmons, two of the best high school players in West Texas, both returned to wear the purple and gold, generate considerable excitement, and incite much anticipation for Pecos's first year in Class AAA.

Ephriam, one of the few Black students who enrolled at Pecos High School after its integration in 1955, was more comfortable in his second year at his new school. Walking the halls of the high school building on South Park Street after Irene Turk's English class or shop taught by Garland Matthews, Ephriam encountered few problems. "I could do no wrong in her class," he said of Turk. "She tutored me. She was concerned about my education." Her son Tom was a junior at PHS in 1956–57 and played football with Bubba for the Eagles.

"A lot of those teachers had a heart," Ephriam said. "They knew where we were coming from. They really, really were helpful. I never had any experiences of discrimination at school."

"Bubba was just one of the kids," 1956 PHS graduate R. C. Christopher said. "He wasn't a bad boy; he wasn't a good boy. That wasn't something we thought of. A lot of kids even today are in the same situation. . . . He got along in school."

Ephriam's classmates encouraged him, and his teammates supported him. He was named co-captain with Simmons for the upcoming basketball season, an indication of what was to come in Ephriam's second of two unforgettable seasons with the Eagles. He led his team in scoring in the all-important district games, earned third-team all-state, and extended Pecos's season all the way to the Class AAA state championship game.

Bernice remembers older members of their family in Pecos talking about her brother Bubba. "They would always talk about how good he was," she said. "People were cheering for him. 'Oh, my God, he played so well. He did it. He ran down that court and popped the net.' Or however they said it back in the day."

Christopher, his former teammate at Carver and PHS, said Ephriam was a good basketball player because he "had the best basketball coach that ever graced the city of Pecos, Texas. Bubba was tall. He could get up there.

"He was an all-around athlete," Christopher added. "I remember Bubba blocking shots, the sound of the ball when he hit it.

"And he's a good-hearted person. I remember his daddy and his mama. All of us Black people were in the same boat. Bubba has always been a good person. He's not mean. I doubt that Bubba ever had a fight in his life. Bubba's kind of meek in a way."

Eagles fans in Pecos—while talking over chile rellenos at Ben's Spanish Inn or hamburgers at Al's Burger Bar—were looking forward to the approaching basketball season. In its announcement of the Eagles' schedule for the upcoming season, the *Pecos Enterprise* said on November 19, 1956, "The Pecos Eagles are anticipating a good basketball season."

One week later, November 26, the day before the season opener, the prospects had improved even more, according to the *Enterprise*. "The Tuesday night game will mark the beginning of a season which many of the close followers of the team hope will be the most successful in the school's history."

Before basketball, however, the Eagles played their first season of football in Class AAA in the fall of 1956 for third-year head coach Garland Matthews, an assistant who had replaced head coach Boyd Payne in May 1954. Matthews and Payne had also coached together in Corsicana before coming to Pecos, but Payne resigned in the spring after a season of five wins, three losses, and one tie in the fall of 1953 to become head coach and director of athletics at Seagoville.

Matthews guided the Eagles to a record of 4–6 in his first season in 1954 and followed that with an impressive 8–2 mark in 1955 behind senior quarterback Bill Kelley with wins over Fort Stockton, Seminole, Carlsbad (New Mexico), Wink, Alpine, Monahans, Brownfield, and Andrews and losses to Kermit and Crane. Lineman Al Wilson was the lone Black student who transferred from George Washington Carver School to play varsity football for Pecos High School in 1955 in the first year of integration.

Ephriam and Christopher played for coach Dan McLeod's B team (because Bubba's birth certificate had not arrived by the start of the varsity season, Ephriam said), which had a record of 2–5–1, with its only victories coming over Crane and Alpine.

Guard Jerry Hunter was Pecos's lone representative on the all-District 6-AA first team, and end Billy Jim Simmons, tackle Coy Hudson, and fullback Jerry Creager were second-team selections. The 1955 Eagles football team was honored December 8 at its annual Quarterback Club banquet, which featured Sammy Baugh as its main speaker. Baugh was a former star quarterback at Sweetwater High School, at Texas Christian University, and in the NFL for the Washington Redskins and was, at the time, the coach at Hardin-Simmons University in Abilene.

With Ephriam in the varsity starting lineup in the fall of 1956, the Eagles football team posted another eight-win season in their first year in Class AAA. They won their first seven games of the season over Carlsbad, Wink, Crane, Alpine, San Angelo Lake View, Class AAAA member El Paso Austin, and Brownfield before a 32–12 loss to District 2-AAA champion Andrews at the Mustangs' homecoming game on November 2. They closed the season with a tie with Kermit and win over Monahans for a record of 8–1–1. Pecos's 2–1–1 record in District 2-AAA was good for second behind the 4–0 of Andrews in the small five-team district.

The October 12 win over Lake View came on dedication night for the Chiefs' new stadium in San Angelo. The lone touchdown in the 6–0 triumph came after 156-pound senior quarterback Wayne Wassom directed the "heavily favored" Eagles on a seventy-two-yard drive in the third quarter with 141-pound senior halfback David Wallace scoring on a ten-yard run after what Buz Hudgins of the *San Angelo Standard-Times* said was "a fine bit of fakery by Wassom." Hunter was a defensive star for Pecos.

Hunter, 184-pound senior guard, Wassom, and Wallace were voted first-team all-District 2-AAA by the coaches, and Simmons and guard Mike Dowling were second-team choices. Ephriam was an honorable mention selection at tackle on the all-district team.

Ephriam also was honorable mention on the all-district team chosen by the *Odessa American*.

Eighteen-year-old Billy Jim Simmons's senior year of basketball had finally arrived—the fourth and final year of what the *Odessa American* called "one of the most brilliant high school cage careers ever seen in this area." The *American* called it "a golden era of Permian Basin basketball."

And by the time this six-foot, three-inch forward's career ended on March 9, 1957, in Austin, he had scored a school-career record of 1,744 points in the ninety-five games in which he played, earned all-state twice (unanimous choice as a senior), led the Eagles to the school's first outright district title in basketball and an appearance in the state championship game, made all-tournament at every tournament in which he played during his last three seasons, played in high school all-star games after his senior year in Texas and Oklahoma, and earned sixteen varsity letters in five sports at Pecos High School—basketball, football, baseball, track and field, and golf. The Eagles were 78–21 in his four seasons of basketball.

Elmer Six of Monahans, the coach faced with defending Simmons in his final district game on February 15, told Tom Eastland of the *Odessa American*, "He's the best high school player I've seen anywhere, anytime."

Simmons apparently also impressed Texas Western (now University of Texas at El Paso) coach George McCarty when the Eagles played in El Paso on January 4 and 5. Don Boston, play-by-play announcer for KIUN radio in Pecos, told Tom Eastland of the *Odessa American*, "Coach McCarty saw Simmons play when Pecos made their trip to El Paso for a pair of games with El Paso High. Simmons made 26 points the first night and 27 points the second as Pecos won two games.

"McCarty said he had been lots of places this year and seen lots of high school games, but Simmons was by far the outstanding performer he had seen."

After watching Simmons for four years, Boston added, "He will undoubtedly be one of the most sought-after players in Texas high school basketball with feelers already coming in. . . . He has the speed of a guard, is an excellent driver, and handy around the basket. He got this from playing center as a sophomore.

"However, his trademark is an almost unstoppable jump shot from along the baseline as far away as the corner. He shoots the ball from high over his head, one-handed, after leaping into the air."

Jim O'Brien of the *Pecos Enterprise*, during Simmons's junior season, said his corner shot was "the nearest thing to perfection that fans in these parts will see for many a day."

Simmons was born September 22, 1938, in Pecos to Tom and Edna Simmons, who had moved to this West Texas city from Stephenville in north-central Texas. Tom owned and operated a water-well drilling company, Edna worked at her sister's liquor store on US Highway 285 just north of Pecos, and the family also owned several rental houses.

Billy Jim said his mother delayed his start of school for a year; actually, he was still only five years of age when school started in September 1944 (although he turned six later that month). So Billy Jim was nearly seven years old when he enrolled in first grade at Pecos Elementary School in September 1945. "That helped me be more mature," Simmons said. "Most of my friends were a year ahead of me in school."

Simmons got his start in basketball by playing with neighborhood friends in his backyard while in the sixth grade in 1950–51. They dribbled the ball on a caliche surface and shot at a goal nailed to a chicken coop. "We played there a lot," Simmons remembers. "We had some pretty good games. I kind of thought it was a sissy sport. Football was the name of the game back then—plus baseball always. Pecos was such a football area all that time."

The following year, Simmons was introduced to organized basketball. His seventh-grade club team was coached by F. L. "Tooter" Green. "He kind of got me started," Simmons said.

"I began to think, 'Well, maybe there's more to this game than I give it credit for.' I scored forty points in one game against Andrews. That got me started really good."

Simmons was a shy, lanky fifteen-year-old freshman when he reported for his first basketball practice at Pecos High School in November 1953. Eagles' coach Richard C. "Dick" Burris quickly recognized that Simmons was too talented to be exiled to the junior varsity as most freshmen were.

Simmons justified Burris's decision by earning a spot among the starting five on the varsity during his rookie season, and he scored 230 points (11.5 per game) in his first campaign with the Eagles. He scored 424 points (20.2 per game) during his sophomore season in 1954–55 (with his initial all-state recognition), and another 461 points (18.4) as a junior in 1955–56 when Pecos finished 24–3 and tied Seminole for the District 6-AA championship.

It marked only the second time in Pecos history that the Eagles shared the district title in basketball (also in 1946 with Monahans), but both times tie-breaking procedures denied Pecos's hopes to represent the district in the UIL playoffs.

Kenner, who coached Simmons his junior and senior seasons, said, "He was quick, he was intelligent, and he liked to play. He was a competitor. He just had what you call natural ability, which goes a long way. You can teach and teach lots of things, but unless you are just kind of built for it, so to speak, you're going to have problems being a star.

"He was a leader. He led not by voice or 'cheerleader type' but more by example on the floor. He was the 'it' really," Kenner added. "He was a good kid. Mischievous as he could be."

When the Eagles had the ball, Simmons often started from a wing position and rolled across the top of the post in the circle, according to Kenner, but he would step back for a fadeaway jump shot. "They talk about how that's new today, but he had it back then," Kenner said. "I told him how to plant his feet and fade back for a shot. And he was good at it."

Ephriam also vividly remembers Simmons's jump shot. "He had a real good jump shot, especially from the baseline," Ephriam said of his teammate.

The *Odessa American* called Simmons "a speedy youngster with a bag of tricks and a devastating outside jump shot." Simmons was "considered by most coaches to be the outstanding college prospect in West Texas."

Simmons's scoring burden declined in his junior season of 1955–56 after the arrival of Ephriam, an equally talented six-foot, four-inch center who transferred to Pecos High School from Carver where he had played on coach Sidney Sadler's skilled teams. Ephriam joined the Eagles' roster and matched Simmons virtually point-for-point, helping attract capacity crowds to Eagle Gymnasium. Ephriam scored 458 points (only three fewer than Simmons), also earned all-tournament at Monahans and Andrews, and received all-District 6-AA honors in his first season in the purple and gold.

The *Odessa American* acknowledged Ephriam's contributions and said Simmons's role in vaulting Pecos to the top of the district in basketball was "not single-handed by any means."

But Simmons had saved his best for last. Three days after football season ended, he was among about thirty players who reported Monday, November 19, 1956, for the first meeting with second-year coach Kenner. The first practice was held the following day for varsity and junior varsity teams. The senior season that awaited Simmons produced 629 points (a career best 21.7 scoring average)—a PHS season scoring record for the third consecutive year—and justified selection on the ballot of *every* all-state voter. The Eagles won seventy-eight of ninety-nine games during his four seasons (winning 78.8 percent of their games), and he had a four-year career scoring average of 18.4 points per game.

On Thursday, November 22, after only two days of practice, the Eagles traveled to Fort Stockton for a scrimmage against the Panthers before opening the season with a home-and-home series against Marfa. The schedule also included a two-game series in El Paso against El Paso High School, tournaments in Monahans and Andrews in addition to the Eagles' own tournament in Pecos, two spirited games against talented District 7-A champion Big Lake, and home-and-home matches against new District 2-AAA foes Andrews, Brownfield, Kermit, and Monahans.

Guard Bill Mitchell, a six-foot junior, was the only other letterman on the Pecos team, which had lost three starters from the previous season—R. C. Christopher and Bill Kelley at guards and Dick Patrick at forward.

The Eagles believed they had some unfinished business awaiting them in 1956–57 after a disappointing end to the 1955–56 season. Ephriam and Simmons picked up where they left off the previous year. They looked sharp in the first week of practice. Simmons was hitting his jump shot with his accustomed accuracy, and Ephriam now carried 195 pounds on his six-foot, four-inch frame to make him an imposing player. He was bigger and stronger—enabling him to dominate the paint with his deadly jump hook and control the backboards with forceful rebounds.

The *Odessa American* called Ephriam a "mild-mannered Negro who earned a maze of publicity last year after Pecos school integration made him eligible." The *American* added, "His height carries 195 pounds and makes him a powerful rebounder. He scores with a better-than-average hook shot and an excellent jump shot from close in."

Joining the two stars and the left-handed Mitchell in Kenner's starting lineup were the five-foot, ten-inch guard Royce Cassell and six-foot-two forward Eugene Walker, a transfer from Big Spring who had battled six-foot-two senior Jimmy Martinez for a starting assignment early in the season. Mitchell and Cassell had the potential to add improved outside shooting to the Eagles' attack—which the *Pecos Enterprise* said was lacking the previous year in two losses to district co-champion Seminole—and Walker was expected to add rebounding strength inside after recovering from the bumps and bruises he accumulated as a lineman during the Eagles' 1956 football season.

Kenner was optimistic about the season. The *Enterprise* said he hoped his veterans and newcomers would jell by midseason. "It's just a matter of getting three juniors ready to give our two seniors adequate help," he said. "If these three boys come through, then we'll be okay."

In the opening series, the Class A Shorthorns proved to be no match for Pecos, an emerging power in West Texas basketball. In each game, one on Tuesday, November 27, in Marfa and one a week later in Pecos, Ephriam led all players with twenty-seven points to pace Kenner's team to a promising 2–0 start to the season.

On its home court, Marfa had challenged the Eagles in the first game. They trailed Pecos by only eight points late in the third quarter, but two Shorthorns fouled out in the final period, and Pecos pulled away for a nineteen-point victory at 66–47. Ephriam was the best player on the court, hitting eleven field goals in his twenty-seven-point performance.

In his first varsity start, Cassell scored eleven points to go along with Simmons's nineteen. The *Enterprise* said Cassell was "a pleasant surprise."

The Eagles were more dominant in the rematch in Pecos a week later—winning by thirty-three points with a final score of 63–30. Ephriam continued to hit with "unerring accuracy," according to the *Odessa American*, as the hosts jumped out to a 33–16 lead by halftime. Ephriam connected on twelve field goals and again led all players with twenty-seven points. The *Pecos Enterprise* said Pecos "looked smoother and a little sharper in shooting than in the first game with Marfa."

Simmons scored eighteen points, but the *Enterprise* said he "missed enough short shots to go away a disappointed boy. He had trouble with the easy ones at Marfa too." Ephriam and Simmons combined to outscore the entire Shorthorn team by fifteen points, forty-five to thirty. In the two games, Ephriam and Simmons outscored Marfa ninety-one points to seventy-seven.

After the first two games, the *Enterprise* added, "Although the Eagles need more bench strength, they could develop into one of the best teams in the state."

Kenner had an ambitious schedule lined up for his team for the month of December. After their home opener against Marfa on December 4, the Eagles faced three consecutive weekends of tournaments—Monahans, Andrews, and Pecos—before taking their holiday break with a record of 11–2. They played twelve games in eighteen days in December with wins in ten of those twelve games and losses only in the finals of the Monahans and Andrews tournaments.

Pecos started the weekend in Monahans with easy wins of 50–28 over Alpine in the quarterfinals on Friday, December 7, and 55–34 over Van Horn in the semifinals early Saturday. Simmons led the Eagles in scoring in both games, with twenty Friday and twenty-four in Pecos's semifinal game. Ephriam turned in games of thirteen points against Alpine and eighteen against Van Horn.

In the championship game, Pecos scored only five points in the opening period to fall behind the hosting Loboes, who had a reputation as spoilers after upsetting eventual state champion Seminole two seasons earlier in the Odessa tournament. They led the Eagles 10–5 after the first quarter, 22–16 at intermission, and 32–23 to start the fourth quarter.

But the scoring of Simmons and reserve forward Martinez sparked the Eagles, who outscored Monahans 20–11 in the final period to force overtime. Pecos actually led, 43–41, in the final minute before Lobo center Jimmy Muldrow connected on a hook shot to tie the score at forty-three. The Eagles missed their final two shots in an attempt to win in regulation.

Simmons started the scoring in the two-minute overtime with another successful jumper, but Monahans tied it at forty-five to force a second "sudden death" overtime, where the first team to score was declared the winner.

Ephriam won the opening tip of the second overtime for the Eagles, but Pecos missed its ensuing field goal attempt. On the Loboes' following possession, Martinez was whistled for a foul, and Monahans's Brooks Franklin made his first free throw to give his team the victory, 46–45, and deny the Eagles a chance to defend their tournament championship in Monahans. Simmons again led Pecos with twelve points, and Martinez and Cassell added eleven each. Ephriam was held to his lowest total of the season (five points).

Monahans connected on sixteen of twenty-two free throws in the game to only seven of sixteen for the visiting Pecos Eagles.

Simmons and Ephriam were joined on the ten-man all-tournament team by Monahans's Franklin and Muldrow, who had led all scorers in the championship game with thirteen points.

Writing in the *Odessa American*, Tom Eastland called the Monahans win an upset. "If not an upset, it was indeed a rather surprising development," he said. "Pecos is supposedly the cream of the West Texas Class AAA crop. Pecos plays an explosive, fast-breaking game that is both spectacular and point-producing."

The Loboes' deliberate style, Eastland wrote, "can evidently turn a fast-scoring outfit like Pecos to mild frustration with their change-of-pace basketball." They limited Pecos's two stars to a total of eighteen points—well under their usual combined total of about forty points a game.

Pecos faced even better competition the following weekend in the superb twelve-team field in Andrews. Among the entries were Class AAAA teams Midland, Odessa, San Angelo, and Jefferson High School from El Paso, along with 1955 Class AA state champion Seminole. The Eagles would have to win four games in three days to earn this weekend's first-place trophy.

And they were almost up to the task, but for the second straight weekend, despite record scoring from Simmons, Pecos fell in a tournament championship game.

The Eagles opened the tournament on Thursday, December 13, with a relatively easy 65–42 triumph over the San Angelo Bobcats to set up a rematch the next day in the quarterfinals against nemesis Seminole. But this time, Pecos came away the winner over the previously undefeated Indians by the narrow score of 45–43 behind Simmons's twenty-six points in what the *Pecos Enterprise* called "the biggest upset."

Seminole had knocked off tournament favorite Odessa in its first game before falling to the Eagles in the quarterfinals.

In the semifinals early on Saturday, Simmons poured in a tournament-record thirty-eight points in Pecos's 74–55 win over Kermit to improve to 7–1 and reach the championship game against El Paso Jefferson, which was looking for its second straight Andrews title. Pecos and Jefferson battled to a 30–30 tie at intermission, but Simmons fouled out midway through the third quarter after scoring 19 points, and Jefferson pulled away for a 62–53 decision in Saturday night's final.

Simmons scored a tournament-record eighty-nine points in four games in three days to claim outstanding player honors and the first spot on the all-tournament team. Ephriam, who scored sixty-three points in the four games, was also named to the all-tournament team and received the sportsmanship award. Simmons was all-tournament in Andrews for the third consecutive year after victories over San Angelo, Seminole, and Kermit and the loss to El Paso Jefferson.

"It was a tired group of boys who took the floor for the final game with Jefferson," the *Enterprise* said, "after they had run what seemed an almost impossible gauntlet." Mitchell and Cassell continued to improve the Eagles' guard play, and Walker and Martinez had "some bright moments at forward."

The Eagles' solid performance established them as co-favorite with El Paso High School, one of three teams from El Paso, for their third consecutive weekend tournament, scheduled for December 20–21 in Pecos.

But first there was a date with undefeated Big Lake, which had defeated host Del Rio, 54–41, in its tournament final on December 15 behind six-foot, four-inch center Tommy Reese on the same night Pecos was falling to Jefferson. The 5–0 Owls were reigning champions of District 7-A.

Big Lake was the final remaining undefeated high school team in West Texas before coming to Pecos on Tuesday, December 18. But Ephriam's twenty-five points and twenty-one from Simmons sparked an Eagles fourth-quarter comeback as Pecos handed Big Lake a 64–53 loss to improve to 8–2.

Pecos's inside defense, led by Ephriam, held Reese to fourteen points after he had registered twenty-two in his team's win over Del Rio.

Two days later, eight teams gathered in Eagles Gymnasium for what the *Enterprise* called "one of the finest tournaments ever held in Pecos." Joining the Eagles and three teams from El Paso—El Paso High, Bowie, and the two-year-old El Paso Tech—were San Angelo Lake View, Presidio, Alpine, and Sonora, Kenner's former team.

In Thursday's quarterfinals, the Eagles blasted Lake View 83–41 after erupting to leads of 22–2 after the first quarter and 54–14 at intermission. Simmons scored eighteen, and Ephriam added sixteen before the Eagles' two stars retired to the bench after two quarters. Cassell and Mitchell also scored in double figures as nine Eagles saw action for Coach Kenner.

Friday morning in the semifinals, Pecos turned in another impressive performance with an 83–54 victory over El Paso Tech. Ephriam led his team with twenty-six points to reach the championship game that night against the surprising Alpine Bucks, which had eliminated El Paso Bowie in the quarterfinals and El Paso High in the semifinals.

After losing in the tournament championship game the previous two weekends, the Eagles were determined to claim the title in their own gymnasium. Pecos held a narrow 31–25 lead over Alpine at intermission. But Ephriam's dominant rebounding and the scoring of the Simmons, Ephriam, and Cassell trio fueled a 14–5 burst for the hosts in the third quarter to produce a much more comfortable advantage of 45–30.

Simmons finished with thirty-two points, and Ephriam scored seventeen. Both were unanimous choices on the all-tournament team, and they were joined on the select group this time by teammate Cassell.

After that stretch of twelve games in eighteen days in December and with a record of 11–2, Kenner's "tired" Pecos team enjoyed ten days off before practice resumed after Christmas on Monday, December 31.

Awaiting the Eagles were four additional non-district games in January before the start of their first campaign in District 2-AAA.

The four non-district games included two against the Odessa High School junior varsity in Eagles Gymnasium and a two-hundred-mile trip west to play twice against El Paso High School on Friday and Saturday, January 4–5, 1957.

After the holiday break, Kenner conducted one practice before returning to the court on New Year's Day against the Odessa junior varsity. Pecos sprinted to a halftime lead of 42–13 before settling for a forty-point victory at 66–26. Simmons scored twenty-five, Ephriam added fifteen, and Mitchell chipped in twelve as every varsity player saw action.

In advance of the Eagles' weekend series in El Paso, the *Herald-Post* wrote about "a visit by mighty Pecos to play El Paso High Friday and Saturday at Austin Gym." In the first game, the Eagles (with only fourteen field goals) were outscored from the field by the Tigers (eighteen field goals), who were tuning up for the start of play in District 1-AAAA the following week. But Pecos hit twenty-three free throws to only twelve for the hosts. Coach C. D. Jarvis's team had been the district champion for two of the past three years, but it couldn't stop Simmons (twenty-six points) and his teammates, who built an early lead and held on for a 51–48 win.

Pecos was a more decisive winner the next night. Simmons scored twenty-seven in his team's twenty-point victory (61–41). The Eagles never trailed and poured in twenty-one points in the third quarter to build on their 24–15 nine-point lead at intermission.

In the *El Paso Herald-Post*, sportswriter Ray Sanchez wrote, "Pecos is a truly loaded squad."

After the Eagles' El Paso trip, the Odessa junior varsity returned to Pecos for a game on Tuesday, January 8. This time, Kenner held out his two stars, Simmons and Ephriam. They watched from the sideline as Pecos escaped with a narrow 39–38 win. It was the last game before the start of District 2-AAA action, and the Eagles proudly owned a record of 15–2. Finally, the next game on the schedule was the much-anticipated district opener at Brownfield on Friday, January 11.

EIGHT

BUBBA, BILLY JIM, AND THE GOLDEN ERA OF PECOS BASKETBALL

Eagles Win District 2-3A Basketball Title—Pecos's First

Eagles Preparing to Enter Second Half of Season
Pecos Enterprise, Dec. 31, 1956

Pecos Slaughters Kermit 64–26 in 2-AAA Contest
Odessa American, Jan. 23, 1957

Pecos Nips Kermit, 75–71 Nears 2-AAA Cage Crown
Odessa American, Feb. 10, 1957

Pecos Rips Ponies, 58–18; Captures First Cage Crown
Odessa American, Feb. 13, 1957

District Cage Championship Captured by Eagles Team; Eyes Now on Regional Playoff
Pecos Enterprise, Feb. 14, 1957

BUBBA EPHRIAM

I'm gonna write a little letter
Gonna mail it to my local DJ
It's a rockin' rhythm record
I want my jockey to play
Roll over Beethoven, I gotta hear it again today . . .

You know she wiggles like a glow worm
Dance like a spinnin' top
She got a crazy partner
Oughta see 'em reel and rock
Long as she got a dime the music will never stop . . .

Roll over Beethoven
Roll over Beethoven
Roll over Beethoven
Roll over Beethoven
Roll over Beethoven and dig these rhythm and blues

—Chuck Berry (1926–2017)

Friday, January 11, 1957, was an important day for the basketball team at Pecos High School. An eight-game winning streak had propelled the Eagles to a record of fifteen wins against only two losses. The news was spreading in West Texas of the accomplishments of Bubba Ephriam, Billy Jim Simmons, and their teammates. They hadn't lost a game since the championship of the Andrews tournament on December 15. But it was now time to start the District 2-AAA basketball season. Wins in their previous eight games weren't going to put the Eagles in the Class AAA playoffs. It was the next eight games that would decide their playoff fate.

And they appeared to be ready for the challenge.

But first, there was time to jam in one more trip to the Dukes Club, a teenage canteen operated by Ephriam with help from his sister Ora Lee and their cousins in Uncle Bob's café near the Ephriam home on East Thirteenth Street. Bubba and his friends often went to the Dukes Club for lunch, even on weekdays while school was in session. "Every day that we could, we went to the Dukes Club," Ephriam remembers. "Most of the time, we were just going to dance. It was a hangout for my little gang."

Bubba said occasionally there were as many as two dozen teenagers at the Dukes Club. "I remember at lunch, we had about eight minutes to get there from school and eight minutes to get back," he said. "They would dance before we had to go back to school. . . . [The parents] trusted me with their daughters. I would bring them to the Dukes Club where they would rendezvous with their boyfriends."

So while the jukebox was playing Chuck Berry's "Roll Over Beethoven" and "Maybellene," Little Richard's "Tutti Frutti" and "Long Tall Sally," Elvis Presley's latest number one hit, and favorites from young rhythm and blues stars such as B. B. King, Jackie Wilson, and Johnny Ace, Bubba and the Dukes Club crew were cooking hamburgers, chili dogs, and french fries and making ham-and-cheese sandwiches for the lunch crowd—all washed down with bottles of Coca-Cola, Orange Crush, and Delaware Punch.

It was an early-day fast-food restaurant. One of Bubba's former classmates from Carver, Eddie Lynn Walker, and his cousins Robert Ephriam and Evelyn Faye "Mickey" Jackson shared cooking duties, and Ora Lee often remained to wash dishes and clean the kitchen and dining room after Bubba and his friends hurriedly returned to class. Like Bubba, Ora Lee missed school often while she was growing up. She remained at their nearby home to care for the younger siblings while their parents worked.

Bubba's sister Bernice remembers that he occasionally instigated games of "spin the bottle" at the Dukes Club as a way to meet girls.

"Bubba loved jazz," longtime friend and Carver classmate Donnie Lee Hall said. "He liked to listen to Nat King Cole. He had a nice personality. He was on the smooth side.

"Me and Bubba, we come a long ways," Hall added. "I thought he was my big brother. . . . We used to go run the girls—not wild or nothing like that. Bubba thought he was a playboy. We had a lot of fun together. He kept a smile on his face. He was always trying to be cool."

The café and canteen were housed in the former home of his grandparents Mattie and Dan Ephriam, and it was Walker who first traced and then painted an outline of Bubba's fist and forearm on the front door welcoming visitors to the Dukes Club (as in "Put up your dukes!" or "Duke it out!"). The club also was often open on weekends, occasionally at night after football and basketball games, and other times outside the café's normal operating hours when adults weren't around.

Ephriam believes the Dukes Club was one of the first integrated teenage canteens in the state. He opened it about 1954 at the age of sixteen. The crowd often included African American, Anglo-American, and Hispanic teenagers—many of them members of one of Pecos's gangs. Ephriam's pack was known as the Dukes, and there also were Leonard "Catman" Tyler's Chain Gang (yes, they wore chains), the Black Lagoons, the Pachucos, and a group of White teenagers from Anglo neighborhoods west of US Highway 285 known as the West Side Gang.

"The gangs would get together at the Dukes Club to dance, play cards, and shoot dice," Bubba explained. "And after football and basketball games, we'd all go down to the Dukes Club. I would open it up or my cousin would open it for me."

The opening line from Johnny Ace's 1955 number one R&B hit "Pledging My Love" ("Forever my darling, our love will be true") was still lingering in Bubba's head as he returned to the PHS campus after lunch to board the bus with his teammates and coaches John Kenner and Jerry Cook for the three-hour ride to Brownfield for the District 2-AAA opener.

Now it was time to get serious. The Brownfield Cubs provided the opposition for the Eagles that Friday night. The Eagles remembered what had happened the year before when they tied for the District 6-AA championship but failed to advance to the playoffs.

So after win-loss records of 1–0 in November, 10–2 in December, and 4–0 in the first week of January, the Eagles were eager to start their first season in District 2-AAA.

The *Pecos Enterprise* established the Eagles as "the clear-cut favorite to gain the championship," but the Cubs were "potentially dangerous" because on January 5, they narrowly lost to 1955 Class AA state champion Seminole by only two points in the championship game of the Brownfield tournament.

The *Odessa American* said that in the first quarter of the district opener, Brownfield set its defense to stop the six-foot, four-inch Ephriam and six-foot, three-inch Simmons, but Billy Mitchell and Eugene Walker began the game with success shooting from outside. "The Cubs were forced to loosen their defense to stop the outside shooting," the *American* reported as the Eagles built a lead of 18–7 over the hosts in the first period.

Brownfield trimmed its deficit to only five points, 27–22, by intermission, but the visitors turned back the challenge in the third quarter by outscoring the Cubs 19–9 to take a commanding 46–31 advantage. Ephriam started district play by leading all scorers with twenty-three points, and Simmons added nineteen after what the *Enterprise* called "a cold night from the floor." Mitchell had twelve points, and Walker added eight points and "did an outstanding job of rebounding" in the 66–50 victory.

It was a forecast of things to come. Ephriam went on to lead his team in cumulative total points for the entire eight-game district season.

Lesley Butler with fifteen points and Johnny Raybon with fourteen paced the Cubs in their opening 2-AAA game.

"If they play like that all the way," Brownfield coach Farris Nowell told Tom Eastland of the *Odessa American*, "they'll have [the district title]. . . . We were stopping Simmons and Ephriam in the first quarter, and then this Mitchell and Walker got hot shooting from the outside. We had to let Simmons and Ephriam go.

"Pecos really got on that board," Nowell continued. "We put both our tall boys in under the board, but they still out-rebounded us."

In the words of Chuck Berry, the Eagles were rockin'. Put another dime in the jukebox.

Pecos was now 16–2 for the season, but more importantly, it was off to a 1–0 start in District 2-AAA. With multiple open dates in a district with only five teams, the Eagles had ten days to prepare for their next district game on Tuesday, January 22, at home against co-leader Kermit.

And apparently, Kenner was eager to begin those preparations. Perhaps unhappy with Ephriam's recent offensive slump (his scoring average had declined to 16.5 points per game after the El Paso trip and before District 2-AAA play started) and his lack of rebounding against Brownfield, Kenner summoned Ephriam to the gymnasium Saturday morning. "I want to see you in the gym tomorrow morning," Bubba said Kenner told him after the game. "I want to teach you a thing or two about basketball."

The next morning, Ephriam arrived at the PHS gym, stood at the door, and looked inside the empty gym for Kenner. "I see you didn't chicken out," the coach said. "I see you made it. Come over here."

As Ephriam walked across the gym floor toward Kenner, the coach threw the basketball at his starting center. "He hit me in the gut with it," Ephriam remembers, "but I shot and made two points."

The two began a rough game of one-on-one basketball, and Ephriam said, "He just wanted to try to hurt me. He plowed over me, hit me in the midsection and kind of folded me a little bit. He was trying to knock me out of bounds. . . . He was trying to stop my shot. I let him have a good elbow."

Ephriam stopped to address his coach. "Listen, I don't need this. I don't need you. I don't need your school. I don't need your basketball team." Ephriam put his clothes on, left the gymnasium, and returned home determined not to return to Pecos High School on Monday. "To this day, I don't understand how it is that a man could hate a kid."

Bubba stayed home on Monday and Tuesday, when Kenner came to the Ephriam home. "I saw him," Bubba remembers. "I told my sister [Ora Lee] to tell him if he didn't get off my porch, I would blow his brains out." So Kenner left.

Kenner returned Wednesday, according to Bubba, but this time he sat in his car. "He had to do the one thing he hated to do most of all," Ephriam said. "He had to go to Coach Sadler to try to get him to come talk to me to try to get me to come back."

Around one o'clock, Sadler came to the Ephriam home. "He had heard I wasn't in school," Bubba said. Sadler knocked on the door. "Open up this door," he said. "I know you're in there."

Sadler grabbed his former player by the collar. "What's this I hear about you quitting school, not being in school?" Then Ephriam explained his absence to his former coach.

"I've been expecting to hear something like this," Sadler said, as Ephriam remembers today. "I knew something would happen, but I didn't know it would be him. You know, Bubba, if I could take your place, I would gladly do it. But it just so happens that you have to be the one it falls upon.

"Think about your sisters and brothers and all the rest of the kids coming along behind you. This is just a tryout to see if integration will work in the state of Texas. If anything like this happens out here, if there was a flare-up, it was just like a candle, they can snuff it out. It could set integration in the state of Texas back twenty years. The eyes of Texas are upon you. They're watching you.

"You don't understand what's going on. When you get older, you will understand things. You can put the puzzle together. The more you handle the pieces, you can put it together."

Ephriam told his former coach and mentor, "I'll go back."

Bubba returned to Pecos High School on Thursday—still five days before the Eagles' next game. He said, "Nothing happened at school," and apparently Ephriam received no counseling or other discipline for missing three days of classes.

Bubba's son, Ira Earl, says, "I remember my grandmother talking about sometimes he would come in and he would be upset. They would say, 'This is something that's started, and you've got to finish it.' At first, they weren't for it, but once it started, 'You're all in now.'

"The uncles said, 'Go on and let the boy play. That's what you've decided to do. Now that you're here, you're not going to quit.'"

The *Odessa American* said Pecos was the center of attention Tuesday, January 22, "when the conference's two unbeaten teams, Kermit and Pecos, clash for the lead in the week's top cage game." Kermit had opened with wins of 71–57 over Brownfield and 59–55 over Monahans to sit atop the standings at 2–0 ahead of Pecos's 1–0 despite the fact that the Eagles were the winningest team in West Texas with sixteen victories.

Jackie Probst, Gene Williams, and Sammy Cates gave the Yellow Jackets a dangerous three-man scoring attack.

But after the opening tip before a capacity crowd at the PHS gymnasium, the question of who would emerge as the District 2-AAA leader was quickly answered. The Eagles put on "an awesome display of power," according to Eastland in the *American*, to smash Kermit 64–26. The hosts dominated the opening period and led 20–2 after the first eight minutes.

Guard Royce Cassell opened the scoring with two long set shots to give the Eagles a quick 4–0 lead. His fourth field goal at 7:27 of the first quarter extended the shutout to 18–0 before Kermit finally scored in the final half-minute of the first quarter with two free throws by Probst. Eastland said Cassell was "the key to the first-period runaway."

Again, Pecos's opponent was forced to abandon its strategy of concentrating its defense inside on Ephriam and Simmons to press the Eagles' outside attack. That opened the lane and enabled Simmons to drive to the basket and hit jumpers from the baseline. In the second quarter, Cassell and Ephriam scored four points each, and the Eagles went to their dressing room at intermission with a comfortable margin of 32–10.

Simmons finished with twenty-one for high-point honors, Ephriam scored sixteen, and Cassell finished with twelve for Pecos. Of Simmons, the *American* said, "The amazing Eagle was all over the court, rebounding and shooting with uncanny accuracy." Pecos's lead grew to forty-two points, 58–16, midway into the fourth quarter before the winners settled for their thirty-eight-point win. The winning streak reached double figures at ten games.

J. L. Davis led Kermit with eight points as the high-scoring trio of Probst, Williams, and Cates combined for only eighteen.

In a follow-up column in the *American* two days later, Eastland wrote, "Pecos looked as perfect turning the trick as any basketball team composed of humans can. The way the Eagles handled Kermit made it look easy. That couldn't be farther from the truth. Nobody 'handles' a team like Kermit easily. It takes a superb brand of basketball to thump a good team. Pecos did it with rebounding and accuracy. . . .

"Perhaps Andrews or Monahans has some new method of stopping the Eagles short of shooting them," Eastland added. "It's up to those two if anybody's going to stop them in the first go-around in District 2-AAA."

But neither Andrews nor Monahans had an answer for the Eagles in their next two games despite the fact that Monahans had defeated Pecos on December 8 in double overtime, 46–45, for the championship of the Monahans tournament. Pecos smashed last-place Andrews by twenty-six points, 80–54, on January 25 in Andrews as the Eagles reached at least eighty points for the third time this season, and the district leaders scored a forty-two-point victory, 79–37, over Monahans on January 29 in a return to Eagle Gymnasium before a standing-room-only crowd.

Pecos had completed the first half of district play with a twelve-game winning streak and records of 19–2 for the season and 4–0 in district play.

In Andrews, Ephriam scored thirty-six points—all from the field—as the Eagles left the winless Mustangs little chance to escape the District 2-AAA cellar (0–3). In the *American*, Eastland said Ephriam "hawked the basket throughout the contest, tipping in rebounds before they reached the outstretched arms of the shorter cagers."

Pecos had leads of 23–11 after the first quarter, 47–25 at halftime, and 65–36 entering the final quarter. Simmons added to the Pecos offense with twenty-one points, and Cassell scored eight.

Four Eagles scored in double figures as Pecos wrapped up the first half of 2-AAA with the revenge victory over Monahans. Simmons led the balanced scoring attack with twenty-two points, followed by Walker with nineteen, Mitchell with seventeen, and Ephriam with twelve. The Loboes never recovered from a 24–4 deficit after the first quarter.

The Eagles registered winning margins of sixteen, thirty-eight, twenty-six, and forty-two points (average margin of 30.5 points per game) in their first half of the District 2-AAA schedule.

Pecos started the second round of 2-AAA games at home on Friday, February 1, by winning its twentieth game of the season. For the third time in the last four games, Ephriam and Simmons outscored the Eagles' opponent by themselves. Pecos whipped Brownfield 83–55 to stretch its record to 20–2 for the season and 5–0 in district action.

Pecos erupted for thirty-one points in the first quarter and added twenty-two points in the second quarter for a halftime lead of 53–27. The Eagles were on pace to score more than one hundred points, although that pace did not continue. Ephriam finished with thirty-three points, and Simmons added twenty-eight to combine for sixty-one points. The *Odessa American* reported that Simmons's season total now stood at 466 points to eclipse his own school record of 461 set the previous season.

Fortunately for the Eagles, Pecos enjoyed a week off before its next game, a rematch on the road against Kermit on Friday, February 8. The Yellow Jackets, very familiar foes for the Eagles, were still contenders for the 2-AAA title with only one district loss (5–1), but a win for Pecos (5–0) would give the Eagles at least a share of the 2-AAA championship and guarantee them the right to represent the district in the Class AAA playoffs—a first for Pecos High School.

But early the week of the Kermit rematch, the pressure of performing at his best every game, keeping the Eagles at the top of the standings, satisfying his coach, and representing the African American community as one of the first Black students to compete in high school sports in Texas finally began to show some visible effects on Ephriam.

"Kenner was always nagging me," Ephriam recalled. "I avoided him in the halls at school. I hated to see that man coming. He always had something degrading to say, but I wasn't going to let him stop me from achieving my goals.

"I was depressed from that kind of animosity. I lost my appetite and hadn't eaten in about a week. I lost my smile, my enthusiasm, everything. And it began to show. My demeanor had changed. I was just going through the motions. My mom got concerned because I wasn't eating at home, either, and she called the school."

The "cure" was to treat Bubba to breakfast and lunch at Ben's Spanish Inn, a Whites-only restaurant where his cousin Earline Williams was a cook. Ben's Spanish Inn was a popular local diner operated by Ben Matta and his wife, Chuy. At breakfast the first day, Bubba says he just sat there—still without an appetite. "I didn't want the food. I just didn't want nothing."

He told his friends, "Just take me on to school."

Simmons and several Eagles were taking an interest in the plight of their teammate. "Simmons and several of the guys would be there," Ephriam said. "They were all worried about it. They had just about given up. They wanted to see me eat. But I was suppressing things that were happening and not letting it go. I knew if my daddy and uncles knew that this was happening up there or knew about the fight between me and Kenner, I knew what would happen."

Finally, on Wednesday, two days before the Kermit game, Ephriam began to regain his strength after eating lunch at Ben's Spanish Inn. "I remember seeing Earline in the kitchen looking at me through that little serving window," Bubba said of his cousin.

"What's going on?" she asked. She paused and then continued, "I know what to do for him. Just leave him alone."

Earline put her hand on Bubba's head and began to pray. "She had a strong belief," Bubba recalled. She returned to the kitchen, prepared ham, green beans, and red potatoes and brought a plate of food to the dining room to place on the table before Bubba.

All eyes were on Bubba now. "They were watching me," he recalled. "I picked up my fork and forked some beans to my mouth. I ate a few green beans and picked up my knife to cut the ham." There were cheers and sighs of relief among the small crowd gathered at the restaurant. "They were carrying on; they were excited to see me eat. I sat there and began to eat. They were talking to me and encouraging me.

"I had to put that all out of my mind," he continued. "It triggered all of those thoughts. It stopped me from loving the sport."

Bubba said he remembers even Coach Kenner was there to watch as Earline brought Bubba a second plate. "Someone called the school to let them know I was eating," he continued. The celebration continued the following day at the PHS pep rally for the game against the Yellow Jackets.

Friday arrived for the Kermit game, and Ephriam was back with his team. "But I hadn't gotten all my strength back," he said. "I didn't have no energy."

Despite playing at less-than-full strength in the Eagles' most serious challenge in district, Ephriam sparked the Eagles to a narrow overtime victory after first Simmons (with 3:40 to play in the fourth quarter) and then Mitchell (1:15) were disqualified after being charged with five fouls each. Ephriam's free throw shooting late in regulation and in overtime provided what proved to be the Eagles' margin of victory. He led all scorers with thirty-five points—the third time in the last four games he had scored at least thirty points.

Pecos outscored Kermit by sixteen points in the first half after taking an early 10–0 lead. Ephriam scored eleven points in the first quarter as the visitors took a cushion of 18–10. But in the third period, Kermit began to chip away at Pecos's 40–24 halftime advantage behind the scoring of Cates and Williams.

Pecos led by eleven points, 57–46, to start the final quarter, but Kermit continued its rally despite also losing two players with five fouls. With Pecos's lead shrinking at 67–61, Kermit then closed to within three at 67–64 on free throws by Williams (one) and Gene Smith (two). In the final minute, with Simmons and Mitchell on the bench, free throws by Cassell and Ephriam gave Pecos its sixty-eighth and sixty-nineth points.

Ephriam still remembers standing at the free throw line and the referee handing him the ball with twenty seconds to play in regulation for what was to be a decisive free throw—to return that all-important two-point lead to the Eagles (69–67) to likely assure them of at least a tie at the end of regulation time.

But despite Ephriam's heroics, Cates, who led his team with twenty-five points, answered with a jumper from the left corner as the final seconds ticked off the clock to tie the game at sixty-nine and send the two teams into overtime. Kermit had outscored Pecos by sixteen points in the second half.

In overtime, Ephriam with four free throws and Walker with two handed Pecos its 75–71 triumph. Ephriam was exhausted. "I had used up all my energy," he said. "The guys had me up on their shoulders celebrating. The school was in an uproar. I could see Mrs. Carter [Daisy Lee Roquemore, Billie Sadler's niece], one of our elementary school teachers at Carver, running toward me in her brown fur coat, but she never got to me because all the others swooped in around me.

"I think I blacked out. What little energy I had built up, I had used it all up during the game. I didn't get a chance to participate in the celebration after the game because I was totally zapped. The next thing I know, I was in the locker room on a table, and they were talking to me and giving me water," he said. "I had made the tie-breaking score. I knew that put us in the regional tournament."

Daisy Lee Carter was one of Bubba's most ardent fans, so it's no surprise he remembers her on the court after the thrilling win over Kermit. "She encouraged me to play better and use my height to my advantage. She told me, 'Bubba, you can be the high-point man. You can be the star of the team.'

"She had been around Prof," he continued. "She watched our practices and told me to straighten up, reach higher, and release the ball at the peak of my jump. She inspired me. . . . I have to acknowledge that part of my ability to her. She had that effect on me, and I thanked her for it."

Bubba said in later years she told him, "You better not come to town without visiting me."

That pivotal game was the seventh time Pecos and Kermit met on the basketball court during Ephriam's two years with the Eagles. And the overtime win left Pecos with a perfect 7–0 record in the series. This was the only game among those seven that Pecos's margin of victory was less than ten points.

In the four games during the middle of the 2-AAA season—propelling Pecos from 2–0 to a commanding lead of 6–0 atop the district standings—Ephriam led his team with 116 points (29.0 points per game). For the first time in the history of Pecos High School, the Eagles would play a basketball playoff game.

But there was the matter of two more district games in the final week of the regular season. Pecos fans would have slept more peacefully had they known that there were no upsets on the horizon for the celebrating Eagles.

Ephriam started the final week of district play by watching a game, however, instead of playing in a game. He said he made the seventy-five-mile drive east on Highway 80 to Odessa on Monday, February 11, with Sidney and Billie Sadler and another teacher to watch the Harlem Globetrotters. They played the Washington Nationals in Broncho Fieldhouse at Odessa High School and escaped with their usual victory—this one by the score of 72–63. The *Odessa American* said Meadowlark Lemon, Leon Hillard, Clarence Wilson, Woody Sauldsberry, and their teammates entertained the crowd with their usual assortment of basketball antics, tricks, and stunts.

Ephriam said he believes Sadler talked to Globetrotter officials about the possibility of Bubba playing for their team after his high school career ended. The Globetrotters were leaving the following day for a trip to El Paso, where they were to play their next game, and Sadler apparently invited them to stop in Pecos to watch Ephriam play Tuesday night for the Eagles.

Pecos easily captured another decisive victory, but Ephriam said he made an abbreviated appearance. "The night Harlem stopped to talk to me and see me play," Ephriam said, "[Kenner] took me out in the third quarter." Ephriam said he saw Harlem representatives enter the gym, then Kenner quickly pulled him from the lineup, cursed Sadler, and pushed him to the locker room.

"He hid me from them," Ephriam said. "They never got to see me play."

Ephriam dressed—he put on his clothes over his uniform—and was escorted to the school cafeteria, where custodian Chico Rodriquez was assigned to watch the disappointed player. "He ushered me off the floor back to the locker room. He made me put my clothes on over my sweaty uniform, still cursing Prof Sadler and me, and asking, 'Who do you think you are? I know who's responsible for this. I'll give him a piece of my mind. I'll teach him to mess with my team. . . .'

"Harlem never got a chance to talk to me or see me play," Ephriam continued. "He destroyed my chance of playing with the Harlem Globetrotters."

Despite Ephriam's early exit, the Eagles proved that they were the best team in District 2-AAA and a worthy playoff representative with another forty-point victory, 58–18, over Andrews on February 12 in the final home game of the season at PHS gym. And they followed that with an equally impressive 71–33 triumph over Monahans on the road three days later to complete the 2-AAA season.

The win over Andrews gave Pecos sole possession of the district trophy. (The Eagles had tied for district basketball titles in 1946 and 1956 but both times failed to advance to the playoffs.) The *Odessa American*, in its report of the Andrews game, made no mention of Ephriam's early departure. Perhaps it wasn't noticeable in the easy victory.

After Simmons scored eleven points in the first quarter to spark Pecos to a 13–4 lead, Andrews tried to stall in the second quarter. The tactics backfired, however, and the Mustangs failed to score with Pecos taking a 17–4 lead to the dressing room.

Then Pecos erupted for seventeen points in the third quarter and twenty-four points in the fourth quarter to claim the victory. Ephriam scored sixteen points before his exit.

Before the next game Friday, Kenner admitted to the *Pecos Enterprise* that he was worried about what he called "a natural letdown" by his team against Monahans on February 15. "Monahans has already beaten us once this year and is capable of doing it again," the coach said. "I just hope the boys don't have a letdown."

Simmons led the Eagles in scoring both games of the final week with twenty-three against Andrews and twenty-four against Monahans, and Ephriam added twenty points at Monahans to conclude the regular season.

And with Andrews's stunning 71–55 upset of Kermit on the final night, that left Pecos with a three-game lead in the final district standings at 8–0, followed by Kermit at 5–3, Monahans at 4–4, Brownfield at 2–6, and Andrews at 1–7. The Eagles had won twenty-three of their first twenty-five games of the regular season, owned a sixteen-game winning streak, and produced an average margin of victory in eight district games of a whopping 29.0 points. The Eagles scored 576 points in eight 2-AAA games (72.0 per game average) to only 344 for their opponents (43.0) in those eight games.

Coach Kenner scheduled a warm-up game for the Eagles before the Region I-AAA tournament in Lubbock. His team would play another rematch—this time against the winningest team in West Texas. The Big Lake Owls were 30–1 and champions of District 7-A. Their only loss? They fell 64–53 to Pecos on December 18 in Eagle Gymnasium with Ephriam (25 points) and Simmons (21) leading their team to a come-from-behind victory.

But the host and outcome were different this time. The rematch was scheduled in Big Lake for Saturday, February 23, one week before Pecos's regional final. In the earlier game between these two teams, Pecos came from behind in the fourth quarter to win, but this time, the rally belonged to the Owls. Pecos led 35–23 at intermission and 48–41 entering the final quarter before six-foot, four-inch Tommy Reese (19 points) and Bill Connally (18) sparked Big Lake's comeback.

Connally scored his team's final six points. He tied the game at fifty-five with a free throw, then added five more points for the 60–56 victory. Ephriam and Mitchell each scored fourteen for Pecos, and Simmons added twelve despite playing with four stitches to close a cut over one eye that he had suffered in the game against Monahans on February 15.

Ephriam had edged his teammate Simmons in scoring in the eight District 2-AAA games, 191 points to 184, and both were named to the ten-man all-district team. Simmons beat Ephriam in balloting for the outstanding player award ahead of two other contenders, Gene Williams of Kermit and Curtis Hart of Andrews.

In district play, Ephriam averaged 23.9 points, and Simmons scored 23.0 per game.

The other six members of the all-district team were Bobby Powers and Jimmy Muldrow of Monahans, Jay Sharrard of Andrews, Kenneth Cary of Brownfield, and Jackie Probst and Sammy Cates of Kermit.

NINE

EAGLES SECURE AUSTIN BERTH WITH REGION I-3A TITLE

Eagles Triumph over Snyder and Vernon to Advance to State

Pecos Justly Proud of Eagle Cage Club
Odessa American, Feb. 24, 1957

Eagles Meet Snyder in Texas Tech's Municipal Coliseum
Pecos Enterprise, Feb. 28, 1957

Pecos Tops Snyder; Vernon Pulls Upset
San Angelo Standard-Times, Mar. 2, 1957

New Faces to Dot State Tournament; Pecos Baffles Vernon
Lubbock Avalanche-Journal, Mar. 3, 1957

Eagles Will Leave This Week for State Tourney in Austin after Snyder, Vernon Wins
Pecos Enterprise, Mar. 4, 1957

Coach John Kenner's team—referred to as "Kenner's iron men" by the *Odessa American* and *Pecos Enterprise* because the starting five boys played most of every game—made history at Pecos High School. The

1956–57 team was the first ever at the school to qualify for the playoffs in basketball after winning a district championship outright.

March arrived on the calendar in Pecos, and for the first time, the Eagles were still playing basketball. Postseason basketball. Fans in Pecos believed the Eagles could make the "final four" in Austin.

The *Enterprise* called it "the golden era" of Eagle basketball.

On Sunday, February 24, 1957, a day after Pecos's final regular season game, the *Odessa American* reported, "This year's championship was a fitting climax to four years of outstanding basketball built around 6'3" Billy Jim Simmons and 6'4" Iria (Bubba) Ephriam, a pair of all-staters.

"Simmons has been outstanding for four years, but it was the big stretch made by Ephriam, a mild-mannered Negro who came along two years ago following integration, that really put the spark to an otherwise run-of-the-mill cage game. . . .

"Pecos fans, like most citizens in cities that are fortunate enough to have a winner, are high on this team. They feel it is the type of team that might get a trip to Austin, but they are not packing their bags yet. They have, however, packed the overnight cases to Lubbock."

There still were two must-win games in Lubbock before a trip to Austin for the final four.

"I knew we had to win both games to go to state," Simmons said. "It was my last chance. . . . For me to get to this point was what my life was all about—to make the state tournament."

Joining the Eagles (who had a 23–3 season record), champions of District 2, in the Region I-AAA tournament were the playoff veteran Phillips Blackhawks (20–3) from District 1, the Snyder Tigers (15–6) from District 3, and the Vernon Lions (14–12) from District 4. Phillips, like Pecos, was in its first year in Class AAA after being promoted from AA due to growing enrollment, and the Blackhawks were favored to capture their first Region I-AAA title and advance to Austin for the second straight year after their narrow two-point loss (70–68) to Jacksonville in the 1956 Class AA state championship game.

Superintendents, principals, and coaches from the four schools met at Texas Tech in Lubbock on Saturday, February 16, to decide the format and pairings for the I-AAA playoffs. Snyder and Vernon reportedly wanted individual bi-district games (districts 1 vs. 2 and districts 3 vs. 4) followed a few days later by a regional final game between the winners of the two bi-district games to determine the Austin qualifier. Kenner and the Phillips coach, Billy Hughes, wanted a two-day regional tournament with coin flips to determine the pairings.

"I'd like to have the tournament," Kenner told reporters. "It would mean less traveling for everyone involved."

The *Pecos Enterprise* reported that "there was quite a hassle" at the Region I-AAA meeting in Lubbock. And after a coin flip favored a regional tournament, "another dispute developed in the manner of seeding the teams." A telephone call to Dr. Rhea Williams, director of athletics at the University Interscholastic League in Austin, revealed that the usual procedure was to draw, although that was not mandatory.

Kenner remembered the Phillips representatives "as the hot dog of the bunch" at the meeting. "Hell, you guys down in 3 and 4 are afraid to play us," one shouted. "You are trying to get rid of us."

The *Snyder Daily News* told of an "ill-fated statement made by the Phillips principal who went on record as saying the 3-AAA and 4-AAA champions were afraid to play the 1-AAA and 2-AAA champs."

The *Pecos Enterprise* said the Region I-AAA chairman (from Brownfield) voted with Pecos and Phillips for a coin flip, which resulted in the semifinal pairings of Pecos versus Snyder at 7 p.m. and Vernon versus Phillips at 8:30 p.m. on Friday, March 1, at Lubbock Municipal Coliseum.

Texas Tech, coached by Polk Robison, was playing its first season in its new coliseum and its final season before entering the Southwest Conference in 1957–58. Robison's team was coming off three straight Border Conference titles. The *Pecos Enterprise* called the coliseum "the most comfortable basketball arena in the nation."

Known to fans as "the Bubble," the city-owned coliseum on the Tech campus opened with 7,500 theater-style seats, scoreboards at each end of the arena, heating and cooling systems to control the temperature for fan comfort, and all-weather parking for 1,900 cars.

The four schools decided to divide gate receipts equally from the three I-AAA games after paying the coliseum rental fee of six hundred dollars. Ticket prices were set at one dollar for adults and fifty cents for students.

Superintendent Ray Whitley and principal L. R. Hudson were hoping Pecos's share would cover expenses for their team's trip to Lubbock and a possible trip to Austin.

The I-A and I-AA tournaments also were scheduled in Lubbock that same weekend—all six of their games on Saturday, March 2—so the AAA final game was set for 5 p.m. on Saturday. Twelve boys teams were in Lubbock for a dream weekend for West Texas high school basketball fans.

The *Odessa American* called it "one of its biggest weekends of state playoff basketball in the city's history. Previously, only Class AA and A tournaments have been in the Hub City." The *Lubbock Avalanche-Journal* also reported it was the first time for the Region I-AAA tournament to be played in Lubbock.

Saturday's I-A schedule called for semifinal games at 8 a.m. and 9:30 a.m. and a final at 7 p.m., and the I-AA plan was for semifinal games at 11 a.m. and 12:30 p.m. with a final at 8:30 p.m.

In the *American*, after the officials from the four schools met, sports columnist Tom Eastland wrote, "Pecos got the first break of the tournament before it even started. . . . Pecos got the best deal conceivable under the circumstances."

Eastland added, "Phillips, Pecos and Vernon are considered by the experts as the three strong teams in the meet with perhaps Phillips being given a nod by the statewide experts. Snyder, on the other hand, District 3-AAA's representative, is looked upon as the weakest team of the four. . . .

"In all probability, if Pecos could have had its choice of the four teams to meet in the first round, the Eagles would have selected Snyder.

"That would have enabled the two other strong teams, Phillips and Vernon, to have the dubious honor of attempting to knock one another off," Eastland continued.

And that's exactly what happened. Coach Bob Percival's Vernon team overcame a three-point deficit in the final three minutes to deny Phillips a return trip to Austin with a 56–54 victory in Friday's second semifinal game. "The upset story of the year," according to the *Lubbock Avalanche-Journal*, followed Pecos's 64–53 win over Snyder in the first semifinal match to set up Saturday's regional final featuring Pecos and "unheralded" Vernon.

The Eagles now were less than twenty-four hours away from earning their ticket to the Class AAA state tournament at Gregory Gymnasium on the campus of the University of Texas at Austin.

"We didn't take anything for granted," Ephriam said. "We knew we had to get out there and play the ball we knew how to play. That's something Coach Sadler taught us. That's the spirit we went in there with. Nobody's going to give you anything. You've got to play for it."

"Did you do your best?" Sadler frequently asked his players at Carver.

"Yes, sir, we did," Ephriam and his teammates answered.

The coach replied, "That's all you can do. That's what makes you a winner."

"Bubba never backed off from anything," Simmons said. "He knew only one way, and that was to play. I felt like that's what our whole team was. We worked good as a team. Bubba fit right in."

Another teammate, Humberto Baez, promoted from the B team for the regional and state tournaments, added, "Bubba was very athletic, and he worked very hard."

First on the Eagles' agenda in Lubbock, Ephriam, Simmons, and their Pecos teammates had to contend with the troublesome Snyder Tigers. Both teams were coming off losses to other playoff teams in regional warm-up games—Pecos fell 60–56 at Class A Big Lake on February 23, and Snyder lost 62–56 to Class AA Seminole in Andrews on February 26.

And like Pecos, Snyder was undefeated in district games thanks primarily to Milton Ham, a six-foot-two all-state end in football who was averaging nineteen points per game with honorable mention all-state honors in basketball, and six-foot-five center Dwayne Prince.

"We didn't know much about them," Simmons said. The Eagles and Tigers had not met in basketball in either of the last two seasons. But the Eagles were familiar with Ham from his reputation in football and from competing against him in baseball (including a 1–0 loss to the Tigers).

Before Friday's game, as the Eagles were leaving their automobiles with gym bags in hand and walking to the coliseum, a crowd gathered to point at Ephriam, take photographs, and talk to the players. Ephriam, Simmons, and teammate Eugene Walker, as usual, walked at the back of the group. "We always brought up the tail end," Ephriam said. They were accustomed to the attention. It had happened before.

On this occasion, Ephriam recalled, Kenner shouted at the crowd, "Stop. He's only a boy." And he brought Ephriam and Simmons from the back to the front to walk with him into the coliseum—perhaps to offer a bit of protection to his African American star center and his newly named first-team all-state forward. Ephriam said he didn't think about Kenner's motive until later when "some of the fellows started talking about it. They said he was mad because they weren't taking pictures of him—just kids talking silly stuff. He wanted to be 'the big coach' walking between his two spark plugs."

Ephriam said people were also already waiting inside the coliseum. "They had their cameras," he said. "It looked like they were camped out in there. They knew we were coming."

Donnie Lee Hall, a teammate of Ephriam's at Carver who followed the Eagles in person and on the radio, recalled, "A gym would be packed when Bubba got there to play. They came to see this Black guy play basketball with White guys. They wanted to see what we had. They found out we had something special."

In the first semifinal game, Pecos lived up to its reputation as a two-man team. Simmons and Ephriam combined for fifty-two of Pecos's sixty-four points before a crowd of 3,500. Simmons led all scorers with twenty-eight points after recovering from his injury from two weeks earlier in the Eagles' final district game. Fifteen of his twenty-eight points came in the first half, and he finished with twelve rebounds before leaving the game in the fourth quarter with another injury—this time a sprained left ankle. The *Lubbock Avalanche-Journal* called it "a non-serious ankle injury."

Ephriam was especially dominant in the second half. He scored his team's final three points of the third quarter and its first ten points of the fourth quarter in a span of about four minutes to give his team a cushion of 53–40 with 4:35 to play. "Ephriam, first Negro to play in the regional meet, took over at this point," the *Lubbock Avalanche-Journal* said, "and all Tiger hopes faded." He disposed of Snyder with twenty-four points and a game-high sixteen rebounds.

Pecos led 14–10 after the first quarter and by as many as ten points in the second quarter before settling for a 29–22 lead at half. The score was tied four times in the first half—the fourth at twenty-two—but Snyder failed to score in the final 3:20 of the second quarter after that 22–22 tie.

Kenner's team regained its ten-point lead in the third quarter at 34–24. But behind the scoring of Ham, Prince, and six-foot, three-inch forward Robert Dabbs, Snyder pulled to within two points, 38–36, just 1:44 before the period ended. That's when Ephriam almost single-handedly sparked Pecos by scoring his team's next thirteen points.

"Ephriam took over and boosted the Eagles out of danger," Jimmy Browder wrote in the *Abilene Reporter-News*. "The tall Negro hit 13 straight points as the fourth quarter got underway, putting the Tigers in a hole they could never climb out of. Ephriam scored 24 points and stole much of the thunder from his heralded teammate, Simmons, who wound up as high-pointer with 28."

Pecos led 42–36 to start the fourth quarter and 53–40 with 4:35 to play, thanks to Ephriam. Snyder got only as close as seven, 60–53, in the final minute of the game. Prince scored seventeen points to lead the Tigers, and Dabbs added ten. Not to be overlooked in the Eagles' winning effort was the defense of Walker, the six-foot, two-inch forward who limited Ham to only seven field goal attempts and ten points.

The *Odessa American* said Walker "badgered and hawked the speedy Ham throughout the contest, holding the 19-points-per-game star to only 10" in the 64–53 triumph.

Pecos topped Snyder in rebounds, 48–36, and shot 40 percent from the field (Ephriam was 9 of 17 for 53 percent) to 36 percent for Snyder. Ephriam grabbed sixteen rebounds, and Simmons got twelve. "Ephriam and Simmons hurt the Tigers as much on rebounding as they did with their scoring punch," Browder wrote.

Simmons especially enjoyed the win over Ham, who he said had intentionally fouled him during the game. "I stole the ball and was going down for a layup. He tackled me just like a football player. That's all he was, a football player. Beating him was really good."

Simmons said when the two first basemen crossed paths in Snyder's 1–0 win over Pecos in baseball, Ham suggested they room together at

TCU (Ham was going to play football for the Horned Frogs, Simmons basketball). "I've already got a roommate," Simmons told Ham. Years later, Simmons remembers, "I wouldn't have roomed with him. I hated that guy so bad."

Saturday came with cool, cloudy weather featuring some fog and drizzle. It dipped down to thirty-eight degrees that morning and warmed to only fifty-five. The Eagles needed another victory, but their leading scorer was nursing a swollen left ankle. "We had to win the second game," Simmons said. "That's the only way we could get to state. I wasn't going to miss that for anything. I still couldn't jump off my left foot. It was pretty bad. I was worried, but we had to do it."

The Texas Tech athletics trainer, Delmer Brown, treated Simmons's ankle on Saturday, but the swelling remained. The *Pecos Enterprise* said Brown offered the option of injections to deaden the pain. The *Enterprise* said Simmons played "a courageous game" despite "a serious handicap."

The newspaper added, "Few of the fans and apparently none of the sportswriters knew that Simmons was playing with a deadened foot. He received an ankle injury with about three minutes left in the first game. The ankle swelled badly, and Texas Tech's trainer Delmer Brown worked on it most of Saturday. They were unable to get the swelling down, and Brown recommended deadening shots. He received four shots to deaden the pain, and he played brilliantly."

Simmons said, "I was just so tickled to death that deadening my foot worked and I could play. I didn't believe it would work. I thought, 'Well, this is for nothing, dang it.' I was dead-footed. I don't know how I played. I've got to be able to shoot off that foot. It was a tough game. We knew we were going to play a good team. They won their first game. I was still able to make it work and score.

"I knew what I had to do," he continued. "I knew what the team expected me to do. Everything worked out great. I had two real good games there. Bubba did, too. He always did."

In the introductions before the regional championship game, the spotlight in Tech's darkened coliseum focused on Simmons and Ephriam. And in the spotlight between them stood Baez, the Eagles' five-foot, seven-inch, 135-pound sophomore who was born in Mexico and grew up in Balmorhea. "I was just awed by all the people in the big gym," Baez said. "Oh, man, I couldn't believe it," he added about Kenner adding him to the varsity roster for the playoffs.

The Eagles faced upset-minded Vernon, a team that the *Lubbock Avalanche-Journal* called the tournament's "crowd favorite." The Lions "threatened to pull off the greatest double upset in regional history."

But Simmons and Ephriam—this time with an added spark from five-foot, ten-inch guard Royce Cassell—spoiled Vernon's plans for another upset. Simmons had a remarkable start. He scored twelve points in the first eight minutes as Pecos built a lead of 23–16 after the first quarter.

But Vernon remained in contention. Jack Phillips, who finished as his team's leading scorer, connected for the Lions near the end of the second period to pull Vernon within three at 33–30. But Cassell hit from long range just before the horn sounded to give Pecos a five-point lead at 35–30. It gave the Eagles important momentum going into the dressing room at half and prevented Vernon from inching closer.

Kenner called it "the shot that probably sent us to Austin."

"I taught Royce that fundamental shot," Kenner said. "I said, 'Royce, they're going to be sagging back on Bubba and Billy Jim. They're not going to be pressing you much. If they get so far back and you get anywhere near the top of the circle, be sure you go ahead and take that shot. Just let that ball fly.'

"It was a nip and tuck ball game," Kenner continued. "As he crossed the center line just before half, it was about tied up. They all sagged. They just knew we were going to throw the ball in to Bubba or Billy Jim. He just let that ball go, and it went through the net.

"He shot I don't know how many of those a day," the Eagles' coach added. "I told him, 'You just shoot and shoot. That's your preworkout. You just keep shooting.' And he did. He got that shot down."

But Vernon still would not go away. The Lions scored the first six points of the third quarter, and midway through the period, they grabbed their only lead of the game, 36–35, on a layup by all-tournament selection Mac Percival.

Pecos responded. Ephriam, Cassell, and Bill Mitchell scored six straight points as the Eagles regained control at 41–36. They never trailed again and had a margin of 43–40 to start the final quarter. Vernon did tie the score twice, at forty-seven (by Jack Phillips) and forty-nine (by John Rollans), but then Pecos went on a 12–1 run to take a 61–50 lead and put the game away. The final margin was nine points at 62–53.

In that twelve-point streak, Mitchell and Simmons each contributed four, and Ephriam and Walker each made two. After scoring twelve in the first quarter, Simmons faced a double-team from the Lions' defense most of the remainder of the game. He was scoreless in the third quarter.

Simmons finished with twenty-five points, Ephriam added seventeen, Mitchell scored ten, and Cassell had eight for the Pecos offense. The two teams battled evenly with forty-three rebounds each, and Pecos hit 46 percent of its field goal attempts to 36 percent for Vernon.

Phillips led Vernon with fifteen, and Percival had fourteen points and fifteen rebounds. The *Lubbock Avalanche-Journal* called Percival "probably the most valuable player in the tournament." He scored sixteen in Friday's upset of the Phillips Blackhawks.

Simmons, Ephriam, and Percival were joined on the Region I-AAA all-tournament team by Snyder's Prince and Phillips's David Bennefield. The Tech coach, Robison, who coveted Simmons to add to his Red Raiders roster, presented the Region I-AAA championship trophy to the victorious Eagles after the game and sent them on their way to Austin. The Eagles succeeded Amarillo Palo Duro (which moved up to Class AAAA in 1956–57) as Region I-AAA champions.

"I knew then we were going to state," Simmons said. "Since we're going, we might as well try to win."

"We celebrated," Ephriam said. "We knew the next stop is Austin. But we also knew we had to get back and go to work."

Many years later, after Ephriam had moved to Abilene, he took his mother, Loraine, to Lubbock to visit his sister Ora Lee, who was ill and had been hospitalized. While in Lubbock, he also returned to the coliseum where the Eagles had achieved one of the proudest moments in Pecos High School history and realized their dream of qualifying for the state tournament. The visit took him back to "the golden era" of Eagle basketball.

Ephriam found an unlocked door, entered the quiet coliseum, and explained to an inquiring custodian the reason for his visit. He told Ephriam, "You go right ahead. Take as much time as you want to."

Those emotional moments from the scene of a much earlier visit to "the Bubble" resurfaced from deep in his memory. Ephriam relived the triumphs over Snyder and Vernon. He experienced again the cheering fans, the sights and sounds and thrills of rousing playoff basketball. "It sounded like I could hear the roar of the people," Ephriam recalled. "It really did bring back memories."

Region I-AAA Tournament

Lubbock Municipal Coliseum

Lubbock, Texas

Semifinal Game

Friday, March 1, 1957

Pecos 64, Snyder 53

	1Q	2Q	3Q	4Q	Total
Pecos	14	15	13	22	**64**
Snyder	10	12	14	17	**53**

Pecos	Field Goals Made	Free Throws Made	Total Points
Billy Jim Simmons	10	8	28
Eugene Walker	0	2	2
Bubba Ephriam	9	6	24
Bill Mitchell	1	2	4
Royce Cassell	2	0	4
Wayne Wassom	1	0	2
Team Totals	***24***	***18***	***64***

Snyder	Field Goals Made	Free Throws Made	Total Points
Milton Ham	5	0	10
Robert Dabbs	5	0	10
Dwayne Prince	7	3	17
Powell Berry	4	0	8
Ronnie Smith	3	2	8
Tommy Prichard	0	0	0
Bill Phillips	0	0	0
Team Totals	***24***	***5***	***53***

Championship Game

Saturday, March 2, 1957

Pecos 62, Vernon 53

	1Q	2Q	3Q	4Q	Total
Pecos	23	12	8	19	**62**
Vernon	16	14	10	13	**53**

Pecos	Field Goals Made	Free Throws Made	Total Points
Royce Cassell	4	0	8
Bill Mitchell	5	0	10
Billy Jim Simmons	10	5	25
Bubba Ephriam	7	3	17
Eugene Walker	1	0	2
Team Totals	***27***	***8***	***62***

Vernon	Field Goals Made	Free Throws Made	Total Points
Jack Phillips	7	1	15
Mac Percival	6	2	14
Ted Ferguson	3	0	6
Curtis Beard	1	0	2
Richard Christopher	4	0	8
Dan Adamson	1	0	2

John Rollans	3	0	6
James Bolton	0	0	0
Team Totals	***25***	***3***	***53***

All-Tournament Team

Billy Jim Simmons, Pecos; Bubba Ephriam, Pecos; Dwayne Prince, Snyder; David Bennefield, Phillips; and Mac Percival, Vernon

TEN

BUBBA'S "HOOK SHOT ARTISTRY" PROPELS EAGLES TO FINAL

Bubba Leads Pecos to Victory in Class 3A Semifinal Game

Pecos in First State Meet
Odessa American, Mar. 6, 1957

It's Smiley, Pecos in 3-A
Austin American-Statesman, Mar. 9, 1957

Ephriam Leads Pecos Eagles to 71–62 Win
Odessa American, Mar. 10, 1957

Decades later, he still remembers the exact amount: $22.68.

Twenty-two dollars and sixty-eight cents.

The morning of Wednesday, March 6, 1957, arrived in Pecos, Texas—time for the Eagles to leave for Austin to compete in the 37th annual UIL boys basketball state tournament. After twenty-eight games in the 1956–57 season, they had earned the right to play in the final four.

From his home on South Walnut Street, William Ephriam prepared to take his younger brother to the gym to meet nine teammates and three coaches for the four-hundred-mile drive to Texas's capital city by way of

Sonora. But first, Bubba wanted to say goodbye to his mother and pick up some clothes. No one from the Ephriam family traveled to Austin to see Bubba's games because they had to remain in Pecos to work; they could not afford the five-day, four-night trip.

Bubba could hear his mama singing when he walked through the front door at her home on East Thirteenth Street that memorable morning. As he almost always did, Bubba was careful not to let the screen door slam behind him. And as she often did, Loraine was singing a gospel hymn as he entered her gleaming, welcoming kitchen, a favorite place of her children. *Have we trials and temptations? Is there trouble anywhere? We should never be discouraged. Take it to the Lord in prayer.* She was washing breakfast dishes before leaving for her domestic chores at the home of Dr. Byron and Mary "Dib" Lackey.

Certainly, she was delighted to see her oldest son. "I just knew you would come this morning," she said, "and I'm so glad you did. Mrs. Lackey told me y'all were leaving this morning for Austin.

"This is all I have," she told Bubba as she handed him some dollar bills and coins. "I wish I had more to give you."

"No, Mama, you keep that. Just give me the change." Bubba knew his father had made a payment on his truck note at the bank that week.

"You go ahead and take it," she insisted. "I get paid the day after tomorrow. You'll have some money in your pocket when you go down there.

"And bring that championship trophy home to Pecos. I know the Eagles can do it, and I know you will play your best. You always do. We are so proud of you, Bubba."

"Bless her heart," Bubba said later. "My mama gave me twenty-two dollars and some change."

Bubba's son, Ira Earl, said Bubba's family depended on newspaper articles and radio broadcasts of games to follow Bubba and the Eagles. "A lot of them heard games on the radio," Earl said. "They didn't get to go to the games. Travel was hard for them. They didn't have places to stay. A lot of people didn't make the trips.

"Not a lot of family was there at the games. That's the hard part."

The aroma of biscuits, sausage, and bacon that had been cooked for breakfast that morning in Mama's kitchen persisted as Bubba lingered a few seconds at the door and listened to his mother singing about Jesus before returning to William's truck. *What a friend we have in Jesus, all our sins and griefs to bear. What a privilege to carry everything to God in prayer.*

With $22.68 and a savory biscuit from Mama's breakfast table, Bubba began the journey to play what turned out to be the final two games of his high school basketball career.

Sports columnist Jim Cope, writing in the *San Angelo Standard-Times* a few days before the state tournament, noted Ephriam's selection that week to the Class AAA all-state third team. And Cope proved to be prophetic when he added, "He'll bear out the faith of the choice with his play in the tournament."

Undeniably, Ephriam did just that. The Eagles did not return to Pecos with the championship trophy they so desired, but Ephriam excelled in the biggest games of his career. He courageously disregarded the pressure of being the first African American in the state basketball tournament in Austin, he scored forty-two points in two games to lead the Eagles (including thirty in a dominating performance in the Eagles' victory in their semifinal game), and he was the co-scoring leader and outstanding player of the 1957 Class AAA state tournament and leading vote-getter on the all-tournament team.

On Monday of the state tournament week, Dr. Rhea Williams, the director of athletics at the University Interscholastic League, announced the pairings for the upcoming games at Gregory Gymnasium on the campus of the University of Texas at Austin.

The Class AAA competition was set to open Friday afternoon at 3:10 when the Eagles (25–3) took the court against the Dragons from Nacogdoches High School (23–5). The second semifinal game at 4:45 p.m. also featured a history-making player. Lewis Qualls, the state tournament's first seven-foot player, led the Golden Eagles (30–7) from Smiley High School in Houston against the Edison High School Bears (14–13) from San Antonio.

The winners were scheduled to battle for the title of state champion the following day, Saturday, March 9, at 8:55 p.m. before another capacity crowd of 7,500 fans. A third-place game matching Friday's losers was scheduled for Saturday morning at 8:45.

"The AAA openers established a precedent," Joe Heiling wrote in the *Corpus Christi Caller-Times*. "Ira [*sic*] (Bubba) Ephriam of Pecos became the first Negro to ever compete in the state meet. And two hours later, Smiley's Lewis Qualls became the tallest."

The Eagles were a "slight favorite" to win their semifinal contest, according to the *Pecos Enterprise*, but the Golden Eagles from Smiley High School, led by seven-foot Qualls, were expected to take the AAA title after earlier eliminating Killeen and Bay City in their regional tournament. Smiley's fourteen-man roster featured eleven players who were at least six feet tall, including nine over six feet.

Smiley coach Herbert T. Beard told reporters he liked his team's chances. "I'd rather have my chance of winning the state tournament than anyone else's. Why should I be worried about this meet?

"I know we have a good team so I'm letting our opponent do all the worrying. We'll run or walk with any of them. We can play close or rough."

Beard should have been worried, however, about his team's game Friday after he watched Pecos defeat Nacogdoches in the first semifinal. The inspired Bears, smaller but quicker and faster than Smiley, led after the first quarter and trailed by only three points at half and two points entering the final period. It took two dunks in the final minute by Qualls to deny Edison's upset bid with a narrow one-point victory in what sportswriter Kirk Hill of the *Houston Post* called "a thriller that had an overflow crowd in Texas University's Gregory Gym on its feet. . . . The Smiley–Edison battle left little to be desired as far as excitement was concerned."

Despite the loss of their tallest players, six-foot, two-inch Billy McLaughlin and six-foot, four-inch Claud Fest, who both fouled out in the fourth quarter, the Bears almost accomplished the upset. Edison started with a scoring advantage of 18–17 after the opening eight minutes, but coach Paul McCarley's stalling tactics in the second quarter backfired. His team scored only six points in the period and fell behind 27–24 at intermission because Qualls broke the stall with three field goals.

McCarley hoped his team's stall would bring Smiley out of its zone defense. "For five minutes by the scoreboard clock, Smiley stood complacently in position," Tom Eastland wrote in the *Odessa American*. "Finally, Smiley came out, and Edison went into action. However, Edison had its troubles and didn't try the stall again."

Smiley pulled away during the third quarter to a lead of 34–26, but Edison continued to battle, increased the tempo, rallied, and trailed only by two, 39–37, to start the fourth quarter. "The San Antonians swept back to the lead in the third quarter by using a blazing running game," Eastland wrote. In the final period, a jumper by Edison's Jimmy Allen tied the score at forty-two with 5:35 to play, and the score was tied on four more occasions before the game ended.

Allen's free throw at 1:25 gave his team a lead of 51–50 (after his two free throws had tied it at fifty a few seconds earlier), but Qualls scored again at 0:35 to put Smiley back on top at 52–51. Jimmy Hammel connected on a set shot from side court as Edison regained the lead briefly at 53–52 with twenty-five seconds to play.

With under twenty seconds to play, Qualls took another lob pass while standing under the basket and dunked the ball at 0:13 to give his team its final lead, 54–53. Hammel's last-second drive was unsuccessful (the *San Antonio Light* said "10 feet from the goal the ball bounced off Hammel's foot and out of bounds") as the Golden Eagles held on to the win.

The *Light* added, "The buzzer went off to end the game, and the Bears trudged off the court with a tumultuous ovation for their gallant effort ringing in their ears."

Coach McCarley told sportswriter John Trowbridge of the *Light*, "My boys played their hearts out, but that big guy was the difference."

George Breazeale of the *Austin American-Statesman* observed, "Qualls proved rather conclusively that the Golden Eagles couldn't have made the finals without him."

In a column in Sunday's *Odessa American*, Eastland said a majority of the approximately twenty sportswriters at the game believed "Edison would have beaten Smiley badly if the San Antonio players had been in good condition and could have kept up the torrid pace."

Qualls led all players with nineteen points (he connected on nine of fourteen attempts from the field), and he added twelve rebounds to help Smiley to a decisive advantage of 31–19 on the backboards. His teammate

Leo Runnels, a six-foot-three senior, added thirteen points with eleven rebounds. Smiley hit only 44 percent of its field goal attempts (22 of 50) and 43 percent of its free throws (10 of 23) to keep Edison in contention.

McLaughlin led Edison by scoring thirteen points before he exited with five fouls, and Hammel added twelve. Edison hit 54 percent of its field goal attempts (20 of 37) and 76 percent of its free throws (13 of 17) to keep alive its hopes of upsetting Coach Beard's team and joining the final.

Parents, fellow students, and fans had assembled at the school that Wednesday morning to applaud and encourage the Eagles as they prepared to leave for what the *Pecos Enterprise* called the town's "greatest weekend in sports." A dream was becoming a reality.

"The school was excited," Ephriam remembers. "All the guys were talking. We were focusing on training and conditioning and making sure nobody was getting out and doing something silly. We didn't want anybody to get hurt. We told the guys working on farms and ranches not to go ride no broncs.

"Practice was about the same that week. It wasn't too much different. We just wanted to stay in shape."

A few hundred Pecos fans rode charter buses early Friday for roundtrip fare of eleven dollars each to join the Eagles in Austin and support their team. Radio station KIUN, with Don Boston announcing play-by-play, broadcast the Eagles games back to Pecos.

Joining the hometown fans were former Pecos High School students from the University of Texas, Southern Methodist University, Texas Christian University, Rice Institute, Sul Ross State, Southwestern University, Baylor University, Hardin-Simmons University, and St. Edward's University and other alumni from San Antonio, San Marcos, Schulenburg, and Big Spring to witness the Eagles' historic appearance at the state tournament.

The Eagles played the majority of the 1956–57 season with an eight-man varsity consisting of Ephriam along with teammates Royce Cassell, Robert Hinson, Bill Mitchell, Billy Jim Simmons, Frank Vasquez, Eugene Walker, and Wayne Wassom. Promoted from the B team for the state tournament were Humberto Baeza and Bart Bullock to give Pecos a ten-man squad in

Austin. The Eagles' hard-working manager was Robert Cole, a sophomore who played center on the Eagles' football team.

The *Enterprise* said head coach John Kenner, in his second year at Pecos, was joined on the trip by two other members of the PHS coaching staff: Garland Matthews, the director of athletics and head football coach, and Wilburn Booher, a junior high coach. The team traveled that day in automobiles, including a station wagon the school issued to Matthews and a new 1957 Chevrolet ("the hottest thing on the road," Kenner remembers) that was used for driver's education classes at PHS.

Ephriam avoided riding in the same vehicle with Coach Kenner. He joined teammates Baeza and Vasquez in Matthews's station wagon for the noon departure to Sonora, where Kenner had coached for three years before moving to Pecos. They practiced in the Sonora gymnasium on Wednesday afternoon, spent the night, and resumed their trip Thursday morning. In Austin, they resided at the State Motel, 2500 South Congress, twenty-five blocks south of the capitol and across a bridge over the Colorado River.

(In interviews more than sixty years later, neither Kenner nor Ephriam remembered if the State Motel was the only hotel in Austin that would accommodate the Pecos team with its lone Black player. After Junior Coffey of Dimmitt High School became the second Black player at the UIL state tournament in Austin three years later [discussed more in Chapter Twelve], team members later told the *Lubbock Avalanche-Journal* that only the State Motel in Austin would house Black visitors.)

As he occasionally did, Kenner took the team to a cafeteria to eat upon their arrival in Austin. "I always put Bubba in the middle of the line with a few guys in front and a few guys behind," Kenner said. "I was in front, and the B team coach was at the back. That would keep down the chances of anything that might happen.

"I knew how people felt back in 1957, for crying out loud."

But this day, something did happen, and it reminded Kenner and the Eagles that they were no longer in the more tolerant West Texas.

Kenner described the incident. "As we were going through this big cafeteria line, there was a little old guy there. I can still see the little man. I guess he was about five-foot-eight and dressed in his suit and tie. He was right behind Eugene Walker, who was our last boy in line. That guy looked up, saw Bubba, and slammed his tray down."

The man screamed, "I'm not going to eat anywhere there's a goddamn nigger!"

Kenner said he turned to see the six-foot, two-inch Walker, also a lineman on the Eagles' football team, grab the man by the lapels of his coat and lift him off the floor. Kenner shouted, "Eugene, put him down."

The man started to speak, but Kenner interrupted. "Mister, let me tell you something right now. Hush. I know how you feel, but we can't help this. You feel the way you do, but you see what these kids think of that guy. They'd kill you in a minute for him.

"We can't help what Mr. Eisenhower did. This was forced on us, so this is the way it's going to be. We're going to live with it."

Kenner said the man straightened his coat, abandoned his tray, and quietly left the cafeteria, and the team members continued ordering their meals as they anticipated their state semifinal match the following afternoon against Nacogdoches.

The Class AAA semifinals were conducted on the middle day of the tournament. High school basketball fans were treated to twenty games in three days in five divisions (B to AAAA), including a state tournament record of fifty-one points by Buna's Don Stanley in his team's convincing 74–43 triumph over Seminole in the Class AA championship game Saturday just before the Pecos–Smiley finale for the AAA title.

No doubt Ephriam and his teammates could barely contain their exhilaration as they walked into Gregory Gymnasium on the university's central campus near the main building with its famous 307-foot tower. "I remember walking in," Ephriam said. "We were excited about getting to the school. We saw several of the games."

"I had never seen that many people at one time in my life," Baez said of the packed Gregory Gymnasium. In their dressing room before the game, Ephriam helped the five-foot-seven Baez pin up his warm-up pants to fit because the varsity warm-ups issued to the sophomore were too long.

Kenner also liked his team's chances of winning. "We blew in there for that first game against Nacogdoches, and we thought we had a pretty good chance of winning this thing. We were scoring seventy-something points a game, and that was in 1957.

"I had changed the offense we were running, so that's the reason we were doing so well. And with Nacogdoches, we had no problem."

After a sluggish start, at the end of the first period Pecos trailed 14–13 on the scoreboard after Nacogdoches's Monroe Brewer connected from the corner in the final seconds. The Dragons had come in with a perfect district record of 12–0 for coach Edgar Johnston and a playoff win over highly-regarded Waxahachie (the Class AAA state champion the following year in 1958 led by UIL third-team all-century player Phil Reynolds). Center Monroe Brewer (five points) and guard Billy Wayne Holloway (four points) combined for nine of Nacogdoches's first fourteen points and four of its first five field goals in the first quarter. The Dragons jumped out to a quick 4–0 lead over Pecos in the first minute.

Nell Pouns, society columnist for the *Pecos Enterprise*, said, "The first half of our game with Nacogdoches was such a close race that I found my heart thumping terrifically."

The obstacles Ephriam faced early in that semifinal game weren't limited to the players on the court from Nacogdoches. He was carrying other burdens. "I remember the crowd," he said. "When I got the ball, the whole gym would be booing. 'Kill him, kill him, trip him, trip him.' There were lots of slurs. I heard everything. I never heard my name called the right way."

"The people were booing him when we first hit the floor," Baez said. "They were wanting us to lose."

Ephriam continued, "I remember running down the floor and driving to the bucket. There came some toilet tissue (thrown from the crowd) plastered against my face as I was about to shoot. I went on in and made the bucket. On my way back down the floor, I remember saying to myself, 'If this is what integration is all about, I don't want no part of it.'

"I never did wipe my face. I was crying, really."

Despite his arduous personal challenge, Ephriam fueled the Eagles' comeback. Herb Owens wrote in the *Fort Worth Star-Telegram*, "Ephriam put on quite a show in Pecos' march past Nacogdoches. He hooked spectacularly, leaped high with agility, and blocked numerous shots with his long arms."

After scoring six points in the opening quarter, Ephriam connected on four field goals and a free throw in the second quarter for nine points as the Eagles outscored the Dragons 23–17 to take control with a 36-31 lead at halftime.

In what the *Star-Telegram* called "a wild 15 minutes," the lead changed hands fifteen times and the score was tied seven times before Pecos took a lead it never relinquished a minute before the torrid first half ended. Ephriam's twelfth and thirteenth points of the game gave Pecos a cushion of 32–30, and the Eagles never trailed again.

Additional field goals by Ephriam and Simmons expanded the margin to five points, 36–31, as the teams left the court for their locker rooms at intermission. Putting their slow start behind them, the Eagles had outscored the Dragons 23–17 in the second quarter. Ephriam now had half of his eventual thirty points and Simmons had ten as the two superstar Eagles combined for twenty-five of their team's thirty-six points.

As the game progressed, Ephriam slowly gained favor from the crowd at Gregory Gymnasium with his remarkable play. Clearly, he was the best player on the court that afternoon. The derisive comments diminished, and for a while the previously howling gym became quiet.

The only sounds Ephriam heard were the scuffling of sneakers on the court, the bouncing ball, the grunts of the players from their physical exertion, and the clapping and cheering from R. C. Christopher, now a student at Austin's Huston-Tillotson College, who was sitting in the front row near the Eagles' bench. "That's the way to go, Bubba."

Many in the crowd also began cheering for Ephriam, who recalled, "Soon the whole gym was cheering for me. 'Give it to Bubba.'"

Playing in their sparkling white uniforms, the Eagles outscored Nacogdoches 41–29 in the middle two periods of the game. Ephriam almost matched the Dragons in those sixteen minutes with seventeen points of his own in perhaps his finest game as an Eagle. Pecos led 54–43 after three quarters and 71–62 as the clock expired. It was his team's fiftieth win in Ephriam's two seasons at Pecos High School.

"Nacogdoches' speed and outside accuracy were no match for Ephriam, a wiry, loose 6'4" Negro who showed no signs of stage fright that might be expected of an eighteen-year-old playing under such circumstances," Walter Robertson of the *Dallas Morning News* wrote.

In his account on the wire, Ed Overholser of the Associated Press said, "The Pecos Eagles, powered by the hook shot artistry of Iria Ephriam, pushed to the finals of Conference AAA with a 71–62 win over scrappy Nacogdoches. Ephriam, using a fallaway hook shot and deadly tipins, wound up with 30 points. He was the first Negro to play in a Texas state schoolboy basketball tournament."

George Breazeale of the *Austin American-Statesman* added, "Ephriam displayed a masterful scoring touch plus the ability to move well in spurring Pecos to its win over Nacogdoches. Showing tremendous ability to go up for lob passes to the baseline, Ephriam hit on 11 of his 20 field goal attempts."

The *Register*, a Black weekly newspaper in San Antonio, headlined its story, "Negro in State High Cage Meet, First Time." They wrote, "For the first time in the 37-year history of the annual Texas state high school basketball tournament, a Negro player participated last weekend and was one of the top performers of his division. . . .

"He scored 30 points as the Pecos Eagles took a torrid 71–62 decision from Nacogdoches. Ephriam used a fall-away hook shot and deadly tipins that just could not be stopped."

Bubba's son, Ira Earl, later said of his father, "He was a specimen of physical fitness."

But Ephriam wasn't preoccupied with being the first African American to play in the Texas state basketball tournament. "I really wasn't aware of it," he said. "The realization came when people were talking to me after the game. 'Do you know that you were the first Black to do this?' I never focused on that or thought about that."

Ephriam finished with thirty points and thirteen rebounds, and his more celebrated teammate, first-team all-state selection Simmons, playing on a sore left ankle, recorded fourteen points after a scoreless third quarter and matched Ephriam with thirteen rebounds. Walker added a season-high twelve points, Cassell scored nine, and Mitchell got six as only five players saw action for Kenner in his team's first game in Austin.

Pecos connected on 45 percent of its field goal attempts (29 of 64) and held Nacogdoches to 36 percent (24 of 66). Pecos led in rebounds, 40–31.

In the *Morning News*, Robertson added of Ephriam, "He scored 30 points with a wide variety of shots around the net and cleared the backboards with untimid authority." And Odessa's Eastland wrote, "The game against Nacogdoches was all his. It was made for Ephriam since the Dragons were short and not exceptionally fast, giving the 6'4" Eagle an opportunity to take lobs under the basket and dump them in. He did dump them, too, hitting 30 points."

The *Odessa American* said Simmons was "getting the ball very little and finding room to shoot rarely."

"That first game is like a blur to me," Simmons recalled. "I wasn't right. I remember that Bubba and Eugene pulled us through." Asked by reporters after the game if the double-team defense Nacogdoches employed against him caused problems, Simmons said, "No. Not that so much as the fact that I couldn't move."

In her society column in the *Enterprise*, Pouns added, "The last half was just as exciting, but with a much better margin in the score in our favor. Pandemonium broke loose in our group when our team finished out in front. We had actually reached the finals."

Cassell played despite a fever of 102 degrees, according to Kenner. The coach told Cassell's mother before the game, "Royce is trying to back me down and saying he's going to play. Ma'am, I'm not going to play him. The little fellow is sick. He's vowing that he is going to play."

"Well, here's what I think," Mrs. Cassell answered. "If he wants to play, you let him play."

"Okay, if that's the way you want it, but I'm going to be watching him."

Kenner later said of Cassell, "He gutted it out."

Holloway led yellow-clad Nacogdoches with fourteen points, forward Darrell Brandon scored thirteen points, and Brewer finished with twelve before leaving with five fouls.

After the game, the Eagles rejoiced in their locker room—for the moment, at least, not worried about the challenge awaiting them Saturday night. Wassom, a senior who played forward in basketball and quarterback in football, congratulated Ephriam during the celebration with a hug and a handshake. And while they were shaking hands, Wassom slipped money into Ephriam's big fist.

"Don't tell anybody," Wayne whispered. "We'll get in trouble." Ephriam said Wayne's father had given the money to Wayne with instructions to "make sure and get this to Bubba."

Ephriam immediately put the money in his bag. "I forget exactly how much it was. It was either forty or fifty dollars or something like that. And that was a lot of money back then."

So the Eagles became the first team to advance to the 1957 Class AAA championship game, and they were joined within a couple of hours by Houston's Smiley High School. Both finalists were making their first appearance in the state tournament.

The *Dallas Morning News* summarized, "It was Iria (Bubba) Ephriam, the first Negro ever to play in this storied schoolboy tourney, and sophomore Lewis Qualls, the first seven-foot player in the history of Texas high school basketball, who drew the most attention.

"Ephriam powered Pecos to an impressive 71–62 victory over Nacogdoches in the AAA opener. Immediately afterward, the towering, lumbering Qualls boosted highly-favored Smiley of Houston over a surprisingly tough hurdle, San Antonio Edison, 54–53."

Ephriam's appearance on the University of Texas campus came seven years before the first African American student competed for the UT Longhorns. According to Dwonna Goldstone's book, *Integrating the 40 Acres: The 50-Year Struggle for Racial Equality at the University of Texas*, the first African Americans to compete as UT Longhorns were James Means and Oliver Patterson at a track and field meet on February 29, 1964, at Texas A&M University in College Station. The UT regents had voted about four months earlier, November 9, 1963, to desegregate all student activities at the university, including intercollegiate athletics.

UT first accepted African American undergraduate students in the fall of 1956 after regents adopted this new administrative policy: "Beginning with the fall semester of 1956, the University would . . . admit qualified applicants on all levels without reference to race." That fall there were

101 African American undergraduate students (63 men, 38 women). The first graduate student was Herman M. Sweatt in September 1950 after a favorable ruling in June in the landmark case *Sweatt v. Painter* in the US Supreme Court. He had applied for admission to the UT law school in 1946.

And it was not until May 15, 1964, that the UT Board of Regents voted six to one to completely integrate all facilities, including dormitories, the following fall.

37th annual UIL Boys Basketball Tournament

Gregory Gymnasium

Austin, Texas

Semifinal Game

Friday, March 8, 1957

Pecos 71, Nacogdoches 62

	1Q	2Q	3Q	4Q	Total
Pecos	13	23	18	17	**71**
Nacogdoches	14	17	12	19	**62**

Pecos	Field Goals Made (Attempted)	Free Throws Made (Attempted)	Total Points
Billy Jim Simmons	5 (17)	4 (8)	14
Eugene Walker	6 (12)	0 (1)	12
Bubba Ephriam	11 (20)	8 (15)	30
Bill Mitchell	3 (4)	0 (1)	6
Royce Cassell	4 (11)	1 (2)	9
Team Totals	***29 (64)***	***13 (27)***	***71***

Nacogdoches	Field Goals Made (Attempted)	Free Throws Made (Attempted)	Total Points
Bill Spears	4 (9)	1 (3)	9
Darrell Brandon	4 (5)	5 (7)	13
Monroe Brewer	5 (12)	2 (4)	12
Billy Wayne Holloway	7 (19)	0 (0)	14

Troy Don Burch	1 (7)	4 (6)	6
John Sutton	1 (2)	0 (1)	2
Victor Bane	2 (2)	2 (2)	6
Team Totals	***24 (66)***	***14 (23)***	**62**

REBOUNDS: Pecos 40 (Simmons 13, Ephriam 13, Mitchell 5, Walker 4); Nacogdoches 31 (Spears 8, Brewer 7, Brandon 4)
FOULS: Pecos 13, Nacogdoches 17
FOULED OUT: Brewer
OFFICIALS: Lee and Watson

ELEVEN

HISTORY-MAKING PLAYERS CLASH IN CHAMPIONSHIP GAME

Ephriam and Pecos Battle Qualls and Houston Smiley for Class 3A Title

Smiley Beats Eagles, 52–35, for AAA Title
Odessa American, Mar. 10, 1957

Smiley Pops Pecos for State AAA Title
San Angelo Standard-Times, Mar. 10, 1957

Pecos Eagles Cage Team Welcomed Home by Citizens after Games in Austin
Pecos Enterprise, Mar. 11, 1957

Negro in State High Cage Meet, First Time
San Antonio Register, Mar. 15, 1957

Bubba Ephriam and Lewis Qualls had at least a few things in common. They were two of the finest high school basketball players in the state of Texas during the 1956–57 season, Ephriam and Qualls played for teams that qualified for the much-anticipated UIL state tournament on March

7–9, 1957, in Austin, and they each led their teams into the championship game Saturday with impressive performances in Friday's semifinals.

And Ephriam and Qualls, both history-making players, were accustomed to being the objects of open-mouthed stares from strangers in public.

Ephriam began grabbing attention two years earlier when he joined the basketball team at Pecos High School after Pecos became one of the first cities in Texas to integrate Black and White students in high school. He transferred to PHS from George Washington Carver School, which was coming off back-to-back state tournament appearances for the Prairie View Interscholastic League in February 1954 and February 1955 under coach Sidney Sadler.

Earlier, he had played on Carver's B team as a sixth grader in 1952–53, and he was an important member of the Wildcats' PVIL state tournament teams for Coach Sadler as a varsity player in 1953–54 as a seventh grader and in 1954–55 as an eighth grader.

Former Pecos coach David A. DeWitt Jr. told reporters in Austin at the 1957 UIL state tournament that he watched Ephriam play on the Carver B team as a sixth grader.

Ephriam still remembers the quality of teams at those PVIL state tournaments. "I had participated in state competition against much better and tougher teams than there was in Austin." So the 1957 UIL tournament actually was Ephriam's third state tournament.

Literally, Qualls stood out in a crowd. In 1959, a month after winning his second state title, he told *Sports Illustrated*, "We'd walk in a restaurant or some place, and people would look at me like they thought I was crazy. But I got to where I talked to people and met people and it didn't bother me. They usually ask, 'How's the weather up there?'

"That gets pretty old. 'Fine' is about all I say."

An honors student at Smiley High School, the fair-skinned, crew-cut, and soft-spoken Qualls led the Golden Eagles to a four-year record of 129–27, including two state championships (1957 as a sophomore and 1959 as a senior). He scored 1,782 points in his final three seasons. When he graduated in 1959, he reportedly had sixty-four college scholarship offers before choosing to enroll at Southwest Conference member Texas A&M. He was elected to the Texas High School Basketball Hall of Fame in 1990.

His coach at Smiley, Herbert Beard, said, "We had a great deal of experience with tall boys here, and they have been very fine basketball players.

"When I picked him up out of a PE class in the eighth grade," Beard told *Sports Illustrated*, "he was 6'10" and weighed 265 pounds. People made fun of him. They said he'd never play ball, that he was too clumsy. I tried to tell him that those people who were laughing at him would be paying some day to see him play."

His scoring average was a modest nineteen points per game, but Beard said the Smiley team didn't intentionally feed the ball to Qualls so he could score. "We used him for defense, as a rebounder and as a decoy. When you have a boy seven feet tall and he sticks his hand up and it reaches 9'7", it throws the opposition's shooting off."

Qualls blocked six to eight shots per game, according to Beard. He told George Raborn of the *Waco Tribune-Herald*, "It takes two men to handle him under the boards. We use him to stop everything in a given area inside the free throw line. That kid has come a long way since we spotted him in the eighth grade when he was nothing but a bashful, awkward boy.

"He used not to like playing before people, but he doesn't mind now. Playing against tall kids has really brought Qualls out."

After his team's victory over Nacogdoches, head coach John Kenner sat in Gregory Gymnasium with the other Pecos coaches watching Friday's second AAA semifinal game matching Houston Smiley and San Antonio Edison. "We actually sat up there and pulled for Smiley," Kenner said. "We had just finished beating Nacogdoches, and we were watching these two. Edison had those little fast Mexican boys, and they were flying up and down the court.

"I said, 'Boy, I don't know how we can stay with them.'

"Smiley had the seven-footer, Lewis Qualls. They were good. When it was all over, I said to the guys that were with me, 'You know what? If we can hold Smiley to sixty points, we can win this thing.' So we held them to fifty-something, but we didn't win."

Pecos's two star players, Ephriam and Billy Jim Simmons, also watched the Smiley–Edison contest, although Kenner usually did not approve of his players watching games of the teams they were about to play. "We saw several of the games," Ephriam said. "The one we remember most was the game with Lewis Qualls. Everybody was oohing and ahhing about him."

Simmons added, "When Bubba and I were watching that seven-foot guy, we both said, 'We can stop that lob [the pass inside to Qualls]. That's not going to be a problem.'

"Well, it was a problem. We couldn't stop that lob. I was especially surprised Bubba couldn't stop that lob. For me to get to that point in my life was what it was all about—to make the state tournament and, certainly, the finals.

"I could see Bubba's arms and hands always above. I don't know how many rebounds he got per game. I know he must have gotten a bunch. We played a lot of double post; we could screen for each other. We both averaged twenty-something points a game, so that was forty-something points in a game. It was a big scoring punch. . . .

"He had that kind of hook shot that he shot. He was dependable. He could make shots, and if he didn't make them, he would get his rebound real good. I had confidence in Bubba being there by me. We'd get the rebound, and we'd score. Between him or me, one of us was going to score.

"So if I was having trouble, Bubba was going to be there. He was a good teammate, a good guy to have."

Another capacity crowd of 7,500 filled Gregory Gymnasium Saturday for seven games—the five state championship games (B to AAAA) and third-place games for classes AAA and AAAA. The Pecos–Smiley AAA game was the seventh game of the day and the grand finale.

Kenner's starting lineup certainly looked very familiar to Eagles' fans. Kenner's "iron men" took the court for the opening whistle of their thirtieth game of the season. Joining the 6'4" Ephriam at center were the forwards, 6'3" Simmons and 6'2" Eugene Walker, and the guards, 6'0" Billy Mitchell and 5'10" Royce Cassell—a relatively tall high school lineup in 1957 averaging 6'1". The Pecos Eagles came to the final with wins in twenty-six of their first twenty-nine games.

However, they faced an even taller opponent. Smiley's starting five for its thirty-ninth game of the season averaged 6'4". For the opening tip by referee James L. "Curly" Hayes of Abilene, Coach Beard sent to the court two forwards, 6'3" Leo Runnels and 6'3" J. B. Watson, and two guards, 6'6" Jerry Graham and 5'10" Dick Beard, with the 7'0" Qualls at center. They had won thirty-one of their first thirty-eight games.

Pecos's reserve guard Humberto Baez, promoted to the varsity from the B team for the playoffs, was startled by the size of the Smiley players, especially Qualls. "When I first saw him, I thought, 'There's no way.' He was a monster to me. He was *big*.

"For the opening tip-off, I had never seen Bubba look up to anybody."

Beard assigned the athletic Graham, the team's co-captain, to defend Simmons, Pecos's leading scorer and first-team all-state player, and called for Qualls and another Smiley teammate to double-team Ephriam when he got the ball.

R. C. Christopher said Smiley double-teamed Ephriam because "Qualls couldn't guard him." Whatever the reason, Beard's strategy worked.

Before tip-off for Pecos–Smiley, four other state championships were decided. Dallardsville Big Sandy defeated Meadow, 80–59, in the Class B title game; White Oak whipped McGregor, 66–51, in Class A; Buna completed an undefeated season (40–0) with a convincing 74–45 triumph over Seminole in Class AA; and Port Arthur Jefferson beat Pampa, 67–51, for the Class AAAA trophy.

It was after nine o'clock when the game finally started. Smiley's Golden Eagles scored the first eight points of the game in the initial 3:29 of play and stretched their commanding 8–0 lead to 14–5 by the end of the first quarter. Against the defense Beard designed, Pecos made only one field goal in the first quarter. Despite his sore left ankle, Simmons was the only Pecos Eagle to score in the opening period (he finally made Pecos's first field goal with seventeen seconds remaining in the opening period), and Runnels led Smiley with six points.

The margin widened in the second quarter, when Smiley outscored Pecos 19–8. Qualls hit six field goals in this pivotal quarter to score twelve of his team's nineteen points. Ephriam eventually did get untracked, scoring six of Pecos's eight points, but Smiley already held a twenty-point lead, 33–13, at intermission.

In the first half, Pecos had connected on only three of its twenty-seven field goal attempts (11 percent accuracy), and Qualls had outscored Pecos's entire team fourteen to thirteen.

"The coach from Smiley saw us, and he went to work to put a defense around me," Ephriam recalled. "I could roll either way and shoot a hook shot. But he had a switching defense to keep me from rolling right or left—a really, really strategic defense to keep me from coming back to the bucket. It was pretty rough. That's why I didn't score like I did in the game with Nacogdoches. They had a defense to box me in and keep me from scoring."

Before the game, Kenner warned Ephriam and Simmons about getting into foul trouble. He told them, "Look guys, if Qualls gets that ball inside, let him go on and score. Let him score. He's going to score that much on us anyway. If he gets the ball inside like that, don't put yourselves in jeopardy."

The coach continued, "But they couldn't stand it. By the end of the first quarter, I had already called three timeouts, and by the end of the second quarter, I had called my fourth one." Ephriam and Simmons each collected three fouls in the first half. "They both had a good foul count on them."

During halftime, Kenner told his players to let him call their fifth and final timeout during the second half. The 6'6" Graham's defense and Simmons's lingering ankle injury combined to restrain Simmons. He hit only three of nineteen field goal attempts, was held scoreless in the fourth quarter, and finished with only nine points before fouling out. Mitchell also was charged with five fouls and was disqualified in the second half. (Ephriam wasn't whistled for a foul in the second half to finish with three.)

Pecos was charged with seventeen fouls in the game to only nine for Smiley. No Smiley player was called for more than two fouls. "Smiley just had those big ol' tall boys, and they were good," Kenner explained. "They had to be, or they wouldn't have beaten Edison.

"Bubba had all those big guys around him," the Pecos coach continued. "That put the clamps on him. And that heavy foul situation in those first two quarters made an impact on us. . . .

"And Bubba, I guess, couldn't take over because of all that height inside. That cut down on all his rebounding and putback that he had been doing." Instead of being the tallest player on the court, as he usually was, Ephriam faced not one but two players on the opposing team taller than he was.

Eight days after his ankle injury in Lubbock, Simmons was still having trouble with it. "Billy Jim made only three of nineteen." Kenner kept calling for Simmons to get the ball on offense. "He had done it all year. I wouldn't have believed it. I guarantee if you had blindfolded him and brought him across there and said, 'Let it go,' he would have scored. It just didn't go that night."

Simmons added, "I still couldn't jump on this left foot, and I was a jump shooter. I was shooting off the wrong foot. In warm-up in that state final game, I was making every damn shot I was shooting. That's what really threw me.

"And I had a really good guy guarding me, about six-foot-six [Jerry Graham]. What I didn't realize was that he really was their best player. He went to Texas, and we played against each other while I was at TCU. I had an idea that helped me alter my shot.

"We were concentrating so much on the seven-foot player. He hurt us real bad, but that six-foot-six boy was a good player. They were well-rounded, and they were well-coached, too. We got down fast, and we couldn't recover."

(Graham played in twenty-two games for the Longhorns in 1959–60 when they finished 18–8, won the Southwest Conference championship with a league record of 11–3, and eventually lost to Kansas in the NCAA Division I regional semifinals.)

Pecos and Smiley battled evenly in the third quarter. Each scored thirteen points (Qualls had eight points, Ephriam three, and Simmons his final two) to put Smiley on top again by twenty points, 46–26, entering the final period.

Ephriam still questions Kenner's decision to continue to design plays for Simmons. "If a man is hurt as bad as he was, couldn't move, then why play him?"

During a timeout called by Smiley in the fourth quarter, Ephriam said Kenner told him not to shoot again. "He called me aside and said, 'Listen, they're giving away some good scholarships here, and Billy Jim is a senior this year. If anybody gets one, I want it to be him, because you with your Black ass will be lucky to pass by a college, let alone go to one. If you shoot the ball one more time, I'll have your ass on the bench next to me.'"

Ephriam began passing to Simmons as instructed by his coach. "But you could see how much activity he had over there around him. Everybody was hollering at me when I got the ball, 'Shoot it,' but I couldn't shoot it. I had to pass it off because coach said.

"I can still hear it echoing in my ears. 'Pass it to Simmons. Pass it to Simmons. Pass it to Simmons.' If I had not been passing to Simmons, it would be a different story."

Ephriam believes that "Kenner lost the state tournament for Pecos. . . . I would get the ball in the key, roll past Qualls, and pass the ball over the top to Simmons over in the corner. He would either miss or get the shot blocked."

Cassell noticed Ephriam had stopped shooting. "What was that Kenner said to you?"

"Coach told me to pass the ball to Billy Jim because they're giving away some good scholarships down here, and if anybody gets one, he wanted it to be Billy Jim."

"What?" Cassell was puzzled.

"That's right. Pass it to Billy Jim and let him shoot."

According to Ephriam, Cassell called the Eagles' final timeout in the fourth quarter, and Simmons joined their conversation on the court. "What's going on?"

Cassell answered, "You know what he told Bubba? He told Bubba to pass the ball to you because he wants you to do all the shooting because they're giving away scholarships down here."

"Come on," Simmons replied. "We came down here to win the game. We didn't come down here to play for scholarships. We're playing to win the game. Let's play ball."

Cassell told Ephriam, "Bubba, we're going to throw the ball in to you, and you shoot."

That prompted Kenner to send Frank Vasquez into the game to substitute for Ephriam. Vasquez ran on the court and tapped Ephriam on the leg. "Coach wants you."

But Ephriam's teammates sent Vasquez back to the bench. "They ain't nobody substituting," one of them said.

"There was no way Frank Vasquez was going to substitute for Bubba," Baez added.

After a low-scoring fourth quarter, Pecos managed to trim its deficit only to seventeen points against Smiley's reserve players to fall by the final score of 52–35. Pecos's total was the fewest points scored by a team in the Class AAA final game in tournament history.

"I saw that game in old Gregory Gym," Christopher remembers. "Bubba gave it the best he had."

"If I had been allowed to shoot," Ephriam said, "I could have made the difference. To stop an able-bodied player from shooting and pass to a tired, hurt player is stupid. And he tried to take me out of the game. . . . The only time Simmons came out of a game was if he fouled out. But Kenner would take me out and let Simmons play and run his points up."

Beard cleared his bench in the closing minutes, and he called two timeouts in the fourth quarter so he could make substitutions. Eleven of Smiley's thirteen players in uniform played in the game.

During Smiley's other timeout in the final quarter, with Kenner kneeling in the middle of the Eagles' huddle on the sideline, a drop of sweat fell from Ephriam's face onto Kenner's jacket. Ephriam said his coach grabbed a towel and "shoved it in my face."

"Wipe that sweat off your face," Kenner told Ephriam.

But sweat wasn't the only thing dripping from Ephriam's face. By now he felt moisture at the corners of his eyes and on his cheeks. Ephriam's sweat was mixed with his tears.

Ephriam said a young girl seated near the Pecos bench noticed his despondence. "I could read her little lips."

She told her friend, "He's crying."

Ephriam covered his face with the towel to hide his tears. "I've often thought about that," Ephriam remembers. "To athletes, sweat is welcome, but just a drop fell on his jacket, he turned around and came all unglued—like I was contagious.

"I really think that having to play under those conditions was a little worse than playing on a sprained ankle." Ephriam remembers asking himself, "What is going on inside of me?" He wanted more than anything to tell someone—to make them understand—the oppression he was experiencing. He wanted to speak about the hurt inside, explain the burden he was carrying and know that they heard him.

"It took me so long to talk about it," he continued. "I wanted to think I was making a difference and that integration meant something. I feel bad not going back to Pecos after I left. Some kids came back, but I couldn't go back.

"Tell me, my friend, how am I supposed to feel?"

During his two years at Pecos, Ephriam's name frequently appears in newspaper articles about the Eagles' games—as it most definitely should have. And occasionally, photographs of the talented player were published. But Ephriam's name rarely appeared in the headlines. A headline in the *Pecos Enterprise* on March 14, 1957, said, "Ira [*sic*] Ephriam, Simmons Placed on 3-A All-Tournament Team." And the *Odessa American* twice in 1956–57 used Ephriam in its headlines—"Ephriam Cans 27, Pecos Rips Marfa" after the season opener and "Ephriam Leads Pecos Eagles to 71–62 Win" after the victory over Nacogdoches in Austin.

A Black newspaper, the *San Antonio Register*, printed these headlines over two of its accounts of the state tournament: "Negro in State High Cage Meet, First Time" and "Ephriam on All State."

Today, Bubba's daughter Iria Loraine Abram says of her father's experiences, "He had to grow up really fast. It wasn't fair, because it wasn't just about kids playing basketball."

In the championship game, Qualls led all players in scoring with twenty-three points, Watson added eleven, and Graham made eight while limiting Simmons to nine. Qualls hit all but four of his fifteen field goal attempts (73 percent accuracy), and he wrestled away fifteen rebounds. Smiley as a team hit 41 percent from the field and commanded the backboards with a sizable rebound advantage of 47–27.

Herb Owens, in the *Fort Worth Star-Telegram*, said, "Qualls isn't agile nor does he have great stamina, but he's likely to be a fine player before he is graduated in 1959."

Walter Robertson of the *Dallas Morning News* added, "Smiley's seven-foot sophomore Lewis Qualls proved to be too much for Pecos, and the Houston team stunned the west Texans, 52–35, to take the AAA title."

The *San Antonio Register* added, "In the championship game, Pecos, ice cold, bowed to Smiley High of Houston, 52–35, as Smiley's seven-foot, one-half inch star dumped in 23 points and dominated both backboards. Ephriam with 12 points was high for Pecos in the title fracas."

Tom Eastland of the *Odessa American* apparently wasn't as impressed. In a follow-up column after the tournament, he wrote, "Lewis Qualls . . . gave the capacity crowds at Gregory Gym on the campus of the University of Texas one of their biggest disappointments of the tournament. Oh, he was 7'0" all right, and looked possibly taller. He could cram the basket all right without even jumping. About the only thing he couldn't do was play basketball."

Qualls was only a sophomore, Eastland reminded, and not yet old enough to use his tremendous height to any advantage. "All the big boy did in the way of basketball was to stand under one basket until the ball changed hands and then run to the other end to stand again. He was invariably the last man down the court."

"Qualls couldn't jump two inches off the floor," Baez said, "and it took him a long time to run down the court." The Smiley seven-footer had forty-two points and twenty-seven rebounds in two games, but he hit only two of nine free throws. He tied Ephriam for most points in two games, led in rebounds, and hit twenty of his twenty-nine field goal attempts (69 percent).

In the final, Ephriam again led his team with twelve points—six in each half—and Mitchell (6), Walker (5), and Cassell (3) completed the Pecos scoring with Simmons's nine. Wayne Wassom and Robert Hinson also played for Pecos in the fourth quarter after Simmons and Mitchell left with five fouls each. Pecos improved its shooting in the second half (9 of 27) to finish at twelve of fifty-four for 22 percent accuracy, but that wasn't nearly enough to overtake Smiley's big early lead.

Simmons wasn't the only Eagle who shot poorly against the Smiley defense. Ephriam was three of twelve from the field, Mitchell was three of nine, Walker hit two of nine, and Cassell made only one of five. Blocked shots were not reported in accounts of the game, but no doubt many of those misses had no chance of connecting because of blocks by the seven-foot Qualls or the six-foot-six Graham.

Ephriam was Pecos's rebound leader with eight.

"I was pretty well embarrassed," Simmons said. "That kind of ruined my whole career by losing in the finals and by the way that I played. It wasn't really good."

In the first game of the day, Saturday morning at 8:45, Edison easily whipped Nacogdoches, 75–45, to earn third place in Class AAA in a game between Friday's two losing teams. Four Bears scored in double figures, and Nacogdoches hit only 24 percent of its field goal attempts (14 of 58). Edison led Class AAA with 128 points in two games.

After the championship game, Ephriam was honored by UIL officials in an awards ceremony as the leading vote-getter on the Class AAA all-tournament team. He and Qualls shared high-point honors; each scored forty-two in his team's two games. Sportswriters from across the state who were in Austin to report on the tournament selected the all-tournament team. In their voting, Ephriam emerged as the top player, followed by Edison's Bill McLaughlin as runner-up with Qualls third and Simmons fourth. Three players—Runnels of Smiley, Jimmy Hammel of Edison, and Monroe Brewer of Nacogdoches—tied for the fifth spot to produce a seven-man all-tournament team.

Fans swarmed the court after the game ended—many, no doubt, to get closer looks at the first Black player and the first seven-footer to play in the UIL state basketball tournament. "Everybody started swooping down to the court," Ephriam said. "I was still in amazement of the game.

"Little kids and people were passing me pieces of paper for autographs. I saw two little White girls coming through the crowd. They reached out and touched me on the arm and congratulated me on the game I played. 'You really did a good job.' 'That was a beautiful performance.' I looked at them and just smiled."

Ephriam said he had lost track of time when suddenly Kenner grabbed his wrist, jerked him away from the crowd, and led him off the court. "Come on. Who do you think you are signing autographs?" His coach abruptly ended Ephriam's autograph session.

According to Ephriam, three men then took him aside, and two led him to a separate room while another went to the Pecos locker room to retrieve his gym bag and clothes for him to dress after a shower. From this room, through the blinds, he could see his Eagle teammates walking on the sidewalk to their waiting automobiles.

But the men closed the blinds. "They told me to get away from the window. They said they were there to protect me," Ephriam said. "They escorted me to our cars."

Now, more than sixty years later, neither Ephriam nor Coach Kenner remembers being aware of a threat made against Pecos's African American player.

"I didn't know if there was a threat on my life," Ephriam said. "It never dawned on me they were there to protect me."

It was after eleven o'clock Saturday night before Pecos's disappointed players and coaches finally departed Gregory Gymnasium. Kenner wanted to reward his players for their splendid season with dinner at an Austin fave, the venerable Night Hawk, Harry Akin's longtime popular restaurant located at the very busy intersection of Congress Avenue and Riverside Drive since 1932.

But what Kenner didn't know was that at the time, the Night Hawk refused to seat African Americans in its dining room. "He can't eat here," the Eagles were told as they entered the restaurant, "but he may eat in the kitchen."

Kenner's first thought was to walk out. "I started to leave. I was mentally and physically drained by that time. I went from about one eighty [pounds] to one seventy. That's the only restaurant in Austin that didn't allow Bubba to eat with us." But Kenner said Ephriam told him he didn't mind sitting in the kitchen. "Are you sure, Bubba?"

"Coach, I don't mind."

So with Ephriam eating in the kitchen, his teammates and coaches ate in the Night Hawk dining room. "At the time," Ephriam's teammate Baez said, "we didn't think anything about it."

Sixty years later, however, Kenner said he still regrets his decision to remain at the Night Hawk. "I don't know why I let my guard down. . . . We came out, and I told Bubba, 'I'm sorry.'"

"That's alright, coach. I met one of my cousins."

Kenner added, "He probably ate better than we did."

According to Dwonna Goldstone, in her book, *Integrating the 40 Acres*, it wasn't until three years later that the Night Hawk integrated. The combined efforts of UT students and local pastors in 1960 persuaded Akin and Night Hawk management to serve African American students "after they identified themselves." The restaurant later agreed to serve "all Negroes without question who are otherwise acceptable as customers."

In *As We Saw It*, a 2018 book from the University of Texas Press that tells the story of integration at the university, the editors say the Night Hawk on "The Drag" (Guadalupe Street on the western edge of the UT campus) was the first restaurant in Austin to integrate. Akin, who later served as mayor of Austin in 1967–69, reportedly attended a conference of one hundred restaurant representatives from Southern states in 1963 in Washington, DC, and heard Attorney General Robert Kennedy urge them to integrate their restaurants. One month later, Akin assembled representatives of eighteen restaurants and hotels in Austin to sign a resolution to desegregate their food establishments immediately.

Nell Pouns, society columnist for the *Pecos Enterprise*, observed after the championship game that for Pecos fans, "The exciting memory will last for years to come. We didn't win, it's true, but everyone was proud of our boys and the way they worked until the closing whistle.

"Tears and cheers marked the end of the game and the awarding of the trophies. This year we got second but everyone from Pecos should be justly proud of the team and its coach."

The spectacle and performance of Qualls were popular topics of conversation. Pouns wrote, "Their seven-foot player seems to be a psychological as well as a physical advantage.We are used to seeing Ephriam, who is not little by any means, but when he stood beside that young giant he looked dwarfed. It must be discouraging to keep reaching for the ball and realizing that it always gets caught 12 inches above your head.

"Tall boy didn't do much leg work, but did most of his playing under the basket. If Pecos had the ball he was there to catch it off the backboard.

He tossed it to one of his teammates who worked back to the other end of the court while he rambled on to get in position again. When it reached him there he got on tiptoe and dropped it in the basket.

"With all fairness to him, he can't help being that tall and probably didn't want to play in the first place. He certainly didn't play with the enthusiasm of his teammates."

The Eagles returned home Sunday and were greeted at the south edge of town near Pecos's famous rodeo arena on US Highway 285 by about six hundred fans with a spirited thirty-minute celebration of the team's accomplishments. They had been alerted by a telephone call when the team reached Fort Stockton about fifty miles away.

"There were lots of people," Baez said. "My family was there; I was really surprised. . . . None of them had ever seen me play. They didn't go to Lubbock or Austin. The only one who ever saw me play was my older brother Lazaro, who played at Balmorhea."

The high school band performed, coaches and players made speeches, and television and radio stations were there to interview players and coaches and record, document, and broadcast the event. The Eagles still were heroes to their families and their fans in Pecos.

And it would be another three years before the next African American player appeared in the Texas state basketball tournament in Austin.

37th annual UIL Boys Basketball Tournament

Gregory Gymnasium

Austin, Texas

Championship Game

Saturday, March 9, 1957

Houston Smiley 52, Pecos 35

	1Q	2Q	3Q	4Q	Total
Pecos	5	8	13	9	**35**
Smiley	14	19	13	6	**52**

Pecos	Field Goals Made (Attempted)	Free Throws Made (Attempted)	Total Points
Billy Jim Simmons	3 (19)	3 (4)	9
Eugene Walker	2 (9)	1 (3)	5
Bubba Ephriam	3 (12)	6 (7)	12
Bill Mitchell	3 (9)	0 (0)	6
Royce Cassell	1 (5)	1 (3)	3
Wayne Wassom	0 (0)	0 (0)	0
Robert Hinson	0 (0)	0 (0)	0
Team Totals	***12 (54)***	***11 (17)***	***35***

Smiley	Field Goals Made (Attempted)	Free Throws Made (Attempted)	Total Points
Jerry Graham	4 (8)	0 (2)	8
Dick Beard	0 (7)	3 (4)	3
Lewis Qualls	11 (15)	1 (3)	23
Leo Runnels	2 (7)	3 (9)	7
J. B. Watson	3 (11)	5 (9)	11
Joe Helton	0 (0)	0 (0)	0
David Grayson	0 (1)	0 (0)	0
Boyce Holland	0 (0)	0 (0)	0
Keith Taylor	0 (0)	0 (0)	0
Maurice Moore	0 (0)	0 (0)	0
Jimmie Emerson	0 (0)	0 (0)	0
Team Totals	***20 (49)***	***12 (27)***	***52***

REBOUNDS: Pecos 27 (Ephriam 8, Walker 7, Simmons 7, Mitchell 3); Smiley 47 (Qualls 15, Graham 9, Runnels 9, Beard 6)
FOULS: Pecos 17, Smiley 9
FOULED OUT: Simmons, Mitchell
OFFICIALS: Watson and Hayes

All-Tournament Team

Bubba Ephriam, Pecos; Billy Jim Simmons, Pecos; Lewis Qualls, Houston Smiley; Bill McLaughlin, San Antonio Edison; Leo Runnels, Houston Smiley; Monroe Brewer, Nacogdoches; and Jimmy Hammell, San Antonio Edison

TWELVE

FROM PECOS TO VIETNAM—BUBBA'S STORY CONTINUES

Bubba's Decade after '57, Including Ten Years in the Navy

Truman Orders End of Bias in Forces and Federal Jobs
New York Times, July 27, 1948

Marines Land to Guard Danang Base
New York Times, Mar. 8, 1965

Marshall Named for High Court, Its First Negro
New York Times, June 14, 1967

Saturn 5 Places Apollo in Orbit in a Smooth Test
New York Times, Nov. 10, 1967

Please don't ask Bubba to show you his scars. That's because, first, yes, he does have scars. And, second, yes, they still hurt. They are painful. They are tender. They are heartrending. Especially the scars you can't see, the ones inside. They remind him of his past. They tell a story.

Belva Hollingshead Williams knows of Bubba's scars. She knows his story. A classmate of Bubba's at Pecos High School, she joined fellow students, parents, former students, and fans at Gregory Gymnasium in Austin,

Texas, in March 1957 to watch the Eagles play in the UIL basketball state tournament. She witnessed the sometimes cruel treatment he experienced as the tournament's first African American player. She admired his courage. And despite the loss in the championship game, she celebrated with other Pecos fans the achievements of Ephriam and his teammates.

Through more than sixty years—since those memorable days as classmates—Williams has shared the story of Bubba Ephriam. "I have told your story many times," she remarked to Bubba. "I told it with pride as if it were my story as well as yours. . . .

"I have always remembered your courage," Williams said in a letter to Bubba dated July 28, 2014, soon after his induction in San Antonio into the Hall of Fame of the PVIL Coaches Association. "I am speaking of your courage not only at the basketball tournament in Austin, but at other basketball games in those two years."

Like Ephriam, she arrived as a freshman at Pecos High School in September 1955 after moving with her family to the city. She attended most of the regular season home games and the UIL state tournament. Bubba, Belva, class officers Bobby Jones, Robbye McCain, Jane Jones, and Dickie Bowlin, and 170 other sophomores are pictured on pages 54–62 in *The '57 Eagle*, the school's yearbook. Belva was "who's who" in English II, Spanish I, and typing, and she was a member of the Spanish club and pep squad.

"We never know how we may influence people by our actions and our words," she told Bubba. "I wanted you to know how your actions influenced me in a positive way. I am sure I am not the only one."

Certainly, she was not the only one. Through the years, Bubba has received dozens of similar cards, letters, telephone calls, and visits from friends, family, classmates, teachers, coaches, and Pecos basketball fans. Another member of the PHS class of 1959, Delinda McDonald Richman, thanked Ephriam for "weathering the sad treatment you received at Gregory Gym at the state meet."

A sophomore class representative on the PHS student council that year, Richman added, "I was at that tournament and couldn't believe my eyes and ears." She had moved to Pecos at age ten from Temple, which she said had a large Black population. "I was taught to treat them like everyone else," Richman said.

She continued, "I am so sorry for all of the discrimination and ugliness you have had to endure in your life. There is no animal crueler than man. . . . You are a good man and deserve much, but will not get what you truly deserve. Life is that way."

Rose Ann Kelton Hatchett, a 1956 graduate of Pecos High School who cheered for Bubba his first year at PHS, told him, "I had no idea that you and R. C. went through so much trouble in basketball, especially later at state finals. We cheerleaders never knew. . . . You have really been through a lot."

Another former PHS classmate, Barbara Frandsen, now of Austin, wrote, "We all remember you. Your presence in the halls and classes at Pecos High School was a demonstration of courage and dignity. Your presence on the basketball court was beautiful. We were awestruck by your talent and hard work."

About two months after his basketball season ended in Austin, Ephriam's playing career for the Eagles also concluded with his final baseball games and track and field meets. In May, the school year ended at Pecos High School, and Bubba turned nineteen years of age. That meant he would be too old for UIL athletics the following 1957–58 school year.

He worked a summer job in packaging and shipping at a chemical plant in Odessa owned by Billie Sol Estes, a Pecos resident, family friend, and well-known businessman and financier. But Ephriam did not return to school in September to resume his high school education. Instead, he continued to work at Estes's plant until deciding later that fall to join the US Navy.

Ephriam said his father's mounting problems hiring crews for his cotton and farming businesses contributed to his decision to join the Navy. After cotton and farming "played out" for Bubba's father, he opened a salvage yard and also worked as a mechanic.

"His crews thinned out," Bubba explained. "People stayed in town. They got jobs in town, and the women did domestic work. There were no crews to pick cotton anymore."

Bubba said trucks began to arrive in West Texas loaded with Mexican laborers who worked for lower wages as negotiated for each field by a foreman who represented a remote landowner ("a lot of those folks never seen any cotton"). "Big trucks came in," Bubba remembers, "and started letting Spanish people out in the fields right next to Daddy's field."

He added, "And don't call them 'wetbacks.' I never have liked that term. They say they swim the Rio Grande to come over here and take these people's jobs. That's the biggest lie ever told. They don't swim the Rio Grande to come over here and take these jobs. They bring whole crews over on the back of a truck.

"We had to venture out and get other jobs," Bubba added. "But there wasn't no jobs. That's why I decided to go into the Navy so I could help my family."

The US Navy that welcomed Bubba in 1957 looked a lot different than it had two decades earlier.

Military historian Dr. Ulysses Grant Lee Jr. said in his book, *The Employment of Negro Troops*, that in the peacetime years after World War I, the US Navy eliminated almost all Black sailors and employees. Dr. Lee, an English professor, Howard University graduate, and former US Army officer who died in 1969, wrote in his book first published in 1966, "The US Navy no longer employed Negroes in peacetime at all except as messboys because of the problem of mixing the races aboard ships."

In July 1940, *The Crisis*, official magazine of the NAACP, published a photograph of military airplanes with the caption: "FOR WHITES ONLY War planes—Negro Americans may not build them, repair them or fly them, but they must help pay for them." (Dr. Lee said African Americans were not accepted for training by the Army Air Corps at any US base at that time.) Later that year in an editorial, *The Crisis* stated, "Of all the shabby dealings of America with a tenth of her citizens, none is more shameful or more indefensible than the refusal to give Negroes a fair chance in the armed forces."

Conditions began to change later that year with the approval of the Selective Training and Service Act on September 16, 1940. It provided for quotas of African American troops in proportion to the percentage of Black citizens in the US population. Of the first four hundred thousand men called to serve after the act became law, thirty-six thousand were to be African Americans. The two provisions for the integration of US troops were:

> Within the limits of the quota determined . . . for the subdivision in which he resides, any person, regardless of race or color, between the ages of 18 and 36 shall be afforded an opportunity to volunteer for induction into the land or naval forces of the United States.
>
> In the selection and training of men under this Act . . . there shall be no discrimination against any person on account of race or color.

And so African Americans began to be admitted into the US armed forces. However, they served in segregated units, according to Dr. Lee, because "the policy of the War Department is not to intermingle colored and white enlisted personnel in the same regimental organizations." And according to Dr. Lee, "A majority of Negro troops were assigned to non-combatant duties."

African Americans across the nation advocating for acceptance into the armed forces adopted the slogan: "Negroes had to fight for the right to fight."

More than nine hundred thousand Black soldiers fought in these segregated regiments in the Army and Navy during World War II (1939–45) to defend a constitution whose protections they did not fully enjoy. Harry S. Truman, who assumed the presidency after the death of Franklin D. Roosevelt on April 12, 1945, appointed the President's Commission on Civil Rights in 1946 because, he wrote in his memoirs, "of the repeated anti-minority incidents immediately after the war in which homes were invaded, property was destroyed and a number of innocent lives were taken." Truman urged Congress to adopt the commission's recommendations issued in 1947 in its report *To Secure These Rights*, but when senators from the South delayed legislation with threats of a filibuster, Truman issued an executive order ending segregation in all branches of the military.

The Truman Presidential Library and Museum in Independence, Missouri, says Truman, who was reared in pro-slavery Missouri and was the grandson of slave owners, was "the first American president to proclaim the equality of blacks." He signed Executive Order 9981 on July 26, 1948, and declared that "there shall be equality of treatment and opportunity for all persons in the armed services without regard to race, color, religion, or national origin." (Truman signed an executive order that same day ending segregation in the federal workforce.)

Although an executive order had been issued, the desegregation of the military happened slowly. It wasn't until after the Korean War (1950–53) that the military was fully integrated. Most of the actual enforcement of Truman's order was implemented during the presidential administration of Dwight D. Eisenhower (1953–61). David A. Nichols, in his book *A Matter of Justice: Eisenhower and the Beginning of the Civil Rights Revolution*, said the last all-Black unit in the US military wasn't abolished until September 1954. And Kenneth Claiborne Royall, secretary of the Army and former brigadier general, was forced into retirement in April 1949 for refusing to desegregate the Army, according to Robert B. Edgerton in his book *Hidden Heroism: Black Soldiers in America's Wars.*

Many soldiers returned home after World War II determined to end segregation. They joined the NAACP, registered to vote, protested discrimination in jobs and housing, and demanded equality for their children in public schools. Howard Zinn, writing in *A People's History of the United States*, says one Black veteran told his college teacher, "The Army jim-crows us. The Navy lets us serve only as messmen. The Red Cross refuses our blood. Employers and labor unions shut us out. Lynchings continue. We are disenfranchised, jim-crowed, spat upon. What more could Hitler do than that?"

In his book *Postwar America 1945–71*, Zinn says, "Donations of blood to the armed forces were separated by race in Red Cross blood banks."

During Ephriam's second term in the Navy, when he was serving in the machinists' division of the engineering department on board the USS *Bennington*, he was assigned to work as a messman in the ship's commissary for about two years before resuming duty in M division.

Ephriam recalls other subtle instances of discrimination in his ten-year naval career. For example, on the USS *Lexington*, Ephriam said, he served under a veteran E-9 officer "who was always going around trying to find something to write me up about. We didn't get along very well."

Zinn, in *People's History*, reprints this "draftee's prayer" from a Black newspaper in January 1943:

> Dear Lord,
> today I go to war:
> to fight, to die.
> Tell me what for?
> Dear Lord,
> I'll fight,
> I do not fear,
> Germans or Japs;
> my fears are here.
> America!

Bubba visited the US Navy's recruiting office at the post office building in Pecos in November 1957. "I went down and talked to the Navy recruiter," he said.

"Sure, we'd be glad to have you," the officer told Bubba.

"I wanted to join a branch of the military where I could travel, go places, see the world," Bubba said. "I wanted to blend in and accept their culture. I didn't want to try to change them."

Bubba's induction process happened quickly after his decision to join the Navy. "I took the test," Bubba continued. "I'm sure a lot of the questions on the test I wasn't familiar with. He reached out to help me and the other guys to help them get in. I'm pretty sure."

Ephriam said he experienced similar opportunities later in his naval career. "In boot camp I saw the need to help these young guys instead of rejecting them," he explained. "I could relate to where they were. I was lenient with the guys in the early stages of my naval career."

During the first of his two terms in a ten-year military career, Ephriam sent money home to his mother from his US Navy paychecks. "I sent money back to Mama for four years," Ephriam said. "Several of my sisters were old enough by then to help her."

In December 1957, Ephriam traveled to El Paso, Texas, for a physical examination to enter the US Navy. He passed the exam, returned home to Pecos, and received orders to report to Albuquerque, New Mexico, after the holidays to begin his naval career. The six-foot-four, 185-pound teenager from Pecos, Texas—with a tenth-grade education and no high school diploma—enlisted January 23, 1958, in Albuquerque, signed the Oath of Allegiance, and pledged to serve four years in the US Navy.

His next stop was the US Naval Training Center in San Diego, California. He was issued his Geneva Convention and US Armed Forces identification cards on February 3 and began eight weeks at Recruit Training Command. Almost one thousand miles from home, Iria "Bubba" Ephriam found himself in boot camp.

He completed training April 7 and reported April 22 to the USS *Lexington* (CVA-16), an Essex-class aircraft carrier built during World War II that was the fifth US Navy ship named in honor of the Battle of Lexington near Boston that launched the Revolutionary War. The ship had been designated as an attack carrier (CVA) in October 1952 following the war after entering the National Defense Reserve Fleet in Bremerton, Washington. After its conversion, the USS *Lexington* was now able to accommodate the most modern jet aircraft.

With Ephriam aboard, the USS *Lexington* departed on April 25 for refresher training in the Pacific. The training was interrupted, however, on July 14, 1958, when the *Lexington* was ordered to embark at San Francisco and sail to Pearl Harbor and then continue to Guam, Philippines, and Japan to reinforce the US Navy's Seventh Fleet during the Second Taiwan Strait Crisis. It arrived at its new station in Yokosuka on August 7—only four months after Seaman Ephriam completed training—and served on a peacekeeping mission there until returning to San Diego on December 19.

The conflict took place between the People's Republic of China (PRC), which had taken control of mainland China, and the Republic of China (ROC), whose government had retreated to the island of Taiwan. The PRC shelled the islands of Kinmen and Matsu in the Taiwan Strait beginning on August 23 in an attempt to liberate Taiwan from the Chinese Nationalist Party and to probe the extent of the United States' defense of Taiwan's territory.

President Eisenhower's administration responded to a request for aid from the ROC and ordered reinforcement of the Seventh Fleet in the region and protection for the supply lines of the Chinese Nationalist government to the islands. Historical accounts of the conflict report that it marked the first use of the US Navy's newly-developed AIM-9 Sidewinder missile in air-to-air combat, which gave the Nationalists a decisive advantage over the Soviet-made MiG fighters used by the People's Liberation Army of the PRC in the skies over the Taiwan Strait.

The US Air Force, Army, and Marine Corps joined the naval forces in the conflict in which hundreds of soldiers and civilians were killed before a ceasefire went into effect on September 22. Numerous MiGs were shot down by Sidewinders, reportedly the first "kills" to be scored in combat by air-to-air missiles.

Young Bubba Ephriam served in the B division of the ship's engineering department. Ephriam, an E-3 fireman, worked in the engine rooms—attending to the steam-generating boilers and turbines that powered the *Lexington* with fellow seamen. Occasionally, he got relief from the 120-degree heat in the engine rooms deep inside the *Lexington* by being posted on level seven above the deck to watch for approaching planes and help them avoid smoke from the engine rooms for safe landings.

A US Navy administrative document dated May 16, 1966, said Ephriam earned the Armed Forces Expeditionary Medal for his service in the Taiwan Strait from October 16 to November 15, 1958, on board USS *Lexington*.

The crew of the *Lexington* fondly referred to their ship as "the Blue Ghost" because of its dark blue camouflage scheme. The Japanese, at least four times in World War II—in propaganda broadcasts by "Tokyo Rose"—erroneously reported the sinking of the *Lexington*, but each time it reappeared, and the Japanese referred to it as a "ghost."

Ephriam's basketball skills were on display early in his naval career. In fact, upon verbal orders from the commanding officer, Ephriam was transferred from the USS *Lexington* during its western Pacific cruise on November 5, 1958, for temporary additional duty. He was sent to the US Naval Air Station at Atsugi on Honshu, the main island of Japan, to play for the NAS Flyers basketball team. The Flyers, whose coach had watched Bubba play, competed against teams from other ships and naval bases and

Japanese universities, and they won the Navy's Far East championship after adding Ephriam to their roster.

Bubba's *Lexington* team also won the Navy's Seventh Fleet basketball championship by defeating teams from other ships in the fleet. They played games in gymnasiums on naval bases, and on the *Lexington*, games and practices were played on a court marked on the ship's deck.

Ephriam departed Atsugi on March 6, 1959, after four months with the Flyers and briefly was assigned to the USS *Fechteler*, a Gearing-class destroyer that also supported the Seventh Fleet as a radar warning ship. He served on the *Fechteler* from March 10 to March 27 before being transferred to an AKA transport ship for the return trip to San Diego to reboard the *Lexington*.

Now the first carrier whose planes were armed with air-to-ground Bullpup guided missiles (on A-4 Skyhawks), the *Lexington* sailed again from San Francisco on April 26, 1959, to support the Seventh Fleet on another Far East tour because of renewed tension in Laos in Southeast Asia through August and September. The *Lexington* exercised with British forces from a base in Yokosuka, Japan, before sailing on November 16 for San Diego (arriving December 2). In early 1960, the *Lexington* experienced an overhaul at the Puget Sound Naval Shipyard in Bremerton, Washington. After time at the shipyard, the *Lexington* was ordered to revisit Pearl Harbor, Guam, Philippines, Okinawa, Hong Kong, and Yokosuka in late 1960 and 1961 to intervene again in the Laotian Civil War.

One of Bubba's younger sisters, Bernice, who was born in 1949, said the younger children weren't well-informed about Bubba's military service. "We didn't know too much," she said. "All we knew was that he was in the Navy and he was on a big ship."

She said when an airplane would fly over their neighborhood, one of the children would look up and say, "Hey, Bubba, when are you coming home?"

Ephriam was scheduled to complete his four years of service in January 1962, but on January 16, he signed a four-month extension so he could remain with the *Lexington* until it completed its western Pacific cruise.

That cruise ended on May 12, 1962, and three days later—on his twenty-fourth birthday—Ephriam was released from active military service after four years, three months, and twenty-three days. He qualified for an honorable discharge and was recommended for reenlistment. Ephriam also was recommended for a good conduct medal even though his record included a few disciplinary actions, including punishment for smoking in unauthorized places, giving a false name, and unauthorized absence.

The USS *Lexington*, the ship that had been Bubba's home for the last four years, was finally decommissioned on November 8, 1991, after old age and mechanical difficulties did what Japanese bombs could not accomplish. It was the longest-serving and third-most-decorated aircraft carrier in US history. Its crew from 1943 to 1963 numbered about three thousand officers and enlisted men. The flight deck of the *Lexington* was 910 feet long and 191.6 feet at its widest part. It could travel up to 33 knots (38 miles) per hour powered by its four propellers, four Westinghouse steam turbines, eight Babcock & Wilcox boilers, and four steam and two diesel generators. Each of its two anchors weighed more than fifteen tons. The total arrested landings of aircraft were calculated at 493,248. (The *Lexington* now rests in the bay in Corpus Christi, Texas, and opened as a museum on October 14, 1992.)

After leaving the USS *Lexington* on May 15, 1962, Ephriam had a decision to make. If he reenlisted within ninety days, he would be credited with uninterrupted service in the US Navy. He spent most of the summer in San Diego with intentions of enrolling in school. He shared an apartment with two other ex-seamen, worked at a pool hall, and considered applying for the newly-formed US Navy sea, air, and land teams (SEALs), special operations forces that had been established in January 1962.

Ephriam also visited with his mother, family, and friends for a few days in his hometown of Pecos. He and his mother had regularly corresponded during his four years of naval service from 1958 to 1962. But while he was home, he was injured in an accident—glass from a broken bottle caused multiple cuts on his hands and arms—which delayed his return to San Diego and prevented his candidacy for the Navy SEALs.

On the ninetieth day after his separation from the USS *Lexington*, August 13, 1962, Ephriam reenlisted for a second term in the US Navy. Ephriam said another reason he delayed his reenlistment was to avoid being assigned again to the *Lexington*, which had been ordered to sail around Cape Horn off the southern tip of Chile and South America to join the Atlantic Fleet, including duty during the Cuban Missile Crisis in October 1962. Ephriam wanted to remain on ships and bases on the West Coast.

His second term was to last six years on the USS *Bennington* (CVS-20) and include three tours of duty in the Vietnam War between 1965 and 1968 and an assignment from the National Aeronautics and Space Administration (NASA) as a recovery ship for the Apollo 4 unmanned space capsule in November 1967. The *Bennington* was the second ship named after a battle near Bennington, Vermont, in 1777 that was the turning point in the Revolutionary War. The ship had been commissioned in 1944, served in several campaigns in the Pacific Theater during World War II, and became an antisubmarine aircraft carrier (CVS) in 1959.

With the six-foot, four-inch, 210-pound Ephriam now on board, the *Bennington*—including a squadron of helicopters—was host ship for training exercises and participated in disaster relief on the West Coast, including a flood in Eureka in Humboldt County in Northern California. In 1963, Ephriam's ship sailed to Seattle, Washington, to serve as the flagship for Seafair, an annual summer festival, and continued to Kodiak and Juneau, Alaska, as part of the Alaskan Command (ALCOM) in the US Northern Command with soldiers from the Air Force, Army, and Coast Guard.

Ephriam worked in the machinists' division in the *Bennington*'s engineering department. But for about two years Machinist Mate Ephriam was assigned to work as a messman in the ship's commissary while it was understaffed before resuming duty in M division. The *Bennington* was home to about 80 to 100 planes, 115 officers, and 1,500 enlisted men. It was 876 feet in length and 191.9 feet at its widest and traveled at speeds of up to 33 knots (38 miles) per hour. It was powered by eight boilers and four propellers.

After Ephriam joined the crew, the *Bennington* made its next western Pacific cruise in 1964 to Pearl Harbor, Philippines, and Hong Kong and to Yokosuka, Iwakuni, Sasebo, Kobe, and Hakodate in Japan. He said that often the crew was not informed of the mission of a trip until the ship left harbor and arrived in international waters.

Vietnam duties began in 1965 during the administration of President Lyndon B. Johnson. And it was also in 1965 that Ephriam married Gwendolyn Howell of Compton, California. The couple resided in Los Angeles.

According to naval records, those three assignments took the *Bennington* to Pearl Harbor, Philippines, Bangkok, Hong Kong, and Okinawa and to Yokosuka, Sasebo, and Hakodate in Japan from March to October 1965; to Pearl Harbor, Philippines, Hong Kong, and Sydney and to Yokosuka and Sasebo in Japan from November 1966 to May 1967; and to Pearl Harbor, Singapore, Hong Kong, and Philippines and to Yokosuka and Sasebo in Japan from May to November 1968.

In March 1965, as the *Bennington* was beginning its first mission in Vietnam, the first American combat boots hit the ground on a beach near Da Nang.

Ephriam qualified for hostile fire pay for five months (December 1966 to April 1967) during his second Vietnam tour and again in June and July 1968 during his third tour. Ephriam, now machinist's mate third class, was awarded a good conduct medal, National Defense Service Medal, Vietnam Service Medal with two bronze stars, and Republic of Vietnam Campaign Medal.

In August 1967, Captain Richard Graffy was notified that the USS *Bennington* had been selected to serve as the primary recovery ship for the Apollo 4 spacecraft from its Saturn 5 launch vehicle after a flight from the John F. Kennedy Space Center on Merritt Island, Florida. Preparations and training began on the *Bennington* immediately and continued for several months because the launch was repeatedly postponed. The "go" orders finally came, and the *Bennington* left California for Pearl Harbor and the ultimate destination about 275 miles from Midway Island to retrieve the command module.

But the Apollo 4 flight was delayed again, and the *Bennington* remained in Hawaii for an additional three weeks. The crew continued to practice with a mock capsule provided by NASA to perfect procedures for the recovery. They conducted simulated exercises to evaluate the flow of information on the day of the flight and to perfect the procedures of contact, approach, and pickup, which rested in the hands of the *Bennington*'s capable, well-trained deck seamen.

Finally, the *Bennington* sailed from Pearl Harbor on November 6 for the recovery area. On the morning of November 9, 1967, around one, according to the clocks on board the *Bennington*, the spacecraft launched from Florida. After a flight of 8:36:59 and three orbits of Earth, at 9:37 a.m., two sonic booms were heard by the crew on the *Bennington*, and a minute later, the spacecraft was sighted suspended from three parachutes.

"We saw it coming down," Ephriam remembers. "We went over and picked it up. I got pictures of it."

Helicopters with swimmers aboard were deployed, and the swimmers jumped into the water, deflated the chutes, and attached a flotation collar to the spacecraft. One of the *Bennington*'s motor whaleboats and its crew were lowered into the water to assist with recovery operations and to retrieve the swimmers after the ship's heavy-duty crane had lifted the spacecraft to the deck.

Apollo 4 was onboard by noon, and the *Bennington* headed to Hawaii to deliver its prize. The *Bennington* then returned to Long Beach, California, and the capsule was taken to the major spacecraft contractor North American Rockwell in Downey, California.

NASA officials said all the goals of the mission were accomplished; it was another successful step in putting an American on the moon less than two years later when Neil Armstrong stepped on the lunar surface on July 21, 1969, after Apollo had landed the previous day.

The Saturn 5 was making its first flight as the largest launch vehicle to ever attempt a flight. The sound from the launch was much stronger than anticipated, and the sound and pressure buffeted the vertical assembly building, launch control center, and media building. Ceiling tiles fell around CBS television anchorman Walter Cronkite, who later admitted he was "overwhelmed" by the power of the rocket and the emotion of the moment.

Cronkite yelled above the noise into his microphone, "Our building's shaking here. Our building's shaking. Oh, it's terrific. The building's shaking. This big blast window is shaking. We're holding it with our hands. Look at that rocket go into the clouds at three thousand feet. You can see it. You can see it. Oh, the roar is terrific."

A few months later, midway through the *Bennington*'s third Vietnam War tour, the six-year term of Ephriam's second tour of duty in the US Navy came to an end. "I was what they call a 'short-timer,'" Ephriam said.

"I got tired of training the younger guys coming in," he added. "When they come out of the academy, they come in with their little cadet stripes on. We had to train those that came into our division—the engineers coming into our division. They come out of the academy as ensigns. We had to train them, teach them. They got to be a pain for the older guys."

He remembers hearing officers say, "Sailor, do you know how to salute an officer when you see one?"

"Yeah, when I see one," came the reply, Ephriam said, "and they would take off running."

Ephriam was discharged under honorable conditions, but this time he was not recommended for reenlistment. He again had been found guilty of unauthorized absence, and his naval records show that in ten years of service, he failed to advance beyond pay grade E-3, he did not improve his educational background by taking additional naval training classes, and sometimes he required "constant supervision to get acceptable results from him." (Bubba disputes the Navy's education claim; he said he took courses that should have qualified him for E-4 or E-5.) He was cited for "unsatisfactory military behavior" and at least once faced court-martial. Bubba's personnel documents added, "His general appearance is adequate, and he gets along well with his shipmates. . . . He has the ability to be a good MM."

So on July 16, 1968, Ephriam's Geneva Convention and US Armed Forces identification cards were destroyed, and he was discharged from the Navy at the US Naval Station on Treasure Island in San Francisco. He had been on active duty with the US Navy in two terms for a total of ten years, two months, and twenty-seven days, including five years and ten months of foreign service.

Bubba collected his travel allowance from the US Navy and flew to Los Angeles to be reunited with his wife of three years, Gwendolyn, at their home on Jarvis Avenue. His first child, a son named Ira Earl, had been born on August 28, 1963, in Bremerton, Washington, to Bubba and Mary Campbell while Ephriam was stationed on the *Bennington* as it was serving in the Pacific Northwest.

In March 1960, while Ephriam was serving in the Pacific Theater, another young Black man, Junior Lee Coffey, played in the UIL state basketball tournament in Austin. But he was not—as has been reported in the intervening years in books, newspapers, and online—the first African American player to participate in the tournament.

Coffey actually played in two UIL basketball tournaments in Austin in 1960 and 1961 for coach John Ethridge of Dimmitt High School. He excelled in football and basketball for the Bobcats in the Texas panhandle town of about four thousand people. He had moved there with an aunt and uncle from Central Texas in March 1957—the same month Ephriam played in the UIL state tournament in Austin—after they found work as migrant farmers in the cotton fields of West Texas.

However, Coffey, a running back who later played in the Rose Bowl for the University of Washington and for an NFL championship team with the Green Bay Packers, missed being the first Black basketball player at the UIL state tournament in Austin by three years. As recently as August 2021, the *Seattle Times*, in Coffey's obituary, said he was "the first black athlete to play in the Texas state boys basketball tournament."

In 2019, Robert D. Jacobus wrote in his book *Black Man in the Huddle: Stories from the Integration of Texas Football* that "Coffey became the first African American to appear in the UIL state basketball tournament." Earlier, newspapers that erroneously reported Coffey's "accomplishment" included the *Lubbock Avalanche-Journal* and *Waco Tribune*, and it appeared in other published reports announcing Coffey's induction into the Texas High School Football Hall of Fame in Waco on May 9, 2015.

Coffey was born on March 21, 1942, in Kyle, Texas. He told the *Avalanche-Journal* in 1999 that moving from San Marcos to Dimmitt "was like an oasis. It was beautiful. I maybe had one or two incidences, but it never came from the kids at school. It was always someone from the city. Otherwise, I had nothing but great experiences there.

"I knew those people really felt that way," he added. "I knew they really cared about me as a person. I have memories of friendship and of truly being a part of the school. They really took an interest in me."

He attended segregated schools for Black students in Central Texas and also in Dimmitt in 1956–57 for eighth grade before Dimmitt integrated for his freshman year in 1957–58 (three years after Friona and two years after Pecos). An eighth-grade teacher, Florence Garrett, encouraged him to enroll at the newly integrated Dimmitt High School in the fall of 1957, he said, and she convinced school administrators that Coffey "had the smarts to go to Dimmitt High School." Otherwise, he said, he would have had to attend a high school for Black students thirty-five miles away in Olton. "That's how the school integrated," Coffey explained to Jacobus for his book *Black Man in the Huddle.*

Coffey said his aunt, Maudie Sanders, "didn't want me roaming the streets," so he decided to participate in organized sports for the first time in his young life. Among his classmates at Dimmitt who introduced him to football and basketball were Hal Ratcliff, later a coach at Lubbock's Coronado High School and TCU and a public schools administrator, and Kent Hance, later an attorney, member of the Texas Senate and US House of Representatives, and chancellor of Texas Tech University.

Coffey told GoHuskies.com in 2013, "I didn't know how to put on pads correctly. I was so embarrassed." In 2015, he explained to the *Waco Tribune*, "Fortunately, the guys didn't laugh at me. They just said, 'Hang in there; you'll pick it up.'"

"So I started playing," he said in Jacobus's book. "I had never played before. I was in a high school where there had never been integration before. . . . I was kind of a natural for football. It required more strength and natural athletic ability rather than skill.

"In basketball, even though I was pretty good, and I kind of liked it better than football, I got by on natural ability. Since I didn't start playing until high school, I was way behind in fundamentals. I didn't know anything about sports. . . .

"I was six-foot-one and two hundred pounds," he added. "There weren't too many players over two hundred pounds back then. When I first went out, the coaches put me at defensive tackle. After I recovered a fumble, though, and knocked people over returning it for a touchdown, that's when they made me a running back."

Coffey ran for 1,294 yards as a junior, and as a senior in 1960, he ran for 1,562 yards and led the Bobcats of coach J. D. Covington to the playoffs with all-state honors.

Coffey said winning smoothed integration. "Winning helped in Dimmitt," he told Jacobus. "They had never won much before I got there so I think winning made integration easier. . . . When I would go into town to buy groceries for my aunt and uncle, people knew me and would compliment me. That was pretty cool. However, even though things opened up a bit in Dimmitt, we still had to get our shopping done before the sun went down.

"Even though I was accepted by my classmates, some of their parents weren't too thrilled about their kid going to school and playing sports with a black kid. One of my friends cried the day he told me his parents wouldn't let him play football because of me. I told him, 'It's not your fault. You don't feel that way.'"

Ratliff told the *Lubbock Avalanche-Journal* in 1999, "The kids always accepted him. I never saw him be anything except for a great sportsman."

Coffey and the Bobcats were even more successful in basketball. Coach Ethridge's team twice advanced to the Class AA championship game, although both times they lost and came away without a state title. In 1960 they lost to undefeated Linden-Kildare, 52–44, in the final despite leading 42–40 entering the fourth quarter.

Ratliff, a 6'3" senior, led Dimmitt with twenty-seven points and was named all-tournament in Austin and all-state. Coffey scored eight points in the final for the 25–10 Bobcats. The winning Tigers—led by 5'9" senior George Hargett and 6'6" sophomore John Beasley—finished 31–0 for coach Tom H. Collins Jr.

The *Lubbock Avalanche-Journal* years later said most hotels and motels in Austin turned the Bobcats away because of Coffey. Ratliff said only the State Motel, the same motel where Ephriam's Pecos team stayed in 1957, would house the Dimmitt team with its Black player. Ratliff told Sam Scott of the *Avalanche-Journal*, "You should have seen the motel we stayed at in Austin. This hotel was called the State Hotel, and it was on South Congress. . . . It was a dump back then, and it was the only place we could stay."

In 1961, the powerful Buna Cougars won the fifth of their seven state championships with a 60–36 triumph over Coffey's Dimmitt team (30–6). M. N. "Cotton" Robinson coached Buna to each of its seven state titles. Three members of the undefeated Buna team (43–0) joined Coffey on the 1961 all-tournament team. Coffey, who scored nineteen points in the final game, also was named to the all-state team.

Coffey's career at Dimmitt earned for him membership in the Texas Panhandle Sports Hall of Fame.

"He was probably better in basketball," Hance said. "He could really jump. He was just a great athlete." Hance, a close friend of Coffey for more than sixty years, recalled his usual assignment from Coach Ethridge on Bobcat basketball road trips of going inside cafes or restaurants to see if they would serve meals to a team that included a Black player.

Hance related one incident, also told in Jacobus's book, when he returned to the bus after inquiring inside a restaurant. "If they wouldn't [serve the team], Hance would make up an excuse so as to not hurt Coffey's feelings," Jacobus wrote. "He would say the place was too expensive or a dump. One time he told Coffey one restaurant was just too crowded."

"Well," Coffey said, "there's only two cars in the parking lot so how could that be?"

Coffey and Hance were co-captains of the Dimmitt basketball team their senior season, and Hance delivered the eulogy at Coffey's funeral. "Those were unusual times," Hance said. "Junior said in later years he didn't realize how much we were trying to protect him."

Because the Southwest Conference was not yet integrated, Coffey reportedly declined offers from nearby West Texas State University in Canyon and also from Minnesota, Illinois, Oklahoma, Kansas, and several other universities. He decided to attend the University of Washington to play for Hall of Fame head coach Jim Owens after being scouted by assistant coach Harold "Chesty" Walker.

Coffey was limited by stress fractures and a hip pointer while playing for the Huskies, and reportedly there was some subtle racial bias for him to overcome. His wife said he was the first Black player at the University of Washington to share a room with a White player.

But Coffey, now six-foot-two and 215 pounds, led the team in rushing in 1962 (581 yards) as a sophomore despite starting only one game and in 1964 (638 yards) as a senior and in scoring in 1962 (eight touchdowns) and in 1963 (six TDs). He played in the Rose Bowl on January 1, 1964, (a 17–7 loss to an Illinois team that featured star linebacker Dick Butkus) and the Hula Bowl on January 9, 1965, and he earned all-coast and honorable mention all-America. The Huskies posted records of 7–1–2 in 1962, 6–5 in 1963, and 6–4 in 1964 in Coffey's three varsity letterman years (19–10–2), and he ranked among the university's top ten in career rushing yards (1,604 with seven 100-yard games) and scoring (sixteen TDs). (He played on the Huskies' winless freshman team in 1961.)

"He had a very unique style with those long legs," University of Washington teammate Ron Medved told *Sports Illustrated*'s "Inside the Huskies."

"He kind of stomped when he ran, and you better not be in the way."

Coffey was drafted in the seventh round of the 1965 NFL draft and was one of only three rookies who played for the Packers that season for a team that won the league championship. He recalled in a Fox television interview in Seattle in 2018 a phone call from legendary coach Vince Lombardi before the draft. "We're interested in you," Lombardi said to Coffey. "Would you like to play for the Packers?"

"Oh, hell, yeah, sure I want to play with the Packers," Coffey responded.

"That Packers team will always be special to me," he told GoHuskies.com in 2013. As a twenty-three-year-old rookie, he appeared in fifteen games in 1965 with only three carries (12 yards) for a team that finished 12–3–1 and defeated defending champion Cleveland Browns, 23–12, in the title game on January 2, 1966, at Lambeau Field. (It was the final NFL championship game before the beginning of the Super Bowl after the following season.)

"The team was stacked with future Hall of Fame players," Coffey said, "and I still made the cut. Green Bay had a similar coaching system to the University of Washington and I could play on special teams. . . .

"It was a different brand of the sport," he told the *Avalanche-Journal* in 1999. "I wasn't the dominant force I'd been in high school. At every different level I went to, I always thought it'd be hard to be a starter. I thought that at Dimmitt; I thought that at Washington; and I thought that when I went to the pros.

"Maybe it's because I was introduced to the game so late that I just continued to improve. I remember I never unpacked when I was with the Packers. I didn't think there was no way I could stick around with Paul Hornung, Elijah Pitts, and Jim Taylor," who were the Packers' trio of talented running backs.

Coffey played only one season with the Packers because he was selected in the 1966 NFL expansion draft by the Atlanta Falcons. He played for the Falcons in 1966 and 1967 and six games of the 1969 season before being traded to the New York Giants (he missed the 1968 season because of a knee injury). In 1966 he ran for 722 yards, caught fifteen passes for 182 yards, and scored five touchdowns, and in 1967, he again ran for 722 yards, caught thirty passes for 196 yards, and scored another five touchdowns. Both years he was among the top ten rushers in the NFL for the Falcons.

He combined for 511 yards with the Falcons and Giants during the 1969 season, and after missing the 1970 season, he finished his career in 1971 by appearing in six games for the Giants. In his NFL career, he played in fifty-nine games for three teams during five seasons with 2,037 rushing yards and fifteen touchdowns.

After his NFL career, Coffey enjoyed a successful career as a thoroughbred racehorse trainer with more than six hundred career wins and one of the highest winning percentages. He got his introduction to horse racing by working during college at Longacres Park in Renton, Washington. While playing for the Atlanta Falcons, he maintained his interest by visiting racetracks at Hialeah Park in Hialeah, Florida, and Tropical Park in Coral Gables, Florida.

He owned, trained, and raced horses at Emerald Downs in Auburn, Washington, after Longacres closed and at Bay Meadows in San Mateo, California, and Golden Gate Fields in Albany, California. Equibase, horseracing data provider for the *Daily Racing Form*, reports that horses trained by Coffey had 3,820 starts with winnings of $5.8 million and 625 firsts, 583 seconds, and 510 thirds. He preferred relatively small stables of runners and trained such horses as Run Away Stevie, Toss the Dice, Missing Flyer, John Paul's Bet, Firetrail, and Raise the Bluff.

Emerald Downs founder Ron Crockett entrusted some of his top horses to Coffey. "Junior Coffey was one of a kind in so many ways," Crockett said to *Thoroughbred Daily News* after Coffey's death. "He was just a solid human being. He was an accomplished athlete, a talented horse trainer, a philosopher, a friend to many and most of all kindhearted. He was a trailblazer."

"My objective is to have a sound and happy horse," Coffey told *Thoroughbred Daily News.* Coffey often was at the racetrack seven days a week, and he incorporated his experience of training for football in physically and mentally training racehorses. His horses and stalls often were decorated with NFL memorabilia. He retired in 2018 with the fifth-best winning percentage (20.13) at Emerald Downs.

"Really, I've had a rosy life even with all these adversities," Coffey once said. "It taught me a lot. What I learned is you stand up for yourself no matter what the consequences."

Coffey died on August 30, 2021, at a hospital in Federal Way, Washington, at the age of seventy-nine. The *Seattle Times* said he had been diagnosed with early-onset Alzheimer's and congestive heart failure.

His wife of fifty-five years, Kathy, also was a longtime employee of Emerald Downs. "He always stood up for himself," she said, "but sometimes he realized it was baby steps."

Coffey is featured in the 2015 book *How Seattle Became a Big-League Sports Town* by Dan Raley, who calls Coffey "possibly Seattle's most misunderstood athlete and underutilized talent."

THIRTEEN

BUBBA TAKES HIS MESSAGE TO PENNSYLVANIA AVENUE

Bubba after '68, Including His Move to Abilene

Martin Luther King Is Slain in Memphis; A White Is Suspected; Johnson Urges Calm
New York Times, Apr. 5, 1968

Jackie Robinson, First Black in Major Leagues, Dies
New York Times, Oct. 25, 1972

Reagan Takes Oath as 40th President
New York Times, Jan. 21, 1981

East Germany Opens Frontier to the West for Emigration or Visits; Thousands Cross
New York Times, Nov. 10, 1989

After Bubba Ephriam's discharge from the US Navy in July 1968 in San Francisco and his airplane flight home to Los Angeles, he wanted to take six months off, delay returning to work, and perhaps write about the experiences of his first thirty years. "But I couldn't focus," he said. His wife, Gwen, an employee of Los Angeles County, encouraged her friends to hire him to also work for the county.

But Ephriam responded, "I'm not looking for a job."

That fall, he did begin working for American Building Maintenance in shops at Hughes Aircraft Company. But the following year, he had to travel home to Pecos because his sister Bernice was seriously injured in an automobile accident. He delayed his return to Los Angeles to remain in Pecos to help his parents, "and [ABM] got somebody else to take my place."

After eleven months at ABM, Ephriam responded to a "help wanted" sign and was hired by Air Treads, a subsidiary of Goodyear Tire and Rubber Company. Air Treads recapped industrial tires, Ephriam said, and operating the heavy equipment "was the hardest work I had ever done in my life. I was so glad when I heard the horn blow for quitting time."

By the time Ephriam got home each workday and sat in his favorite chair, "my whole body was shaking. . . . I was half dead." Gwen, a mother of four whom Bubba married in 1965, had to help him remove his shoes, which were full of tiny pieces of rubber.

In addition to his new job, Ephriam also earned his high school diploma in 1969 by taking courses in Compton, California. But after three and a half years at Air Treads, "an issue" with a foreman led to Ephriam's resignation.

Again, Gwen encouraged him to work for Los Angeles County. One day in 1972, while home for lunch, she said, "They want you to come down and talk to them. Please, just for me." He reluctantly agreed. "I'll be there."

That afternoon, she introduced Bubba to the superintendent of the county golf course, who was aware of Bubba's background in landscaping work for his father. "That's what we need," the official said. They visited the Western Avenue Golf Course, and upon their return to the office, the superintendent announced, "Here's our new employee."

"I haven't put in an application yet," Ephriam countered.

"Don't worry about that," Bubba's new boss said as Bubba began a nine-year career with the parks and recreation department of Los Angeles County in golf course maintenance and landscaping. He enrolled in night classes in turf management at Los Angeles Trade–Technical College and also took courses in industrial law at UCLA, speech at the University of Southern California, and sociology at Los Angeles Southwest College.

After he and Gwen divorced in 1979, Bubba met his second wife, Maggie Brown, in 1980, and their daughter Iria Loraine Ephriam was born on June 23, 1981.

Ephriam suffered a back injury in a workplace accident in 1981, officially retired from Los Angeles County in 1982 with lifetime benefits, and decided to move to Colorado Springs, Colorado, to join his brother, William, in his ministry at the Progressive Church of God in Christ. Maggie wanted to remain in Los Angeles (with Bubba's daughter Loraine), so Bubba's second marriage ended.

In addition to his church ministry, William was active in campaigns for religious freedom, and he and his wife, Ophelia, founded and operated New Hope, a sixteen-bed home for girls ages twelve to eighteen, including court-ordered placements, orphans, runaways, and abused girls.

Bubba managed the home's transportation department, taking the girls to school, church, doctor's appointments, and field trips in a minibus. And what began when Bubba cooked a meal for church members who were stranded during a snowstorm at William's house developed into catering for groups in the community from a commercial grill in a cafeteria at the church building. That helped raise money for the church's mission efforts and enhanced the church's program of feeding homeless people.

"After Wednesday night service," Bubba remembers, "everybody else would be gone, and I'd still be there working in the cafeteria. . . . I stayed busy. And I was going so much." He traveled on behalf of the church to Denver, Kansas City, Albuquerque, Dallas, and Orlando, and once flew to Chicago to drive a diesel truck to Colorado Springs.

Bubba and William studied theology, religious liberty, and world religions with Dr. Joseph C. Paige of Raleigh, North Carolina, and Bubba traveled to Korea in 1984 to assist Dr. Paige at an international conference of CAUSA International, an anti-communist educational organization founded by Reverend Sun Myung Moon. (Dr. Paige, who died in 2002, was president and professor of practical theology at Shaw Divinity School. A crusader for righteousness and justice, he traveled extensively in Europe, Africa, Asia, and South America and was an acquaintance of Reverend Moon.)

Also in 1984, as part of their campaigns for religious liberty, Bubba visited Washington, DC, with other associates from across the nation to advocate for religious liberty and express their concern to congresspeople about what they believed were the government's infringements on the right of US citizens for religious freedom. He was one of several people who agreed to speak on the front lawn of the White House. ("We got word that President Reagan was in the White House.") Bubba said their group brought traffic to a standstill on Pennsylvania Avenue, but none of the other scheduled speakers stepped forward when the moderator called their names. "They all disappeared," Bubba said.

"Ephriam, you're going to have to do it," the moderator said.

"Well, I signed up, didn't I?"

"Yes."

"Well, I'll do it," Bubba said.

Bubba challenged President Reagan's interest in tearing down the Berlin wall to unite a foreign country when, more importantly, there were invisible walls at home in the United States that needed to be removed. The Bible says all men are created equal, Ephriam said, and Jesus died for all mankind—not for only one nationality or one race or one ethnic group of people. Bubba recalled instances of racial discrimination in his own life, and he quoted 2 Chronicles 7:14, when God said he will heal the land of people who turn from their wicked ways.

More than thirty-five years later, Ephriam recreated his remarks from that day in 1984 on Pennsylvania Avenue:

> Mr. President, I admire your interest in tearing down the Berlin wall in a country that's far away. We don't need dividing lines or dividing walls anywhere. We should be uniting countries with the right kind of governing.
>
> But the walls that should be the most important to you are the invisible walls in our own country. I was very glad when our organization told me that I was going to Washington and that I would be speaking here—addressing issues of changes that are needed in this country. My first thought was to make a list of dividing lines.

First of all, this is 1984, not 1684. We still have Native Americans on reservations. And there are vast lines between Black and White people, between Spanish and White people, between Orientals and other nationalities of people. Tell me, Mr. President, when will these lines be erased?

I can't recall a scripture in the Bible where Jesus said he gave his life for only one nationality of people. He died for all mankind. And that means he died for all people. Tell me, Mr. President, who gives any man the right to discriminate against another?

The Bible says all men are created equal. I was taught that in Sunday school. But since my childhood, I have often wondered if that means all men of one color or what?

Mr. President, I have been discriminated against all my life. Just the other day, I was talking about discrimination that I've seen in other countries. I told how I was treated in Austin, Texas, at the state basketball tournament. How awful it was being the only Black boy playing in the tournament. All my listeners were in tears.

While serving in the US Navy, I faced these issues several times. Tell me, Mr. President, when will it end? Racism, divided lines, walls, hatred. These issues are cruel and evil.

I don't vote in elections anymore. And I won't until I see and hear a president, after being elected, lay his hand on the Bible, take the oath, and then open the Bible to the scripture and read to all the nations what God said, that "if my people who are called by my name will humble themselves and pray and seek my face and turn from their wicked ways, I will hear from heaven and will forgive their sins and restore their land."

This is the message that should be shouted from every rooftop, from every mountain peak, throughout the world. Bombs and rockets, guns and fighting. All this wickedness is not the answer to our nation's problems. Jesus Christ is the only—and I do mean only—answer to these problems.

Ephriam returned from Washington, DC, resumed working with his brother, William, in Colorado Springs, and planned a visit to Abilene, Texas, for the following year in 1985 to see his ailing mother, who had moved to the West Texas city in 1967 where two of her sisters resided. (Bubba's father died November 13, 1996, in Pecos.)

Ephriam's aunts encouraged him to move to Abilene, so in 1986, with his new wife, Joyce Miller, whom he married in 1980 after his divorce from Gwen in 1979, and Joyce's two children, he moved from Colorado Springs.

His mother worked for the family of James Minor "Jim" and Jerri Hills Alexander at their home in Abilene and on their ranch north of the city in Jones County. She fished in the Clear Fork of the Brazos River on their ranch. "They gave her the combination to the lock," Ephriam said. "She called it her 'fishing place.' . . . They paid her a lot of visits when she was sick."

Loraine Ephriam Walker was very active with her church, first at Southside Church of God in Christ on Willow Street and later at Praise Temple Church of God in Christ on Ambler Avenue after the congregation moved, and she assisted its pastor, Samuel E. Tabor.

Tabor, born in Calvert, Texas, who was a military chaplain and graduate of Abilene's McMurry University, said Ms. Walker already was serving as the pastor's aide at Southside when he moved to Abilene in March 1988. She helped raise money to support the pastor and fund his travel, and she prepared the pastor's robes and pulpit attire.

"She talked to the women, prepared communion and church dinners, and served guests at church and in her home on Fannin Street," Tabor continued. "Her red velvet cake was very popular. When I told her I needed something, I didn't have to tell her anything else."

Tabor described Ms. Walker as serious and fashionable. "She loved to talk to the ladies about how to act, how to dress, and how to raise their children. She was good at hospitality at church dinners and funerals and weddings. She could decorate the church for any occasion.

"And she loved her family and tried to support them as much as she could," Tabor said. "She loved her grandchildren."

Bubba said his mother eventually decided to have surgery because of what he called "circulation problems" in her legs, and later she had to have one leg amputated just above the knee. She died on April 19, 2006, at the age of eighty-six, and Tabor officiated at her memorial service. Bubba said the Alexander family paid for her funeral and burial in Elliott-Hamil Garden of Memories in Abilene.

Laura "Laurie" Alexander Eagle of Abilene, the oldest of three children of Jim and Jerri Alexander, said Ms. Walker "was a joy in our home. She was a witness for God. She was a saint. Her faith was transformative. My sister would say, 'She prayed me into the kingdom.' We didn't have an inkling as we look back now of the effects she had on our family.

"Mother adored her and so did Dad. He would say she was part of our family. . . . We visited her in her home."

Bubba's younger sisters Linda and Bernice, both of whom lived in Abilene at the time, said the Alexanders helped their mother financially. Linda said they purchased a car for her. "She cooked and cleaned and took care of their kids," Bernice said. "She was pretty much their nanny. And she took care of Laurie's kids."

Bernice said her mother occasionally fished until dark at the Alexander ranch on her days away from work. "We would be wondering where she was," Bernice said.

According to Laurie Eagle, Ms. Walker also helped care for her grandmothers, Ruth Guitar Alexander and Mildred Morris Austin, later in their lives "when they were sick and needed care." And she worked for Laurie and her husband, Bob, after their first child was born in 1981. "Our children adored her," she said.

Laurie added, "She loved the Lord. She talked about God like he was right there. Her sweet spirit drew us closer to the Lord. . . . If you asked her how she was, she would say, 'I'm blessed.'"

Bubba's second daughter and third child, Lawuance, was born in Abilene on February 3, 1988. He operated a series of small restaurants near the Taylor County courthouse, including the Rib-It at South Seventh and Oak Streets and the City Café at South Fourth and Butternut. Attorneys, judges, and reporters from the *Abilene Reporter-News* were frequent customers.

Joyce eventually returned to Colorado Springs with her three children, including Bubba's daughter Lawuance, but Bubba remained in Abilene and later accepted an invitation to open a café at the Veterans of Foreign Wars post on North Third Street. They called it Bubba's Kitchen ("I was going to call it something else"), and he also became the VFW chaplain, performed weddings and funerals, and started a hospital ministry while continuing to help care for his mother. "I almost wore myself out," he remembers. "People wanted me to go to Hendrick [Medical Center] to visit their relatives too."

Because of his busy schedule, he was forced to leave Bubba's Kitchen. After his mother died in 2006, Bubba bought five acres of land west of Abilene near Tye, boarded a few horses, and lived there for several years before returning to Abilene.

Today, Bubba enjoys watching NBA games on television, and he's a faithful fan and season ticket holder for men's and women's basketball teams at Abilene Christian University. He befriended several players and coaches and followed the Wildcat men's and women's teams to NCAA March Madness Division I national tournaments in 2019 and 2021. He talks frequently to former classmates and friends from Pecos and to his siblings, children, grandchildren, nieces, and nephews. He also continues to minister to friends, acquaintances and even strangers during visits to local coffee shops, cafés, restaurants, and nonprofit organizations such as New Beginnings–Big Country, a faith-based transitional housing program founded in March 2010 for women leaving incarceration by Missy Denard, a women's chaplain at Taylor County jail and past winner of the Volunteer Citizen of the Year award for Abilene.

"I'm not a pastor," he said. "I'm an evangelist. I've got to go."

Bubba's sister Bernice, now a resident of Arlington, called her brother "a guy of wisdom. Anytime I asked him to explain something to me, he could explain so you understood.

"He was a perfect gentleman," she continued. "He's just a good guy. I never heard him use profanity. He was well-liked, and he has respect for the elderly and for his friends.

"He would teach us how to play ball. He loved his sisters, and he loved his whole family. We were a close-knit family."

Bubba's daughter Dr. Iria Loraine Abram, who now resides in a suburb of Atlanta, Georgia, and teaches at Beulah Heights University, wrote to him, "You are such a blessing to everyone you meet, and I am so glad that I too am blessed by being able to call you my father. I love you so much. You're the best Daddy in the entire universe."

Abram started her college career at Spelman College in 1999 after Bubba and her mother, Maggie, drove her from Los Angeles to Atlanta. She graduated from Beulah Heights and later earned a master of arts in Christian education and a doctor of ministry. An author, businesswoman, consultant, and life coach, she and her husband, Vincent, have three sons: Isaac, Elisha, and Caleb.

Abram said Bubba was thirty-eight years of age when she was born, "So my recollection is him in his older years. . . . He took parenting very seriously and the job of preparing youth very seriously. He's dependable. He was a master storyteller. He could pull a story out of nowhere and make the people so real and down to earth, so relatable."

William's granddaughter Nicole Ephriam fondly recalls, "Uncle Bubba likes to talk. That has never changed."

"His character is larger than life," Loriane continued. "He literally loves everybody. He never meets a stranger. And he's loved by everyone."

Bubba's life story was unscripted. It developed in real time. Bubba created pivotal, compelling moments that echoed for decades. And those moments continue to play out in real time today—long after he made history on the basketball court, excelled in his purple and gold uniform for the Eagles of Pecos High School, endured an often harsh life with his migrant farm family, triumphed over the poisons of racism and discrimination, served with the US Navy in the Vietnam War, and conscientiously ministered to his family and many others, both young and old, from all walks of life who crossed his path.

His story—a story that began on the cotton fields of West Texas and took him to the capitals of his state and his nation, to the Pacific Theater in wartimes, to ministry opportunities in Los Angeles, Colorado Springs, and Abilene—is much more than words on a page. It happened. And it is happening today. Bubba's powerful story creates and preserves history, and it vigorously resists being forgotten or erased.

His daughter Loraine tells us, "He wants more than anything for his story not to be forgotten, for his story to be told."

FOURTEEN

BUBBA'S SACRED CONVERSATIONS WITH CHILDREN

Bubba and the Kids

I pledge allegiance to the flag
of the United States of America
and to the republic for which it stands,
one nation, under God, indivisible,
with liberty and justice for all.
—Francis Julius Bellamy (1855–1931)

Four-year-old Nicole Ephriam was sitting at one of her favorite places—her grandmother's dining table at the home of Ophelia and William Ephriam in Colorado Springs, Colorado. On this particular morning in 1984, Nicole was enjoying Ophelia's delicious breakfast with her sister Shantel and cousin Sparkle along with her "favorite uncle," Bubba Ephriam.

Today is the day, Bubba was thinking, for the energetic Nicole to show what she had learned from her scheming Uncle Bubba. William was missing from the breakfast table, as he usually was, already busy preparing for his day's activities in their various ministries. But Nicole's audience grew by one as her grandfather William was called to the table.

She didn't pronounce all thirty-one words correctly, but Nicole proudly recited the pledge of allegiance to the US flag. "I pledge allegiance to the *fwag*," she proclaimed—much to the surprise of the members of the Ephriam family who had gathered at the breakfast table that morning.

William cast a suspicious glance at his brother Bubba. "You taught her that, didn't you?"

"Sure." Bubba didn't deny his guilt. "I wasn't going to let that time go to waste. She could be learning something." And Nicole didn't shy away from her familiar position as the center of attention.

Nicole often accompanied Bubba as he drove a church van or minibus while serving in their ministries in Colorado Springs. He was taking members to church events, transporting girls from New Hope—a residence for homeless girls—to school and doctor's appointments, and visiting other local attractions such as a pumpkin patch at Halloween. With her pencil and notepad, she occasionally pretended to be Uncle Bubba's secretary. "He would recite the pledge and have us repeat it," she remembers. "He made a little song with it to help us learn. I didn't realize that I knew the words to the pledge of allegiance."

Now a nurse's assistant for an endocrinologist in Houston, Nicole added, "He always had a love for kids. He was a role model for us. He was my favorite uncle. He would always go and pick up the kids. He took me on a trip to California to visit his daughter Iria Loraine and Aunt Maggie and to the amusement park. It was the longest trip ever, but I thought it was the coolest thing ever."

"He was really something with kids," William said of his brother. "He had a heart for kids. He did those things. I was busy, but he took care of those kinds of things. He always took care of the kids. . . .

"Nicole stayed with us," William continued. "We raised her. We all lived together. Bubba took them around, took them to school and other places."

William said once he and Ophelia discovered Crayola marks on a wall in their home. "Who did this?" they demanded.

In her youthful innocence, the mischievous Nicole quickly replied, "Nicole did it."

Bubba often monitored children in the church cafeteria while adults were in worship or class elsewhere in the building, and on weekdays, he kept the Ephriam children and grandchildren during the day while the other adults in the family were at work. "I made her my secretary," he said of Nicole. "She had her little pencils and pads. She would bring her lunch on our bus trips, but she treated that as her snack. For lunch she wanted to stop at McDonald's. She wanted to stop at every McDonald's we passed. . . .

"She would say, 'Let's do the pledge. I want to learn that.' And when I would deliberately miss a word, she would say, 'That's wrong. Now repeat after me.' She learned a lot from that. . . .

"I always did have a way with children," Bubba explained. "They take to people who give them attention. You drive down the street today and see yards full of toys. But they don't want that stuff. They want their parents. They want them to be part of their activities. It's very important. I gave a lot of classes at church about that."

Loraine remembers times as a child growing up in South Central Los Angeles when her father gathered her and her friends on small chairs and a table in their yard or sitting on a blanket in a nearby park to hear Bible lessons and stories. "He takes to children," she said. "He loves young people. He loves to try to fill them with hope. He loves people, the gospel, and his faith. He shares the Bible."

She added, "And he's never short of words of encouragement. Every conversation is sacred." Loraine said her father occasionally asks her, "What are you teaching your boys at home?"

Against her father's instruction, Loraine said that once as a young girl, she accidentally started a fire in some towels with a candle while her parents were away from the house. She tried to hide the evidence, but her misdeed was discovered. "Now tell me about this," Bubba calmly said to his young daughter upon his return home.

She confessed to her "accident," but she said her father "never laid a hand on me. He read verses to me from the Bible about obedience. . . . I was in tears because I had disappointed him. . . . That has given me patience with my kids today."

Bubba said Loraine usually was the youngest of the neighborhood children, "but she was real smart when she was little. She would study her Sunday school lessons (from First Evergreen Missionary Baptist Church in Compton) and memorize Bible verses. There would be five or six girls hanging around Loraine. She was the leader.

"We would do little skits," he continued, "and I was teaching them kindergarten stuff using a chalkboard on a tripod. I would start drawing an elephant and let them finish it.

"When they started school, I would get a call from the office saying that they were disruptive. They wanted the other kids to be up with them. I wanted the school to give Loraine more advanced work, but they said they had to give them all the same. Loraine would be at the other kids' desks trying to help them finish."

Bubba said his youngest daughter, Lawuance, demonstrated similar aptitude and behavior after he and her mother, Joyce, moved to Abilene from Colorado in 1986. He taught Lawuance, nieces, nephews Quentin and Joseph, grandson "Little Iria" (Ira Earl's son), and neighborhood kids sitting on blankets in the shade of mesquite trees in Abilene and Tye. He transported them around the city in his Cadillac DeVille luxury sedan ("there were not enough seat belts") and later a used church bus he bought for seven hundred dollars from Hillcrest Church of Christ in Abilene.

For his curriculum, he sometimes made use of lessons, Vacation Bible School materials, and other papers he found that had been left on the Hillcrest church bus. One document he still possesses today is "Bible Drill Questions," which includes 114 questions and answers from the Old and New Testaments. For example:

> **Old Testament**
> What was the ark made from? (gopher wood)
> How many plagues were put on the people of Egypt? (10)
> Which part of the Bible did David write? (Psalms)
> Who built the temple? (Solomon)

> **New Testament**
> Who were the parents of Jesus? (Mary and Joseph)
> Where was Jesus born? (Bethlehem)
> How many apostles did Jesus have? (12)
> How many thieves were crucified with Jesus? (2)

> **Basic Bible Knowledge**
> How many books are in the Bible? (66)
> Name the four gospels. (Matthew, Mark, Luke, and John)
> What is the first book of the Bible? (Genesis)
> What is the last book of the Bible? (Revelation)

Apparently, they learned their lessons well. "Very seldom did I have to tell them to do something twice," Bubba said.

He used a tape recorder at home to teach Lawuance the alphabet and to count to one hundred, and he taught her to pray and "how to bless the food." When the older children came home from school, she corrected them when they made mistakes while practicing their counting.

A nephew, Quentin Walker, son of Bubba's sister Linda, thanked Bubba for "being present throughout my life. I appreciate you for being present throughout my childhood, adolescent, and young adult years. Thanks for the good outings and trips to the parks, zoos, lakes, and remote-controlled airplane strips. I love you very much, and I thank God for you."

On a recent Christmas, his daughter Loraine told Bubba he was "the best gift I've ever received. . . . I honestly can't imagine what my life would be like if I was not blessed to have you in my life." She thanked him for teaching her "how to pray, fear the Lord, be a lady, be professional, and to share the gospel of Jesus Christ."

And on a recent birthday, she wrote to him that "the love, wisdom and knowledge you've shared with me over the years is invaluable. . . . May all the seeds that you've sown into lives across this nation bloom into a fruitful harvest."

"Everywhere I went, kids were drawn to me," Bubba said. "I've always had youngsters in my life."

> *Jesus loves the little children,*
> *all the children of the world.*
> *Red and yellow, black and white,*
> *they are precious in his sight.*
> *Jesus loves the little children of the world.*
> —Clarence Herbert Woolston (1856–1927)

ACKNOWLEDGMENTS

This book is dedicated to Iria "Bubba" Ephriam. No one deserves this tribute more than Bubba, my friend for a decade now. As a youth, he experienced an uneasy life with his family of migrant farmers; as a teenager, he endured troubled years of segregation and integration; and as an adult, he served his nation in the contentious Vietnam War prior to his varied ministries in Los Angeles, Colorado Springs, and Abilene, Texas.

As an eighteen-year-old high school student, he alone persisted through cruel experiences in Austin as the first Black player at the Texas state basketball tournament without his parents or any other member of his family. His first coach and mentor, Sidney Sadler, told him, "Bubba, if I could take your place, I would gladly do it. But it just so happens that you have to be the one it falls upon. Think about your sisters and brothers and all the rest of the kids coming along behind you . . . The eyes of Texas are upon you."

There were times when Bubba must have felt as if he didn't belong in the world in which he was living, but he was destined to help create a new world, a more tolerant world, a world where his race would enjoy more equality and justice and new opportunities.

Now in the ninth decade of his life, he's good-natured, insightful, and cheerful. And patient—an attribute he needed in abundance to sit through many hours of interviews for this book.

I also thought about dedicating this book to four people I believe are most responsible for the man Bubba is today. Those four are his parents, Loraine and Iria Ephriam, his brother, William, and Coach Sadler. Two things I regret most are not knowing his parents and Coach Sadler and not getting to see Bubba play basketball. I think I would have liked Loraine, Iria, and Sidney, and I certainly would have enjoyed watching Bubba play basketball.

The many conversations with Bubba were supplemented with research in public libraries in Abilene, Austin, and Dallas. My thanks also to Darla Bracken at Friona Public Library, Laura Baker at Brown Library at Abilene Christian University, Deborah Brown at Sutton County Library in Sonora, Leah Barbee at Tom Green County Library in San Angelo, Dorinda Millan at West of the Pecos Museum in Pecos, Cindy Slater at Stark Center for Physical Culture at the University of Texas at Austin, Jeremy Maynard at Richardson Library at Hardin-Simmons University, Weston Marshall at the Southwest Collection in the Special Collections Library at Texas Tech University, the Texas State Library and Archives, the Austin History Center, Danny Flanagan of Abilene, Marc English of Marc English Design, and Michael Barrett for the original art on the cover.

And thanks to Elaine Pinkerton Coleman of Santa Fe, Bob Eagle of Abilene, John L. Estes II of Abilene for introducing me to Bubba, Kent Hance of Austin, Michael Hurd of Prairie View A&M University, Alice McSweeney of Los Pinos Ranch in Cowles, New Mexico, Tracy Shaw of Pecos-Barstow-Toyah ISD, Sheryl Taylor Curlee of Dallas for genealogy, H. C. Zachry of Abilene, Bubba's PHS classmate Belva Hollingshead Williams, and the National Personnel Records Center for the US Navy.

At least four people I interviewed for *Bubba Ephriam* have passed away since our conversations. I acknowledge the important contributions to this book of R. C. Christopher, Donny Lee Hall, John Kenner, and Billie Kay Sadler.

And to Johne and R. L. Roberts, Linda Roberts, and Cary Roberts—you are the wind beneath my wings.

—Garner Roberts

SCOREBOARD

1956-57 Pecos High School Boys Basketball

Game	Date	Day	W/L	Score	Opponent	Location	Ephriam	Simmons
1	Nov. 27	Tues.	W1	66–47	Marfa	Marfa	27	19
2	Dec. 4	Tues.	W2	63–30	Marfa	Pecos	27	18
3	Dec. 7	Fri.	W3	50–28	Alpine	Monahans QF	13	20
4	Dec. 8	Sat.	W4	55–53	Van Horn	Monahans SF	18	24
5	Dec. 8	Sat.	L1	45–46	Monahans (OT)	Monahans F	5	12
6	Dec. 13	Thurs.	W5	65–42	San Angelo	Andrews	*	6
7	Dec. 14	Fri.	W6	45–43	Seminole	Andrews QF	*	26
8	Dec. 15	Sat.	W7	74–55	Kermit	Andrews SF	*	38
9	Dec. 15	Sat.	L2	53–62	El Paso Jefferson	Andrews F	13*	19
10	Dec. 18	Tues.	W8	64–53	Big Lake	Pecos	25	21
11	Dec. 20	Thurs.	W9	83–41	San Angelo Lakeview	Pecos QF	18	16
12	Dec. 21	Fri.	W10	83–54	El Paso Tech	Pecos SF	26	16
13	Dec. 21	Fri.	W11	76–55	Alpine	Pecos F	17	32
14	Jan. 1	Tues.	W12	66–26	Odessa B	Pecos	15	25
15	Jan. 4	Fri.	W13	51–48	El Paso High	El Paso	n/a	26
16	Jan. 5	Sat.	W14	61–41	El Paso High	El Paso	n/a	27
17	Jan. 8	Tues.	W15	39–38	Odessa B	Pecos	dnp	dnp

District 2-3A

Game	Date	Day	W/L	Score	Opponent	Location	Ephriam	Simmons
18	Jan. 11	Fri.	W16	66–50	Brownfield	Brownfield	23	19
19	Jan. 22	Tues.	W17	64–26	Kermit	Pecos	16	21
20	Jan. 25	Fri.	W18	80–54	Andrews	Andrews	36	21
21	Jan. 29	Tues.	W19	79–37	Monahans	Pecos	12	22
22	Feb. 1	Fri.	W20	83–55	Brownfield	Pecos	33	28
23	Feb. 8	Fri.	W21	75–71	Kermit (OT)	Kermit	33 or 35	26 or 28†
24	Feb. 12	Tues.	W22	58–18	Andrews	Pecos	16	23
25	Feb. 15	Fri.	W23	72–33	Monahans	Monahans	20	24

Practice Game								
26	Feb. 23	Sat.	L3	56–60	Big Lake	Big Lake	14	12
Region I-3A Tournament								
27	Mar. 1	Fri.	W24	64–53	Snyder	Lubbock SF	24	28
28	Mar. 2	Sat.	W25	62–53	Vernon	Lubbock F	17	25
UIL Class 3A State Tournament								
29	Mar. 8	Fri.	W26	71–62	Nacogdoches	Austin SF	30	14
30	Mar. 9	Sat.	L4	35–52	Houston Smiley	Austin F	12	9

* Scoring for Ephriam is unavailable for individual games of the Andrews tournament on Dec. 13–15. He scored a total of 63 points in four games, including 13 in the final.

† There are conflicting reports in newspapers on scoring for Ephriam and Simmons on Feb. 8.

QF=tournament quarterfinal game

SF=tournament semifinal game

F=tournament final or championship game

OT=overtime

Sources: primarily from the 1956–57 PHS yearbook, *Odessa American*, and *Pecos Enterprise*

SOURCES

Books and Articles

Abrahams, Peter. *Tell Freedom: Memories of Africa*. 1954; reprint, New York: Alfred A. Knopf, 1969.

Agee, James. *Cotton Tenants: Three Families*. Brooklyn: Melville House, 2013.

Agee, James, and Walker Evans. *Let Us Now Praise Famous Men*. Boston: Houghton Mifflin, 1939.

Aguirre, Frederick P. "Mendez v. Westminster School District: How it Affected Brown v. Board of Education." *Journal of Hispanic Higher Education* 4, no. 4 (Oct. 2005): 321–32.

Allen, Bertram L. *Texas Black High School Sports before 1967*. Austin: self-published, 1991.

Barr, Alwyn. *The African Texans*. College Station: Texas A&M University Press, 2004.

———. *Black Texans: A History of* African-Americans *in Texas, 1528–1995*. 2nd ed. Norman: University of Oklahoma Press, 1996.

Barr, Alwyn, and Robert A. Calvert, eds. *Black Leaders: Texans for Their Times*. Austin: Texas State Historical Association, 1981.

Behnken, Brian D. *Fighting Their Own Battles: Mexican Americans, African Americans, and the Struggle for Civil Rights in Texas*. Chapel Hill: University of North Carolina Press, 2011.

Bissinger, Buzz. *The Mosquito Bowl: A Game of Life and Death in World War II*. New York: HarperCollins, 2022.

Brinkley, Douglas. *Rosa Parks*. New York: Viking Penguin, 2000.

Canellos, Peter S. *The Great Dissenter: The Story of John Marshall Harlan, America's Judicial Hero*. New York: Simon & Schuster, 2021.

Carrier, Naomi Mitchell. *"Go Down, Old Hannah": The Living History of African American Texans*. Austin: University of Texas Press, 2010.

Clack, Cary. "The Bout." *Truly*Adventurous*, February 15, 2020.

Cooper, Debbie, ed. *USS Lexington "The Blue Ghost."* Corpus Christi: USS *Lexington* Volunteer Association, 2014.

Cray, Ed. *Chief Justice: A Biography of Earl Warren*. New York: Simon & Schuster, 1998.

Dallas Morning News. *Texas Almanac: 1961–1962*. Dallas: A. H. Belo, 1961.

Du Bois, W. E. B. *The Souls of Black Folk*. Chicago: A. C. McClurg, 1903.

Dunbar, Paul Laurence. "We Wear the Mask." *Lyrics of Lowly Life*. New York: Dodd, Mead, 1896.

Edgerton, Robert B. *Hidden Heroism: Black Soldiers in America's Wars*. Boulder: Westview Press, 2001.

Edwards, Harry. *The Revolt of the Black Athlete: 50th Anniversary Edition*. Urbana: University of Illinois Press, 2018.

Fink, Rob. *Football at Historically Black Colleges and Universities in Texas*. College Station: Texas A&M University Press, 2019.

Florio, John, and Ouisie Shapiro. "Revisiting Jackie Robinson's Major-League Debut Seventy Years Later." *New Yorker*, April 15, 2017.

Foreman, Thomas Elton. "Discrimination against the Negro in American Athletics." Master's thesis, Fresno State College, 1957.

Garza, Ryann D. "One Man's Fight Was a Fight for All: The Story of I. H. 'Sporty' Harvey and His Battle Outside the Ring." *Methods of Historical Research* (spring 2021): 7.

Gillette, Michael L. "Blacks Challenge the White University." *Southwestern Historical Quarterly* 86, no. 2 (Oct. 1982): 321–44.

Goldstone, Dwonna. *Integrating the 40 Acres: The* 50-Year *Struggle for Racial Equality at the University of Texas*. Athens: The University of Georgia Press, 2006.

Govenar, Alan Bruce. *Portraits of Community: African American Photography in Texas*. Austin: Texas State Historical Association, 1996.

Hall, Shirley. *Leadership for Changing Times: The* 40-Year *History of the Texas Association of School Boards*. Austin: Texas Association of School Boards, 1989.

Hawthorne, Bobby. "The University Interscholastic League and the Integration of Texas High School Athletics." In *The Texas Book*, edited by Richard A. Holland, 159–72. Austin: University of Texas Press, 2006.

Henry, Ed. 42 *Faith: The Rest of the Jackie Robinson Story*. Nashville: W Publishing Group, 2017.

Holland, Richard A., ed. *The Texas Book: Profiles, History, and Reminiscences of the University*. Austin: University of Texas Press, 2006.

Holley, Donald. *The Second Great Emancipation: The Mechanical Cotton Picker, Black Migration, and How They Shaped the Modern South*. Fayetteville: University of Arkansas Press, 2000.

Hughes, Alton. *Pecos: A History of the Pioneer West*. 2 vols. Seagraves, TX: Pioneer Book Publishers, 1978–81.

Hull, Mary. *Rosa Parks: Civil Rights Leader*. New York: Chelsea House Publishers, 1994.

Hurd, Michael. *Thursday Night Lights: The Story of Black High School Football in Texas*. Austin: University of Texas Press, 2017.

Irons, Peter. *A People's History of the Supreme Court: The Men and Women Whose Cases and Decisions Have Shaped Our Constitution*. New York: Penguin Books, 1999.

Jacobs, Alan. *Breaking Bread with the Dead: A Reader's Guide to a More Tranquil Mind*. New York: Penguin Press, 2020.

Jacobus, Robert D. *Black Man in the Huddle: Stories from the Integration of Texas Football*. College Station: Texas A&M University Press, 2019.

Jacobus, Robert D. *To Live and Play in Dixie: Pro Football's Entry into the Jim Crow South*. Guilford, CT: Prometheus Books, 2021.

Katz, William Loren. *Black Indians: A Hidden Heritage*. New York: Atheneum Books, 2012.

Kennedy, Kostya, ed. *Jackie Robinson: How He Changed the Game Forever*. New York: Meredith Premium, 2022.

———. *True: The Four Seasons of Jackie Robinson*. New York: St. Martin's Press, 2022.

King, Martin Luther, Jr. *The Autobiography of Martin Luther King, Jr*. New York: Warner Books, 1998.

Klarman, Michael J. *From Jim Crow to Civil Rights: The Supreme Court and the Struggle for Racial Equality*. Oxford: Oxford University Press, 2004.

Kluger, Richard. *Simple Justice: The History of Brown v. Board of Education and Black America's Struggle for Equality*. 2 vols. New York: Alfred A. Knopf, 1975.

Ladino, Robyn Duff. *Desegregating Texas Schools: Eisenhower, Shivers, and the Crisis at Mansfield High*. Austin: University of Texas Press, 1996.

Lee, Ulysses Grant, Jr. *The Employment of Negro Troops*. 1963; reprint, Washington, DC: Center of Military History, United States Army, 1994.

Long, Michael G., ed. *42 Today: Jackie Robinson and His Legacy*. New York: New York University Press, 2021.

Luxenberg, Steve. *Separate: The Story of Plessy v. Ferguson, and America's Journey from Slavery to Segregation*. New York: W. W. Norton, 2019.

McCaulley, Esau. *Reading While Black: African American Biblical Interpretation as an Exercise in Hope*. Downers Grove, IL: InterVarsity Press, 2020.

McGregor, Stuart, ed. *Texas Almanac: 1952–53*. The Encyclopedia of Texas. Dallas: A. H. Bello, 1951.

———, ed. *Texas Almanac: 1954–55*. The Encyclopedia of Texas. Dallas: A. H. Bello, 1953.

———, ed. *Texas Almanac: 1956–57*. The Encyclopedia of Texas. Dallas: A. H. Bello, 1955.

Minutaglio, Bill. *A Single Star and Bloody Knuckles: A History of Politics and Race in Texas*. Austin: University of Texas Press, 2021.

Mooney, James L. *Dictionary of American Naval Fighting Ships*. Vol. 4. Washington, DC: Navy Department, Office of the Chief of Naval Operations, Naval History Division, 1969.

Murphy, Leonard B. *A History of Negro Segregation Practices in Texas 1865–1958*. Master's thesis, Southern Methodist University, 1958.

Myers, Walter Dean. "Brown vs. Board of Education." In *Literature: Timeless Voices, Timeless Themes*. Upper Saddle River: Prentice Hall, 2001.

Neiman, Susan. *Learning from the Germans: Race and the Memory of Evil*. New York: Farrar, Straus and Giroux, 2019.

———. "There Are No Nostalgic Nazi Memorials." *The Atlantic*, September 14, 2019.

———. "Working Off the Past, from Atlanta to Berlin." *The New York Review of Books*, August 26, 2019.

Nichols, David Allen. *A Matter of Justice: Eisenhower and the Beginning of the Civil Rights Revolution*. New York: Simon and Schuster, 2007.

Parks, Rosa. *My Story*. New York: Dial Books, 1992.

Parmer County Historical Commission. *Prairie Progress*. Farwell: Parmer County Historical Commission, 1981.

Pecos High School. *The '56 Eagle*. Pecos: Pecos High School, 1956.

Pecos High School. *The '57 Eagle*. Pecos: Pecos High School, 1957.

Pollard, Edward A. *The Lost Cause: A New Southern History of the War of the Confederates*. 1987. Facsimile of the original, New York: Bonanza Books, 1974.

Powe, Lucas A., Jr. *The Warren Court and American Politics*. Cambridge, MA: Belknap, 2002.

Prairie View Interscholastic League Coaches Association. Hall of Honor and Hall of Fame Banquet. Houston: PVIL Coaches Association, July 19, 2014.

Raley, Dan. *How Seattle Became a* Big-League *Sports Town*. Seattle: Fairgreens, 2015.

Ratliff, Harold V. *Texas Boys Basketball: A History*. Austin: University Interscholastic League, 1976.

Rhoden, William C. *Forty Million Dollar Slaves: The Rise, Fall, and Redemption of the Black Athlete*. New York: Three Rivers Press, 2006.

Robinson, Rachel. *Jackie Robinson: An Intimate Portrait*. New York: Harry N. Abrams, 1996.

Russell, Jan Jarboe. "The Last Maverick." *Texas Monthly*, July 2003.

Rynders, Becky Jacobs, ed. *Texas Bound: Alexander, Guitar, Hills, Related Families*. Abilene, TX: H. V. Chapman & Sons Bookbinding, 2004.

Schutze, Jim. *The Accommodation: The Politics of Race in an American City*. 1986; reprint, Dallas: La Reunion, 2021.

Slaymaker, Richard P., John P. Sullivan, and Walter P. Smiley. *Dictionary of American Naval Fighting Ships*. Vol. 1B. Washington, DC: Navy Department, Office of the Chief of Naval Operations, Naval History Division, 1959.

Solomon, Burt, ed. *King: The Life and Words of Martin Luther King, Jr*. New York: *The Atlantic*, 2018.

Soltero, Carlos R. *Latinos and American Law: Landmark Supreme Court Cases*. Austin: University of Texas Press, 2006.

Stiles, Jo Ann. "The Changing Economic and Educational Status of Texas Negroes 1940–1960." Master's thesis, University of Texas, 1966.

Strum, Philippa. *Mendez v. Westminster: School Desegregation and Mexican-American Rights*. Lawrence: University Press of Kansas, 2010.

Swanson, Ryan A. *When Baseball Went White*. Lincoln: University of Nebraska Press, 2014.

Sweig, Julia. *Lady Bird Johnson: Hiding in Plain Sight*. New York: Random House, 2021.

Tatum, Beverly Daniel. *"Why Are All the Black Kids Sitting Together in the Cafeteria?"* New York: Basic Books, 1997.

Texas Historical Commission. *African Americans in Texas: A Lasting Legacy*. Austin: Texas Historical Commission, 2016.

Texas State Historical Association. *The Handbook of Texas Online*. Austin: Texas State Historical Association. www.tshaonline.org/handbook.

Tisby, Jemar. *How to Fight Racism: Courageous Christianity and the Journey toward Racial Justice*. Grand Rapids: Zondervan, 2021.

Tonatiuh, Duncan. *Separate Is Never Equal: Sylvia Mendez and Her Family's Fight for Desegregation*. New York: Abrams Books for Young Readers, 2014.

Truman, Harry S. *Memoirs: Years of Trial and Hope*. Vol. 2. Garden City, NY: Doubleday, 1956.

"The Type We Seek." *Sports Illustrated*, April 20, 1959.

US Department of Agriculture, Economic Research Service. *Statistics on Cotton and Related Data, 1920–1973*. Statistical Bulletin No. 535. Washington, DC: USDA, 1974.

Vincent, Gregory J., Virginia A. Cumberbatch, and Leslie A. Blair. *As We Saw It: The Story of Integration at the University of Texas at Austin*. Austin: Tower Books, University of Texas Press, 2018.

Walker, Moses Fleetwood. *Our Home Colony: A Treatise on the Past, Present, and Future of the Negro Race in America*. Steubenville, OH: Herald Printing, 1908; reprint, India: Pranava Books, 2019.

Wilkerson, Isabel. *Caste: The Origins of Our Discontents*. New York: Random House, 2020.

———. *The Warmth of Other Suns: The Epic Story of America's Great Migration*. New York: Random House, 2010.

Whitehead, Colson. *The Underground Railroad*. New York: Doubleday, 2016.

Wright, Harry K. *Civil Rights USA: Public Schools, Southern States, Texas*. Washington, DC: United States Commission on Civil Rights, 1963.

Young, A. S. *Negro Firsts in Sports*. Chicago: Johnson, 1963.

Zinn, Howard. *A People's History of the United States*. New York: Harper & Row, 1980.

———. *Postwar America: 1945–1971*. Indianapolis: Bobbs-Merrill, 1973.

Newspapers

Abilene Reporter-News
Amarillo Globe-News
Austin American-Statesman
Brownsville Herald
Chicago Defender
Corpus Christi Caller-Times
Corsicana Daily Sun
Dallas Morning News
Devil's River News (Sonora, TX)
El Paso Herald-Post
El Paso Times
Fort Stockton Pioneer
Fort Worth Star-Telegram
Friona Star
Honolulu Record
Houston Chronicle
Houston Informer
Houston Post
Indiana Evening Gazette (Indiana, PA)
Los Angeles Herald Examiner
Los Angeles Mirror
Lubbock Avalanche-Journal
Mansfield News-Mirror
Miami News
New York Daily News
New York Herald Tribune
New York Times
Odessa American
Pecos Enterprise
San Angelo Standard-Times
San Antonio Express-News
San Antonio Light
San Antonio Register
Seattle Post-Intelligencer
Seattle Times
Seminole Sentinel
Snyder Daily News
Southern School News
Stillwater News Press
Thoroughbred Daily News
Waco Tribune-Herald
Washington Post

Interviews

Loraine Ephriam Abram, Riverdale, GA, Dec. 28, 2021 (phone)
Bertram Allen, Austin, Nov. 8, 2017 (phone)
Humberto Baez, Pecos, Dec. 4, 2017 (phone)
Reginald Claudius Christopher, Austin, Apr. 1, 2018
Laura "Laurie" Alexander Eagle, Abilene, May 5, 2021 (phone)
Bernice Ephriam, Arlington, TX, Aug. 25, 2021 (phone)
Ira Earl Campbell Ephriam, New Baden, IL, Aug. 10, 2021
Iria "Bubba" Ephriam, Abilene, May 6, May 20, July 15, July 29, Aug. 19, Oct. 14, Oct. 21, Oct. 28, Nov. 11, 2015; Mar. 9, July 14, 2016; July 16, Aug. 31, 2017; Feb. 19, Feb. 23, Mar. 27, July 24, 2018; Feb. 21, 2019; Sept. 24, 2021; Apr. 27, May 4, July 1, Sept. 5, 2022
Nicole Ephriam, Houston, Sept. 5, 2022 (phone)
William Roland Ephriam, Colorado Springs, CO, Sept. 1–2, 2016; Sept. 5, 2022
Donny Lee Hall, Pecos, November 2016 (phone)
Kent Hance, Austin, Nov. 16, 2017
John W. Kenner, Powell, TX, May 22, 2017
Kim Parks, Abilene, Mar. 3, 2021
Billie Kay Sadler, Pecos, Oct. 13, 2016 (phone)
Billy Jim Simmons, Fort Worth, Nov. 10, 2016
Samuel E. Tabor, Abilene, May 24, 2021 (phone)
Randy Taylor, Pecos, Nov. 2016 (phone)
Larry Turnbough, Balmorhea, TX, Nov. 2016 (phone)
Linda Walker, Abilene, June 11, 2021

Other Sources

Abilene Public Library, Abilene
American Football Database
Associated Press
Austin History Center, Austin
Balmorhea Independent School District, Balmorhea
Briscoe Center for American History, University of Texas, Austin
Equibase Company
Friona Public Library, Friona, TX
George & Helen Mahon Public Library, Lubbock
GoHuskies.com
Handbook of Texas, Texas State Historical Association, Austin
Husky Maven
Inside the Huskies
Jay-Rollins Library, McMurry University, Abilene

Margaret and Herman Brown Library, Abilene Christian University, Abilene
National Cotton Council of America
National Personnel Records Center (Official Military Personnel File)
National Weather Service, National Oceanic and Atmospheric Administration
Parmer County Historical Commission, Farwell, TX
Pecos-Barstow-Toyah Independent School District, Pecos
Pecos High School, Pecos
Phillips High School Alumni Association, Phillips, TX
Prairie View Interscholastic League Coaches Association
ProFootballReference.com
Reeves County Library, Pecos
Richardson Library, Hardin-Simmons University, Abilene
Stephens Central Library, San Angelo, TX
Sutton County Public Library, Sonora, TX
Texas High School Football Hall of Fame, Waco
Texas Historical Commission, Austin
Texas State Library and Archives Commission, Austin
Texas Tech University Southwest Collection/Special Collections Library, Lubbock
University Interscholastic League, Austin
University of Washington, Seattle
University of Washington Magazine
US Department of Agriculture
USS *Lexington* Museum on the Bay, Corpus Christi
West of the Pecos Museum, Pecos

Pecos, Texas, was the site of the world's first rodeo on July 4, 1883. (photo by the author)

Bubba and the Pecos High School Eagles were awarded this trophy for their runner-up performance at the 1957 Texas Class AAA state basketball tournament. (photo by the author)

Billy Jim Simmons, Coach John Kenner, and Bubba Ephriam admire the state runner-up trophy at Pecos High School. (photo from *The '57 Eagle*, PHS yearbook)

Sidney Sadler (1923–88) was principal, teacher, and coach at George Washington Carver School in Pecos. He taught Bubba the game of basketball. (photo provided by Sadler family)

Bubba scored 33 points in the Eagles' 83–55 win over the Brownfield Cubs on February 1, 1957, in Pecos for their 20th win of the season. (photo from *The '57 Eagle*, PHS yearbook)

Bubba was a sophomore at Pecos High School in 1956–57. (photo from *The '57 Eagle*, PHS yearbook)

Bubba learned to play basketball on this outdoor court at George Washington Carver School in Pecos, Texas. (photo by the author)

Bubba was a lineman for the Pecos High School football team and earned honorable mention all-district. (photo from *The '57 Eagle*, PHS yearbook)

Coach John Kenner (center) and captains Billy Jim Simmons (left) and Bubba Ephriam (right) led the 1956–57 Pecos High School Eagles to a record of 26–4. (photo from *The '57 Eagle*, PHS yearbook)

Members of the 1956–57 Pecos High School basketball team were (back row, from left) Coach John Kenner, Bill Mitchell, Billy Jim Simmons, Bubba Ephriam, Eugene Walker, Royce Cassell, manager Robert Cole, (front row, from left) Frank Vasquez, Wayne Wasson, and Robert Hinson. (photo from *The '57 Eagle*, PHS yearbook)

Gregory Gymnasium on the campus of the University of Texas in Austin, scene of the 1957 state tournament. (photograph courtesy of University of Texas Recreational Sports)

Billy Jim Simmons played for the TCU Horned Frogs after his record-setting career for the Pecos High School Eagles. (photograph courtesy of TCU Athletics)

R. C. Christopher was Bubba's teammate at Carver and Pecos high schools and one of the first—if not the first—Black athletes to graduate from a Texas public high school after integration. (photo from *The '56 Eagle*, PHS yearbook)

Lewis Qualls led Houston Smiley to two state championships during his high school career, including a win over Pecos as a sophomore in the 1957 state tournament. © 2024 Texas A&M University

Bubba was assigned to the US Naval Air Station in Atsugi, Japan, in 1958–59 to play for the NAS Flyers basketball team (photo provided by Ephriam family)

Bubba and the crew of the USS *Bennington* retrieved the *Apollo 4* space capsule from the Pacific Ocean on November 9, 1967. (photograph courtesy of US Navy)

The USS *Lexington* with Bubba Ephriam on board sails on August 16, 1958, with the US Seventh Fleet for its assignment in the Second Taiwan Strait Crisis. (photograph courtesy of US Navy)

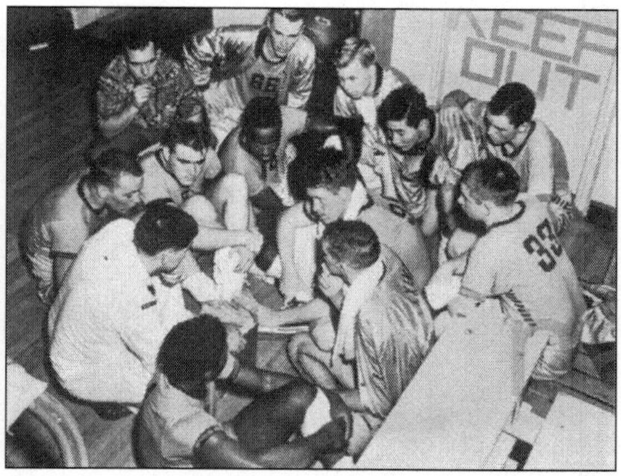

Bubba (14) and his Navy teammates from the USS *Lexington* huddle during halftime of a basketball game in 1958. (photograph courtesy of US Navy)

Bubba spoke at a freedom of religion conference in Dallas, Texas, c. 1985. (photo provided by Ephriam family)

Bubba speaks at a conference in Denver, Colorado, c. 1985. (photo provided by Ephriam family)

Bubba traveled to Washington, DC, in 1984 to deliver letters to members of Congress and speak on the front lawn of the White House. (photo provided by Ephriam family)

Bubba and Alan Inman traveled to Colorado around 1985 to attend a clergy conference. (photo provided by Ephriam family)

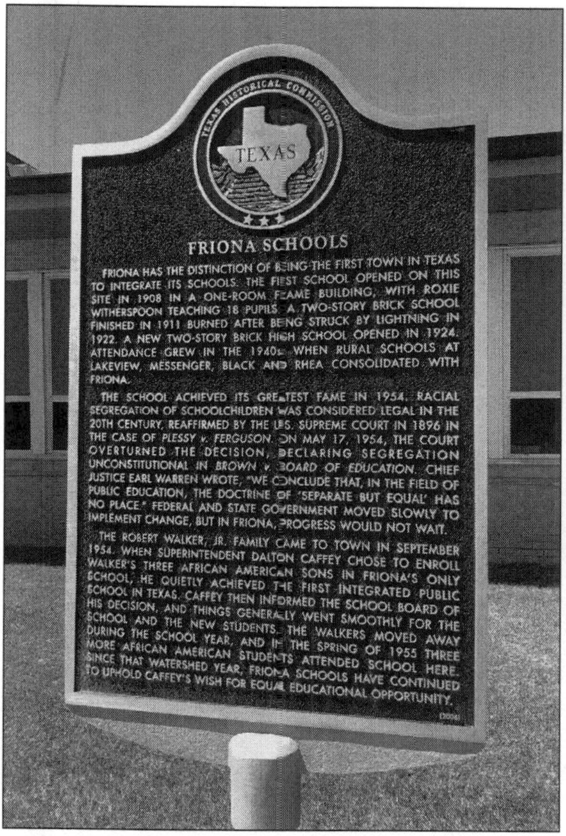

This marker erected by the Texas Historical Commission at Friona Elementary School in 2007 documents the small panhandle town as the first in Texas to integrate its public school in September 1954. (photo by the author)

Bubba's mother, Loraine Ephriam Walker (1920–2006), moved to Abilene in 1967, where she worked for the Alexander family and served at Southside Church of God in Christ and Praise Temple Church of God in Christ. (photo provided by Ephriam family)

Bubba's daughter Loraine and son Earl attended a luncheon in 2014 in San Antonio when their father was inducted into the Hall of Fame of the Prairie View Interscholastic League Coaches Association. (photo by the author)

Bubba wears his Golden State Warriors jacket to a basketball game at Abilene Christian University. (photo by the author)

Bubba talks basketball with former Abilene Christian University player Hayden Farquhar of Throckmorton, Texas, a member of ACU's 2018-19 team that won the Southland Conference championship and earned the Wildcats' first trip to the NCAA Division I national tournament. (photo by the author)

Bubba and his brother William (left) returned to Pecos in November 1996 after the death of their father, Iria Earl Ephriam (1909–96). (photo provided by Ephriam family)